THE SIEGE OF PARIS

Robert Baldick

Robert Baldick, who died in 1972, was a Fellow of
Pembroke College, Oxford, and of the Royal Society
of Literature, and joint editor of Penguin Classics
from 1964–72. He translated the works of many
great French authors including Montherlant, Sartre,
Simenon, Salacrou, Chateaubriand, Flaubert, Huysmans and Verne. He wrote a number of biographies,
a history of duelling and a portrait of the famous
Restaurant Magny, scene of splendid literary gather-
ings. He was married to the American translator and
writer, Jacqueline Baldick, now a literary agent.

Also by Robert Baldick

THE LIFE OF J.-K. HUYSMANS
  Oxford

THE LIFE AND TIMES OF
  FRÉDÉRICK LEMAITRE
  Hamish Hamilton

THE GONCOURTS
  Bowes and Bowes

THE FIRST BOHEMIAN:
THE LIFE OF HENRY MURGER
  Hamish Hamilton

THE MEMOIRS OF CHATEAUBRIAND
  (edited and translated)
  Hamish Hamilton

PAGES FROM THE GONCOURT JOURNAL
  (edited and translated)
  Oxford

DINNER AT MAGNY'S
  Gollancz

Overleaf Unusual Meat

The Siege of Paris

ROBERT BALDICK

NEW ENGLISH LIBRARY
TIMES MIRROR

First published 1964 by B. T. Batsford Ltd.

© 1964 Jacqueline Baldick

*

FIRST NEL PAPERBACK EDITION AUGUST 1974

*

NEL Books are published by The New English Library Limited from Barnard's Inn, Holborn, London, E.C.1. Made and printed in Great Britain by C. Nicholls & Company Ltd.

45002190 4

THE SIEGE OF PARIS

PREFACE

The Siege of Paris in the autumn and winter of 1870–1 was the last full-scale siege of a European capital, the first occasion of the indiscriminate bombardment of a civilian population, the source of immense hardship and suffering, and the origin of a division in the French nation which has still not been healed. Yet for the past 50 years or more it has generally been regarded either as a heaven-sent retribution for the sins of a frivolous society or as an amusing interlude in the grim history of European conflict.

It was in the hope of placing the Siege in its proper perspective that I embarked several years ago on the research for this book. There was, I found, no dearth of material: on the contrary, there was a positive *embarras de richesses*. In the end, confronted with a mass of prejudiced, chauvinistic and often demonstrably false testimony, I decided to present the Siege as far as possible through the eyes and in the words of a number of perceptive and reasonably impartial observers. These include Edmond de Goncourt, who never showed himself a greater diarist than in his record of "the Terrible Year"; Henry Vizetelly, the indefatigable correspondent of the *Illustrated London News*; Henry Labouchère, *alias* "the Besieged Resident", the witty and intrepid representative of the *Daily News* in Paris; and Henry W. G. Markheim, who recorded his impressions of the Siege under the pen-name of "the Oxford Graduate", and was later elected a Fellow of my old College, Queen's.

I should make it clear that this book does not pretend to be a military history of the Siege: I have neither the qualifications nor the desire to write such a work. It is simply an attempt to tell the story of the life of the French capital during some of the darkest and most momentous days of its turbulent history.

I have to acknowledge the gracious permission of Her Majesty the Queen to consult and quote from Queen Victoria's diaries for the period of the Franco-Prussian War.

I must also thank Mr. Robert Mackworth-Young, the Librarian at Windsor Castle, and the Librarians and staffs of the Bibliothèque Nationale, the Bibliothèque Historique de la Ville de Paris, the Bodleian Library, and the Library of the Taylorian Institution at Oxford, for the courteous and unfailing assistance they have given me. For information, books, documents, help and encouragement, I am indebted to more people than I can possibly thank here; but I wish to record my special gratitude to Mr. Helmut Gernsheim, Mrs. Robert Henrey, M. Pierre Lambert, Mr. Iain MacDonald, Mlle. Ursula Pudewell, Mr. Morris Springer and Mr. David Voss.

My greatest debt of gratitude is of course to Paris herself, that beloved city which has given me more than I can ever hope to render.

R. B.

CONTENTS

Preface   9

Acknowledgment   13

Prologue   17

THE FIRST WEEK
Monday, 19 September – Sunday, 25 September
  EARLY ALARMS   27

THE SECOND WEEK
Monday, 26 September – Sunday, 2 October
  BRAG AND BOMBAST   34

THE THIRD WEEK
Monday, 3 October – Sunday, 9 October
  DEMONSTRATIONS   43

THE FOURTH WEEK
Monday, 10 October – Sunday, 16 October
  THE AMAZONS   52

THE FIFTH WEEK
Monday, 17 October – Sunday, 23 October
  GUNS, MORE GUNS, STILL MORE GUNS   63

THE SIXTH WEEK
Monday, 24 October – Sunday, 30 October
  DISASTROUS NEWS   72

THE SEVENTH WEEK
Monday, 31 October – Sunday, 6 November
  INSURRECTION   80

THE EIGHTH WEEK
Monday, 7 November – Sunday, 13 November
  PARIS IN NOVEMBER   91

THE NINTH WEEK
Monday, 14 November – Sunday, 20 November
  PIGEONS AND BALLOONS   101

CONTENTS

THE TENTH WEEK   Page
Monday, 21 November – Sunday, 27 November
THE LULL BEFORE THE STORM   113

THE ELEVENTH WEEK
Monday, 28 November – Sunday, 4 December
THE GREAT SORTIE   123

THE TWELFTH WEEK
Monday, 5 December – Sunday, 11 December
AFTERMATH OF DEFEAT   134

THE THIRTEENTH WEEK
Monday, 12 December – Sunday, 18 December
WAITING FOR NEWS   144

THE FOURTEENTH WEEK
Monday, 19 December – Sunday, 25 December
LE BOURGET   153

THE FIFTEENTH WEEK
Monday, 26 December – Sunday, 1 January
THE END OF THE YEAR   162

THE SIXTEENTH WEEK
Monday, 2 January – Sunday, 8 January
PARIS UNDER FIRE   172

THE SEVENTEENTH WEEK
Monday, 9 January – Sunday, 15 January
HOPE DWINDLES   181

THE EIGHTEENTH WEEK
Monday, 16 January – Sunday, 22 January
BUZENVAL   188

THE NINETEENTH WEEK
Monday, 23 January – Saturday, 28 January
CAPITULATION   197

Epilogue   205

Bibliography   211

Index   215

ACKNOWLEDGMENT

The Author and Publishers wish to thank the following for permission to reproduce the illustrations which appear in this book:

The Mansell Collection, for fig. 2

Fig. 1 is from Armand Dayot, *L'Invasion – Le Siège – La Commune*, 1901; frontispiece from *Mémorial Illustré des Deux Sièges de Paris 1870–1871*, 1874. Chapter headings (An 'absence token') from the Author's Collection.

The Author and Publishers also wish to thank the Oxford University Press for permission to reproduce extracts from Dr. Baldick's *Pages from the Goncourt Journal*, and the Académie Goncourt, holders of the copyright, and the Librairie Ernest Flammarion, publishers of the complete French text, for permission to translate further passages from the *Goncourt Journal*.

Paris, 1870

Chanteloup

RIVER SEINE

St. Brice

Enghien

Montmagny

Pierre

Villetaneuse

ARGENTEUIL

Gennevilliers

ST

Poissy

Bezons

Colombes

Asnières

ST. GERMAIN
en Laye

Chatou

Croissy

FT. VALERIEN

Neuilly

Malmaison

P A R

Bougival

Buzenval

St. Cloud

Sèvres

Issy

Meudon

ISSY

MONTROUGE

VERSAILLES

Clamart

VANVES

BICET

Chaville

Bagneux

IVR

Trivaux
Fme.

Châtillon

Villejuif

Villacoublay

Plessis Piquet

Bicêtre

Sceaux

L'Hay

Abbaye aux Bois

Malabry

Chevilly

Bièvre

RIVER BIÈVRE

Saclay

Massy

Palaiseau

Longjumeau
to Ballainvilliers

14

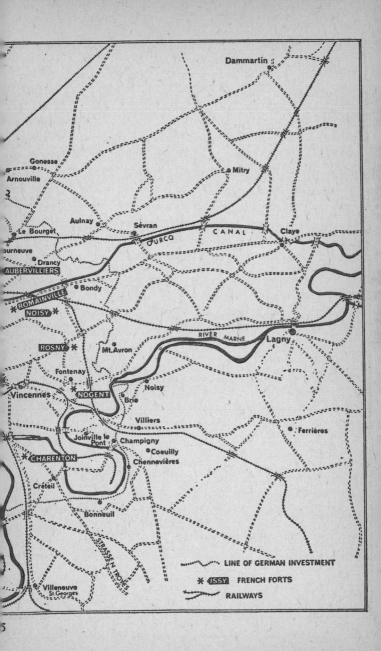

LINE OF GERMAN INVESTMENT

✳ ISSY FRENCH FORTS

RAILWAYS

Prologue

If, in the summer of 1870, some prophet gifted with second sight had foretold that within a matter of weeks Paris would be in a state of siege, he would have been laughed to scorn. For Paris was the *ville lumière*, the centre of civilization, the cosmopolitan capital of the world. Only three years before, in 1867, hundreds of thousands of foreigners, including the Tsar of Russia and the Kings of Prussia, Portugal, Bavaria and Sweden, had flocked to Paris to visit the breathtaking Universal Exhibition, to admire Baron Haussmann's new boulevards, to watch Napoleon III's splendid military parade in the Bois de Boulogne, to wine and dine and dance in an atmosphere of frenzied gaiety, and, inevitably, to go and see Hortense Schneider in *La Grande Duchesse de Gérolstein* at the Variétés, singing: *"Ah, que j'aime les militaires!"* There seemed to be no reason why the world should not go on coming to pay homage to the queen of cities, why this life of brilliance and pleasure should not continue indefinitely.

Even when Bismarck had manoeuvred Napoleon III into declaring war on 19 July, it never occurred to anyone to imagine that Paris might be in the slightest danger. The Minister of War assured the country that the French Army was "ready down to the last gaiter button", while Ollivier, the Prime Minister, declared that the Emperor's Government saw war coming "with a light heart". (He later explained that what he had meant was "with calm confidence", but his first, disastrous phrase was remembered against him.) Only pessimists recalled the Prussian victory over Austria at Sadowa in 1866, or suggested that the French army was fatally ill-organized and under-equipped; the vast majority of Frenchmen were convinced that they had the best soldiers, the best generals and (with the new breech-loading rifle, the *chassepot*, and the *mitrailleuse*) the best weapons in the world. Small wonder, then, that when torchlight processions of singing, cheering Parisians escorted the newly mobilized troops to the capital's stations on their way to the front, the boulevards echoed with the optimistic cry: "*À Berlin! À Berlin!*"

This optimistic mood lasted for over a fortnight, in spite of growing reports of utter disorganization and even mutiny in the army camps. Edmund de Goncourt, who had recently lost his brother Jules and had resumed his *Journal* as a palliative for his grief, recorded an incident on 6 August which demonstrated the population's hysterical eagerness for good news.

"From the Print Room of the Bibliothèque Impériale," he wrote,

I saw people running along the Rue Vivienne; I promptly ran after them. The steps of the Stock Exchange, from top to bottom, were a sea of bare heads, with hats flung into the air and every voice raised in a tremendous *Marseillaise*, the roar of which drowned the buzz of noise from the stock-brokers' enclosure inside the building. I have never seen such an outburst of enthusiasm. One kept running into men pale with emotion, children hopping around in excitement and women making drunken gestures. Capoul was singing the *Marseillaise* from the top of an omnibus in the Place de la Bourse; on the Boulevard, Marie Sasse was singing it standing in her carriage, practically carried along by the delirium of the mob.

But the dispatch announcing the defeat of the Crown Prince of Prussia and the capture of twenty-five thousand prisoners, the dispatch which everybody claimed to have read with his own eyes, the dispatch which I was told had been posted up inside the Stock Exchange, the dispatch which, by some strange hallucination, people thought they could actually see, telling me: "Look, there it is!" and pointing to a wall in the distance where there was nothing at all – this dispatch I was unable to find.

The explanation was simple: the dispatch did not exist. A rumour that the Crown Prince's army had been defeated had been started at the Stock Exchange – with obvious success –

in an attempt to rig the market. The very same evening, however, the Government learnt of two major defeats suffered by the French at Spicheren and Froeschwiller which left France open to invasion. It suddenly became obvious that Paris was in danger of attack, and hurried preparations started for its defence.

Paris had in fact been a fortified city since 1840, when Thiers had taken advantage of the Middle East crisis to provide the capital with a massive defence system: a high *enceinte* wall, 94 bastions, a moat, and, covering the approaches, 15 forts, Saint-Denis, de l'Est and Aubervilliers to the north, Romainville, Noisy, Rosny, Nogent and Charenton to the east, and Ivry, Bicêtre, Montrouge, Vanves, Issy and Châtillon to the south. Unfortunately, despite the Minister of War's assurance to the Empress that "the defence of Paris is assured", the fortifications were in a deplorable state of neglect. As a report by the Government of National Defence published in October revealed,

> the huge *enceinte* of the capital was not only unprovided with any arms but it had neither shelters nor powder-magazines nor cross-bars. Its military zone was covered with countless buildings, and sixty-nine avenues, some as much as eighty yards wide, crossed it in all directions. As for the forts, they were not in a state of readiness either, and the outer works had for the most part been effaced by the passage of time.

Shocked by the condition into which the fortifications had fallen, the authorities set up a committee to put them in a state of defence. Huge obstructions were built outside the city, woods razed, road, rail and river approaches blocked, redoubts constructed and mines laid over a huge area. Over 3,000 heavy guns were brought to Paris and installed in the forts or inside the *enceinte*, while workshops in the city which could be converted into armament factories were set to work producing shells, *chassepots* and *mitrailleuses*. The Louvre was turned into a huge armament workshop, the Gare d'Orléans into a balloon-factory, and the Gare de Lyon into a cannon-foundry. Within a month Paris had been transformed from a city of pleasure into a massive and to all appearances impregnable fortress.

At the same time as the city was being armed and fortified it was also being provisioned on a vast scale. Writing to her mother, Louise Swanton Belloc, on 31 August, Lily Ballot noted that "everything goes on looking much as usual, but Paris is certainly getting ready for a siege. Droves of cattle pass my windows early each morning, and the garden of the Luxembourg is full of sheep." So was the Bois de Boulogne, where a quarter of a million sheep and 40,000 oxen were put to grass. Large stocks of flour and corn were also accumulated in the city, and flourmills were set up in the Gare du Nord. Unfortunately, in this respect as also in the matter of fuel, the authorities underestimated the city's requirements. Since nobody expected the siege to last into the winter, stocks of flour and coal were calculated for 12 weeks at the most. This understandable blunder, like the less excusable omission to bring sufficient milch cows into the capital, was to lead to considerable hardship in the later stages of the siege.

In the midst of all these preparations the French army suffered overwheming defeat at Sedan, where the Emperor surrendered on 2 September with over 80,000 men, and the next day the news reached Paris. "What a sight, that of Paris this evening", wrote Edmond de Goncourt, on the 3rd,

> with the news of MacMahon's defeat and the capture of the Emperor spreading from group to group! Who can describe the consternation written on every face, the sound of aimless steps pacing the streets at random, the anxious conversations of shop-keepers and *concierges* on their doorsteps, the crowds collecting at street-corners and outside town-halls, the siege of the news-paper kiosks, the triple line of readers gathering around every gas-lamp, and on chairs at the back of shops the dejected figures of women whom one senses to be alone and deprived of their men?
>
> Then there is the menacing roar of the crowd, in which stupe-faction has begun to give place to anger. Next there are great crowds moving along the boulevards, led by flags and shouting: "Down with the Empire!" And finally there is the wild, tumul-tuous spectacle of a nation determined to perish or to save itself by an enormous effort, by one of those impossible feats of revolutionary times.

The overthrow of the Second Empire followed inevitably and peacefully on the 4th. While the Empress, who had con-tributed to the downfall of the régime by refusing to allow her husband to return to Paris, slipped out of the Tuileries and took refuge with the American dentist Dr. Evans, the populace invaded the Legislative Assembly, forced the proc-lamation of a Provisional Government, and took the republican leaders to the Hôtel de Ville, where the Third Republic was proclaimed. "All around", wrote Edmond de Goncourt, who was outside the Chamber when he heard the news,

> one could hear people greeting each other with the excited words: "It's happened!" And right at the top of the façade, a man tore the blue and white strips from the tricolour, leaving only the red waving in the air. On the terrace overlooking the Quai d'Orsay, infantrymen were stripping the shrubs and handing green branches over the parapet to women fighting to take them. At the gates of the Tuileries, near the great pool, the gilt "N's" were hidden beneath old newspapers, and wreaths of immortelles hung in the place of the missing eagles. . . .

Oblivious of the terrible defeat which France had suffered and of the growing danger which was threatening Paris, the people went wild with joy at the overthrowing of the Empire. "No words of mine", wrote the horrified Adelaide de Montgolfier, the daughter of the inventor of the balloon,

> can paint the horrible sight I have seen today. Paris drunk with joy – joy because a Republic has been proclaimed! Madmen, madwomen dancing in the streets. As you know, I never cared for the Second Empire; but I am revolted at what is going on now, and I long for a bomb to obliterate me.

Yet the revolution had been a bloodless one, and there was nothing vindictive about the triumph of the Republic. True, the new government, which called itself the Government of National Defence, was such a heterogeneous body that it could scarcely have carried out any sweeping revolutionary measures. It was largely composed of lawyers who had belonged to the opposition in the Legislative Assembly, and included Legitimists and Orleanists as well as ardent Republicans such as Gambetta and the demagogic Rochefort. The President of the Government, General Trochu, had actually been Military Governor of Paris during the last three weeks of the Empire, and had promised the Empress to defend her and the imperial régime "as a Catholic, a Breton and a soldier". He now found himself at the head of a régime of which he could not approve, and committed to the defence of a city in whose garrison and defences he had very little confidence.

It must have been with some trepidation that Trochu learnt of the imminent arrival in Paris of France's greatest Republican and the Empire's most famous exile: Victor Hugo. The poet crossed the frontier from Belgium at four o'clock in the

FRANÇAIS !

Le Peuple a devancé la Chambre qui hésitait. Pour sauver la Patrie en danger, il a demandé la République.

Il a mis ses représentants non au pouvoir, mais au péril.

La République a vaincu l'invasion en 1792; la République est proclamée.

La Révolution est faite au nom du droit du salut public.

Citoyens, veillez sur la Cité qui vous est confiée; demain vous serez, avec l'armée, les vengeurs de la Patrie !

Emmanuel Arago,	Garnier Pagès,
Crémieux,	Magnin,
Dorian,	Ordinaire,
Jules Favre.	E. Pelletan,
Jules Ferry,	Ernest Picard,
Guyot-Montpayroux,	Jules Simon.
Léon Gambetta,	

Hôtel-de-Ville, 5 septembre 1870.

Paris,—Imp. Serrière et Cⁱᵉ, rue Montmartre, 107

Fig. 1 *A proclamation of the Government of National Defence*

afternoon of 5 September, bringing with him a copy of *Les Châtiments*, the ferocious book of poems in which he had scourged the "little Napoleon" and prophesied his downfall, and which was to become the staple reading and reciting diet of the besieged capital. He reached Paris in the evening, to a delirious welcome from the crowds, in the course of which he took the opportunity to disclaim any intention of seizing power.

"We arrived in Paris at 9.35", he wrote in his diary.

A huge crowd was waiting for me. An indescribable welcome. I spoke four times. Once from the balcony of a café and three times from my carriage. When I took leave of this constantly growing crowd, which escorted me to Paul Meurice's, in the Avenue Frochot, I said to the people: "In one hour you have repaid me for twenty years of exile." They sang the *Marseillaise* and the *Chant du Départ*. They shouted: "Long live Victor Hugo!" Every now and then I could hear lines from *Les Châtiments* in the crowd. I gave over six thousand handshakes. The journey from the Gare du Nord to the Rue de Laval took two hours. They wanted to take me to the Hôtel de Ville. I shouted: "No, citizens! I have not come to overthrow the Provisional Government of the Republic, but to support it."

Hugo kept his word. Although in the following months he was repeatedly urged by left-wing Republicans to take over the government from Trochu, he invariably refused. His activity during the siege was largely confined to attending readings of *Les Châtiments* and issuing proclamations in his most grandiloquent style.

It would have been hard for a writer of Hugo's eloquence to resist the temptation to exercise his gift, for he had scarcely arrived in Paris before a positive spate of proclamations began to issue from the Government: a message to Elihu Washburne, the American Minister in Paris, expressing the Government's gratitude to the United States for immediately recognizing the new republic; an announcement from Trochu to the people of Paris, stating that the enemy was marching on Paris and calling on all citizens to show courage and patriotism; and on the same day, 6 September, a circular from Jules Favre, the new Foreign Minister, to the French diplomatic agents abroad, expounding the Republic's attitude to the war.

"The King of Prussia", wrote Favre,

has declared that he was making war, not on France, but on the imperial dynasty.

The dynasty has fallen. Free France is rising to her feet.

Does the King of Prussia wish to continue an unholy struggle which will be at least as baneful to him as to us? Does he wish to give the nineteenth-century world this cruel spectacle of two nations destroying each other, and, oblivious of humanity, reason and science, piling up ruins and corpses?

He is free to do as he wishes; let him assume this responsibility before the world and before history!

If this is a challenge, we accept it. We will not yield one inch of our territory, nor one stone of our fortresses. . . .

Not to be outdone, Hugo published a stirring *Appeal to the Germans* on the 9th, in which he described Paris as "the city of cities . . . in which the beating of Europe's heart is felt", and asked:

Is the nineteenth century to witness the dreadful sight of a nation fallen from civilization to barbarism, abolishing the city of the nations, Germany extinguishing Paris, Germania raising the axe against Gaul?

Like Favre he concluded with a defiant challenge:

Burn our buildings, they are only our bones; their smoke will take shape, become huge and alive, and rise up into the sky; and there will be seen for ever on the horizon of the nations, above us, above you, above all things, above all people, asserting our glory, asserting your shame, this great phantom composed of darkness and light: Paris!

I have spoken. Germans, if you persist, so be it, you have been warned: continue, go to, attack the walls of Paris. Under your shells and your gunfire, she will defend herself. As for myself, an old man, I shall be there, unarmed. It befits me to be with people who die: I pity you for being with kings who kill.

Hugo, like Favre and indeed the vast majority of Parisians, was convinced that if, by some extraordinary mischance, the name of the Republic, redolent of the glory of the first French revolution, failed to work its magic on the Germans, then the name of Paris, the *ville lumière* and city of cities, would. There were only a few sceptics in the French capital who realized that it would take more than a change of régime or the incantation of a place-name to halt the German flood. One such sceptic was Henry Labouchère, the Paris correspondent of the *Daily News*, who became known to the British public through his vivid dispatches as the Besieged Resident in Paris.

When Hugo followed his *Appeal to the Germans* with a no less grandiloquent *Appeal to the French*, he commented sardonically:

> Victor Hugo has published an address to the nation. You may judge of its essentially practical spirit by the following specimen: "Rouen, draw thy sword! Lille, take up thy musket! Bordeaux, take up thy gun! Marseilles, sing thy song and be terrible!" I suggest Marseilles may sing her song a long time before the effect of her vocal efforts will in any way prevent the Prussians from carrying out their plans.

Meanwhile troops were pouring into Paris to man the defences. The core of the defence force consisted of two regiments from General Vinoy's 13th Corps which had been brought back from Mézières with a few thousand refugees from MacMahon's forces; some 3,000 Marines; and 8,000 sailors, most of them hardy Bretons. Two new corps of untrained conscripts completed the regular forces inside Paris, which altogether numbered just over 100,000 men. Over and above this regular garrison there were the Gardes Mobiles, hopelessly undisciplined conscripts from both Paris and the provinces; the aptly named Gardes Sédentaires, or National Guards, a militia composed of all male citizens between the ages of 25 and 35; and a host of minor volunteer organizations formed by every sort of occupational or national group, from Polish exiles to British residents and from journalists to sportsmen.

The whole of this gigantic force turned out on 13 September to be reviewed by Trochu, lining the boulevards all the way from the Place de la Bastille to the Arc de Triomphe. It was an impressive sight, and even the sceptical Edmond de Goncourt found that it roused feelings of hope in him.

"All of a sudden," he wrote,

> in the noise of the drums, a great silence fell and men's eyes met as in a promise to die; then from this concentrated enthusiasm there came a great cry, a cry from the breast of "*Vive la France! Vive la République! Vive Trochu!*" greeting the quick gallop of the General and his escort.

The march-past began of the National Guards, with their rifles decorated with dahlias, roses and bows of red ribbon – an endless march-past in which the *Marseillaise*, murmured rather than sung, left in the distance, behind the slow march of the men, something like the pious, sonorous strains of a male prayer.

And the sight of those grey beards mingled with beardless chins, those frock-coats side by side with smocks, at the sight of those fathers, some of whom were holding by the hand their little girls who had slipped into the ranks, at the sight of this amalgam of working-men and tradesmen turned soldiers who were ready to die together, one wondered whether one of those miracles might not occur which come to the help of nations which have faith.

Trochu, inspecting his heterogeneous forces with a colder eye, was infinitely less confident about their capabilities, and decided that it would be folly to use them in any attack on the Germans. His order of the day to the Gardes Mobiles the next day revealed what he really thought of their fighting abilities, for he wrote:

> If the enemy, by a sudden onslaught or a surprise attack or through an open breach, penetrated the *enceinte*, he would come up against the barricades which are being planned and his leading forces would be thrown back by the successive attacks of ten reserve detachments.

In other words, the huge Paris garrison was to be kept on the defensive, within the city walls, to wait for the German attack and fight if necessary in the streets, where the inexperience of the National Guards would not matter.

The success of this line of action depended on one thing: a German attack. But Bismarck had no intention of launching an attack on the Paris defences, still less of committing the German troops to the hazards of street-fighting. "There is a republic in Paris," he explained in a letter to his son.

> Whether it will last or how it will develop we must wait and see. My desire is that we let the people stew in their own juice and that we make ourselves at home in the conquered departments until we can go forward. If we do this too soon we shall prevent them from quarrelling among themselves. Internal peace cannot last long with this socialistic crowd at the head of affairs. ...

The final orders for the investment of the capital were issued by Moltke from Château-Thierry on 15 September, and on the 17th an encircling movement began, with the Crown Prince of Saxony investing the city from the north and the Crown Prince of Prussia from the south. On the 18th the last mail-train left the city along the Western Line, and on the 19th the last remaining telegraph lines to the west were cut. The Siege of Paris had begun.

THE FIRST WEEK

Monday, 19 September – Sunday, 25 September

Early Alarms

The first official intimation that Paris received that she was completely isolated was a gentle note in the *Journal Officiel* urging the population "not to feel surprised at the absence of telegraphic intelligence from the country", followed by an announcement from the Director General of the Post Office that "as a result of the interruption of railway communications, only *ordinary letters* for the departments and abroad can be accepted".

With characteristic Parisian scepticism, the population, both native and foreign, refused to credit this fantastic news at first. Hundreds of unbelievers streamed out to the western suburbs to challenge the truth of the official announcements, only to return chastened by the sight of the bridges at Sèvres and Saint-Cloud blown up and of disbanded, routed troops pouring into the capital. Not so easily discouraged, a party of four Britons, armed with visas, hampers of food and wine, and a prominently displayed Union Jack, drove off towards the French outposts in a travelling carriage, confident that nobody would stop them. They were turned back by General Ducrot, who told them: "If you English want to get shot, we will shoot you ourselves to save you trouble", but tried again the following day with cheerful stubbornness.

As for the "ordinary letters" which the Post Office agreed to accept "for the departments and abroad", no one had any

clear idea how they were going to be conveyed to their destination, least of all the postal authorities. When Labouchère
asked the postal clerks when and how his letters would leave
Paris, they replied with a shrug-shouldered "Qui sait?" and
in the post office yard he saw postmen perched on the boxes
of their carts at the correct hour for driving away the mail –
but with no horses in front of them. Finally, however, on the
21st, 28 postmen tried to break through the German cordon
on foot; only one, a man called Brare, succeeded, but although he managed to make four more successful journeys,
he was caught at Chatou on his sixth trip and shot on the
spot. After that it was recognized by the Parisian authorities
that the only possible way of sending mail out of the city left
to them was by balloon.

On 24 September the first postal balloon to leave Paris, the
Neptune, rose from the Place Saint-Pierre in Montmartre at
7.15 a.m., carrying over 200 pounds' weight of dispatches on
thin paper. As was only to be expected of the commander of
the newly-formed Balloon Corps, the great balloonist-
photographer-caricaturist-showman Nadar, *alias* Félix Tournachon, there was quite a ceremony to mark the occasion.
The aged Adelaide de Montgolfier had been invited to write
and send off the first letter, and walked over two miles to see
the *Neptune* released ("How delightful", she wrote to Madame
Belloc, "to think that my dear father's invention is now proving of such great value to his country!"); and a large crowd
shouted "Vive la République!" as the balloon rose into the
air. A final touch of showmanship was provided when a
shower of pieces of paper fell from the car of the *Neptune* on
to the Prussian lines. These were 4,000 of Nadar's visiting-
cards, each with one corner turned down in the ritual manner.

Meanwhile the martial enthusiasm of the population was
being maintained at a high pitch, largely by means of parades
and demonstrations. The focus of this enthusiasm during the
early days of the siege was the statue of the City of Strasbourg,
which rapidly became a sort of idol, hidden under heaps of
flowers, with poets declaiming odes in front of it and pedlars
hawking portraits of Strasbourg's heroic defender, General
Uhrich. A more useful form of ceremony – at least in appearance – was enacted in front of the Panthéon, where a platform
had been set up, occupied by various officers of the National
Guard, the local mayor, and a number of clerks, whose

business it was to enrol the names of all Parisians who were willing to join the "marching battalions" of the National Guard. A ribbon of white linen inscribed with the words "Citizens, the country is in danger!" flapped in the breeze; a band played at intervals; and a crowd of parents, sisters and sweethearts stood around applauding as their menfolk marched forward to volunteer for duty. But duty appealed to these citizen soldiers only if it excluded discomfort and danger, and impartial observers expressed grave doubts as to their martial qualities. "Lor' bless you, sir," a British coachman told Labouchère,

> I'd rather have ten thousand Englishmen than the lot of them. In my stable I make my men obey me, but these chaps they don't seem to care what their officers says to them. I seed them drill this morning; a pretty green lot they was. Why, sir, giving them fellows chassepots is much like giving watches to naked savages.

The first encounter between the Germans and the capital's defenders seemed to confirm the coachman's pessimism, for the French troops fled in panic from the Châtillon plateau on the 19th. Edmond de Goncourt, who met a squad of zouaves near the Madeleine, recorded in his *Journal:*

> One of them, laughing nervously, told me that there had been no battle, that it had been a general rout straight away, that he had not fired a single shot. I was struck by the gaze of these men: the fugitive's gaze is vague, shifty, glassy, settling nowhere.

Henry Markheim, who wrote under the pen-name of "the Oxford Graduate", obtained a similar impression from a scene he witnessed in the main avenues leading from Châtillon; a scene of fugitives running between military carts and ambulance-waggons while mounted gendarmes galloped past to cut off their retreat. "Disbanded zouaves", he wrote,

> were explaining to the people, with much gesticulation, how they had "retreated" – not from want of courage, that was simply impossible, but because they had fallen short of ammunition; and some had the barefacedness to show their cartridge-boxes, which, on closer examination, generally proved to be quite full. Young linesmen held forth to crowds of compassionating women; all told one tale: "*Nous sommes trahis;* Trochu has led us to the slaughter. The Prussians have taken our *mitrailleuses*; they will be in tonight; the Fort of Vanves is going to be blown up." "Poor things," the women would say, with the unlimited pity

of the female heart, and they would straightway supply the betrayed heroes with all manner of food and drink. But then National Guards came blustering up and marched the fugitives off to the nearest guard-house. ...

General Trochu promptly issued a circular in his customary grandiloquent style, in an attempt to bolster up the morale of garrison and population. "I call on all good citizens", he wrote,

to react energetically all around them, by their advice and their example, against any attempts at discouragement; to revive faltering spirits by their attitude, and to persuade everybody that only constancy can shorten the duration of this testing period and ensure success.

But the city's morale took another plunge with rumours that Jules Favre had left Paris to negotiate an armistice with Bismarck at Ferrières – rumours which were confirmed on the 21st by the publication of the Foreign Minister's report on these secret conversations. Bismarck, according to this report, had agreed to the election and reunion at Tours of a French National Assembly to negotiate peace, but had insisted on the occupation of Strasbourg, Toul and Phalsbourg as guarantees, whereupon Favre had "nearly fainted" and "choked back his tears". Although the Prussian conditions had been rejected, the left-wing clubs in Paris, particularly in the working-class district of Belleville, felt sure that the Government would capitulate in the near future unless its resolve was stiffened by popular agitation. A large demonstration was accordingly held in the Place de la Concorde on the 21st, and the next day a deputation went to the Hôtel de Ville to ask if the Government was determined to resist to the end and not to negotiate until the last Prussian had been expelled from France. Jules Simon replied that the Government was resolved to die rather than surrender; Étienne Arago, the new Mayor of Paris, declared that the population could rest assured that he would never hand over the keys of the capital to the King of Prussia; and on the 23rd the Government issued an official declaration repudiating rumours of surrender and reiterating its policy of "neither an inch of our territory nor a single stone of our fortresses". But the confidence of the population had been shaken, and the rumours persisted.

In the atmosphere of suspicion and uneasiness reigning in

Paris, spy-mania quickly took hold of the people. As Maurice d'Hérisson, one of Trochu's aides-de-camp, wrote in his memoirs,

> anyone who did not speak French with purity was suspected, the masses being, besides, incapable of distinguishing between the various foreign languages spoken in their midst. Englishmen, Americans, Swedes, Spaniards and Alsatians were arrested alike. A similar fate befell all those people, who, either in dress or manner, betrayed anything unusual. Stammerers were arrested because they tried to speak too quickly; dumb people because they did not speak at all, and the deaf because they did not seem to understand what was said to them. The sewer-men who emerged from the sewers were arrested because they spoke Piedmontese.

Any reason was good enough to justify denunciation and arrest. Thus the famous cartoonist Cham was arrested because his pseudonym was considered suspiciously Germanic. Luckily for him, he was a close friend of Henri Rochefort, to whom he wrote:

> My dear fellow, I have been arrested by the Police Commissioner of the Eighth Arrondissement, who absolutely insists on shooting me straight away in his office, as a Prussian spy, on the pretext that I have an English accent. You would be doing me a kindness if you informed this official that I have never liked working for the King of Prussia.*

Lights appearing in upper windows at night were a favourite object of suspicion, and even the least credulous citizens tended to get excited about mysterious lamps. Thus Victor Hugo noted in his diary:

> At midnight last night I was returning home along the Rue de Richelieu, which was deserted, dark and so to speak asleep at the time, when I saw a window open on the sixth floor of a very high house just beyond the Bibliothèque Nationale, and a very bright light, which appeared to be that of an oil-lamp, appear and disappear several times; then the window closed and the street became dark again. Was it a signal?

Less peaceful folk than Hugo would have taken steps to satisfy their curiosity, and in the early days of the siege there were countless reports of angry crowds bursting into rooms where an unusual light had been seen. Henri d'Alméras records one such incident which occurred on 25 September in the Ternes district. "At a fifth-floor window", he writes,

*A French idiom which means "working without payment".

31

a red and green light kept appearing and disappearing, a sort of portable lighthouse which some criminal hand was doubtless operating. Some worthy citizens climbed up to the fifth floor and rushed into the flat. There they found a very old woman patriotically engaged in making lint bandages, in the company of a red and green parrot in a cage by the window, and who, with great courtesy, asked the intruders if they had breakfasted. The mob refused to recognize their mistake. They did not dare to take the parrot to the police-station, but they forced the old woman to put out her lamp.

The irritation and anxiety of the Parisian population took other, spiteful forms. "Absence tokens", corresponding to the white feathers beloved of patriotic English ladies during the Boer War, were produced to await the return of Parisians who had left the capital before the beginning of the siege: they were metal or cardboard disks with, on one side, a drawing of a Parisian taking to the air with a suitcase in one hand, and on the other an ironical inscription testifying to the Republic's gratitude to such and such a "voluntary absentee". And when a score of infantrymen who had fled from the enemy at Courbevoie were arrested at the gates, they were brought into Paris with their caps and tunics back-to-front, their hands tied behind their backs, and a huge notice hung round their necks reading: "This is a wretched coward who abandoned his post in the face of the enemy. Honest folk are invited to spit in his face."

At the end of the week, however, the people's spirits lifted, and for most Parisians Sunday was a day of outings like any other, with the added spice of a little excitement. "The Champs-Élysées", records the Besieged Resident,

and the Avenue de la Grande Armée were full of people. Monsieur shone by his absence; he was at the ramparts, or was supposed to be there; but his wife, his children, his *bonne*, and his kitchen wench issued forth, oblivious alike of dull care and of bombarding Prussians, to enjoy themselves after their wont by gossiping and lolling in the sun. The Strasbourg fetish had its usual crowd of admirers. Every bench in the Champs-Élysées was occupied. Guitars twanged, organs were ground, merry-go-rounds were in full swing, and had it not been that here and there some regiment was drilling, one would have supposed oneself in some country fair. There were but few men; no fine toilets, no private carriages. It was a sort of Greenwich Park. At the Arc de Triomphe was a crowd trying to discover what was going on upon the heights above Argenteuil. Some declared they saw Prussians, while others with opera-glasses declared that the supposed Prussians were only trees. In the Avenue de l'Impératrice was a large crowd gazing at the Fort of Mont-Valérien. This fort, because I presume it is the strongest for defence, is the favourite of the Parisians. They love it as a sailor loves his ship. "If I were near enough," said a girl near me, "I would kiss it." "Let me carry your kiss to it," replied a Mobile, and the pair embraced, amid the cheers of the people round them. At Auteuil there were *fiacres* full of sightseers, come to watch the Prussian batteries at Meudon, which could be distinctly seen. Occasionally, too, there came a puff of smoke from one of the gunboats. . . .

The sun shone on Paris, and for a few hours Paris forgot that she was encircled by a ruthless enemy, determined to obtain her surrender by force or famine.

Monday, 26 September – Sunday, 2 October

Brag and Bombast

The second week of the siege saw scarcely more military action than the first, but the lull in the fighting was more than compensated for by the din of proclamations and discourses made by prelates and poets, journalists and politicians. Some of these addresses were made to the Germans, such as the philosopher Ernest Renan's letter to Dr. Strauss, reminding him that while it was true that conquerors sat in Valhalla, military virtues were nowhere mentioned in the New Testament among those which gained the Kingdom of Heaven. Most, however, were directed at the writer's fellow citizens. Thus Edgar Quinet appealed to the Government to order a *levée en masse* and organize a determined resistance to the enemy. Bishop Dupanloup sorrowfully announced that Paris was "passing through a period of justice and expiation" and commented that "the hour of chastisement is better than the hour of scandal". And Victor Hugo, infuriated by the lack of response to his *Appeal to the Germans*, published an inflammatory *Manifesto to the Parisians*.

"It seems", he wrote,

> that the Prussians have decreed that France shall be Germany and that Germany shall be Prussia; that I who speak to you, born in Lorraine, am a German; that it is dark at noon; that the Euphrates, the Nile, the Tiber and the Seine are tributaries of the Spree; that the city which for four centuries has illuminated the

34

globe no longer has any reason to exist; that Berlin is enough; that Montaigne, Rabelais, d'Aubigné, Pascal, Corneille, Molière, Montesquieu, Diderot, Jean-Jacques, Mirabeau, Danton and the French Revolution have never existed; that we no longer have any need of Voltaire since we have Monsieur de Bismarck, that the world belongs to the vanquished of Napoleon the Great and the victors of Napoleon the Little; that henceforth thought, conscience, poetry, art, progress and intelligence begin at Potsdam and finish at Spandau; that there shall be no more cilivization, no more Europe, no more Paris; that we are Gomorrah and that they, the Prussians, are the fire of heaven. This decree, Parisians, is being executed on you. To destroy Paris is to mutilate the world. The attack is being made *urbi et orbi.* With Paris extinguished and only Prussia entitled to shine, Europe will be in darkness.

Hugo went on to repudiate this possibility as unthinkable. The old contest between light and darkness, the archangel and the dragon was beginning again, and it would have the same conclusion as of old: Prussia would be overthrown. Yet Hugo went on to predict that Paris would die, and concluded in a disheartening but sublime peroration:

Let Europe prepare for an impossible sight; let her prepare to see the extraordinary city burn. Paris, which amused the world, is going to terrify it. The world will see how well Paris can die. Already the Pantheon is wondering how it can receive beneath its roof this people which is about to earn the right to the shelter of its dome. O Paris, you have crowned the statue of Strasbourg with flowers; history will crown you with stars.

No doubt deciding that after this tirade any further addresses to the Parisians would be superfluous for a while, Louis Blanc turned his attention to the English. In the early part of the war, England's attitude had been openly sympathetic to Prussia, and at the beginning of the investment of Paris *The Times* had speculated with puritanical relish as to how long "the city of luxury and pleasure" would stand up to the afflictions of a siege. Since then *The Times* leaders, closely reflecting the views of the British Government, had repeatedly expressed the opinion that the French should capitulate. "The protests that have been made", it declared,

against all suggestions of peace so long as a Prussian remains within the French frontier do not appear to spring from the virtue of patriotism, which means a passionate attachment to freedom, and the independence of a self-governed people, so much

35

as from the vice of patriotism, which is nothing more than vanity become national.

Now Louis Blanc, in an open letter to the English people, asked them to imagine their feelings if London were besieged and threatened with bombardment, and declared that Prussia's territorial ambitions constituted a danger to other countries besides France.

"The great danger for Europe", he wrote, in a solemn warning which was to be repeated by the French and ignored by the English countless times during the next 70 years,

lies at the moment in the violent character of Prussian militarism; in that spirit which, not content with Alsace and Lorraine, covets Soissons. It is the same spirit which devoured part of Denmark, the same which pillaged Frankfurt, the same which proclaimed the annexation of Hanover as justified by the right of conquest, the same which dismisses as ridiculous the principle that populations are not transferable without their consent and that a people is not a herd of cattle. If the English people understand that our cause is that of the whole world, being that of justice, it is for them to act accordingly; it is for them to consider, in relation to themselves, the consequence of the uncontrolled right of conquest. A nation which sanctions by its indifference the saturnalia of force runs the risk of suffering them, and deserves them.

This open letter, as was only to be expected, had no effect whatever in England, although it did something to modify the suspicious attitude of the Parisian population towards British residents in the capital. *Les Nouvelles* had only recently published an article entitled "English Spies", proposing that to simplify the question of whether they were spies or not, all the English in Paris should be shot; and the correspondent of the *Daily News*, on being denounced by a passer-by as a suspicious character, had been obliged to jump on to a café chair and make an impromptu speech in praise of France in order to escape ill-treatment at the hands of the crowd. Now, however, the newspapers suddenly changed their tune and printed reports of massive pro-French demonstrations in England to which the population gave immediate credence. On 30 September the whole of the Parisian press reported that a meeting of 400,000 people had been held in London, addressed by eminent M.P.'s and leaders of industry, at which resolutions were adopted denouncing Queen Victoria and calling on Gladstone to choose between resigning and declaring war on Prussia. And on 2 October the *Journal Officiel* filled two columns with a letter to Jules Favre from a certain Monsieur de Rohan, "delegate of the democracy of England", informing him that a friend who had arrived from London (he did not specify how) had brought news of a huge meeting in favour of France, and that this meeting represented the opinion of the whole of England. The paper also published Favre's reply, which expressed his sincere thanks for "the sentiments which have been so nobly expressed in the name of the English Nation". For a few days British residents in Paris basked in their resulting popularity, and took care not to voice their conviction that – as Labouchère put it – "Monsieur de Rohan's residence in England is in the vicinty of Tooley Street".

The reports of pro-French demonstrations in England were in fact restrained and well-nigh credible in comparison with some of the lurid inventions retailed every day by the Paris newspapers and greedily accepted by their readers. Two million Germans, Paris was told, had already been killed in battle. Three thousand war-widows, in deep mourning, had demonstrated in Berlin in favour of peace. Moltke, Prince Frederick-Charles, and the Crown Prince of Prussia had died on the field of battle, while Bismarck had been killed trying to repress a revolt of Bavarian troops. King William himself had gone mad, his weak brain having been unable to withstand the excess of his remorse. And at the beginning of October *Le Soir* informed its no doubt surprised but credulous readers that Napoleon III, escaping from captivity, had rejoined the French troops at Sedan, entered Berlin in triumph at their head, and there proclaimed the Republic.

Even more probable, or rather less wildly improbable, pieces of news given by the Paris papers turned out, more often than not, to have no foundation in fact. For example, it was reported that at Versailles the German troops were pillaging the town, raping the women and generally terrorizing the population. In fact, as all neutral observers agreed, the Germans in Versailles were behaving themselves well, flattered and fawned upon by French tradesmen who were making a good living out of their new customers and who deplored the capital's "stupid" resistance. Similarly, every other day there appeared news of some new exploit by the gunboat *Farcy*, which was constantly silencing Prussian batteries at Meudon or Saint-Cloud. But, as was revealed after the war, the *Farcy* was the most useless if also the most decorative element of the Parisian defence system: its gun was so heavy that it could not be fired safely except at very close range, while its hull was so thin that rifle bullets could have pierced it.

In this second week of the siege, however, the people of of Paris were in no mood to submit good news to an over-critical examination. The anxiety of the early days had given way to an almost hysterical optimism, characterized by brag and bombast. As one English correspondent explained to his readers,

> Joseph Prudhomme, that typical representative of bread-and-butter respectability, who the other day was ready for peace at any price rather than endure a siege, is so delighted at having made the discovery, first, that he can do without Madame Prudhomme, his spouse, whom the good soul fondly imagines to be quite safe in the country beyond the reach of Uhlans, and secondly, that he can hold a gun in his hands and mount guard with it:—in a word, he is so enraptured with the proofs of his valour, which he displays by night at the ramparts, and retails by day to his customers, that he is actually developed into a full-blown hero, and he proudly talks of Paris being impregnable.

Another correspondent wrote contemptuously of the military dandies who paraded the boulevards "twirling their moustache with the one hand and holding on to the saddle with the other", while the passers-by gaped at them in admiration. "No contrast can be greater", he declared,

> than that which exists between the Parisian Bobadils and the provincial Mobiles. The latter are quiet and orderly, eager to drill and without a vestige of bluster; these poor peasants are of a very different stuff from the emasculated, conceited scum which has palmed itself off on Europe as representative Frenchmen. The families with whom they lodge speak with wonder of their sobriety, their decency and their simple ways, and in their hearts almost despise them because they do not ravish their daughters or pillage their cellers; and neither swear every half hour to die for their country, nor yell the *Marseillaise*. If Paris be saved, it will be thanks to them and to the working men of the capital. But it will be the old *sic vos non vobis* story; their brave deeds and un-demonstrative heroism will be forgotten, and Jules and Alphonse, the dandies and braggarts of the Boulevard, will swear to their own heroism.

A fair sample of the bragging which was going on all over Paris was given by Labouchère on 30 September. "I went this morning", he wrote,

> into a shop, the proprietor of which, a bootmaker, I have long known, and I listened with interest to the conversation of this worthy man with some of his neighbours who had dropped in to have a gossip, and to congratulate him on his martial achievements, as he had been on guard in a bastion. We first discussed why the Army of the Loire had not arrived, and we came to the conclusion that it was engaged in rallying Bazaine. "I should like to read your English newspapers now", said one; "your *Times* told us we ought to cede Alsace and Lorraine, but its editor must now acknowledge that Paris is invincible." I told him that I felt convinced that he did so regularly every morning. "No peace," shouted a little tailor, who had been prancing about on an imaginary steed, killing imaginary Prussians, "we have made a pact with death; the world knows now what are the consequences of attacking us." The all-absorbing question of subsistence then came up, and some one remarked that beef would give out sooner than mutton. "We must learn", observed a jolly-looking grocer, "to vanquish the prejudices of our stomachs. Even those who do not like mutton must make the sacrifice of their taste to their country." I mildly suggested that perhaps in a few weeks the stomachs which had a prejudice against rats would have to overcome it. At this the countenance of the gossips fell considerably, when the bootmaker, after mysteriously closing the door, whispered: "A secret was confided to me this morning by an intimate friend of General Trochu. There is a tunnel which connects Paris with the provinces, and through it flocks and herds are entering the town." This cheered us up amazingly. My bootmaker's wife came in to help him off with his military accoutrements; so, with a compliment about Venus disarming Mars, I withdrew.

Alas, no flocks and herds were being led through tunnels into Paris, and the food situation was beginning to deteriorate. True, for the rich the only problem which had so far arisen was whether their diet was being adulterated with horse-meat. Thus Edmond de Goncourt wrote in his *Journal* for 1 October:

> Today, at Peters' restaurant, I was served some roast beef that was watery, devoid of fat, and streaked with white sinews; and my painter's eye noticed that it was a dark red colour very different from the pinky red of beef. The waiter could give me only a feeble assurance that this horse was beef.

For the poorer people of Paris, on the other hand, who could not eat out, the problem was of obtaining any meat at all. To begin with, the butchers had refused to sell at the prices fixed by the authorities, and there had been some ugly demonstrations. On 28 September the Government announced that 500 oxen and 4,000 sheep would be slaughtered every day and sold to the butchers at a price enabling them to make a profit of 20 per cent. But the amount of meat involved was so small that the butchers opened their shops only every fourth day – the day when their allotment was delivered – and found themselves besieged, not only by their regular customers, but by the customers of other butchers whose shops were shut. The result was the formation of lines of customers – or *queues*, to use the new French word for this phenomenon – as early as two or three o'clock in the morning. There was constant squabbling between those who had to wait standing and those who had folding stools, those whose feet froze into the pavement and those who were provided with foot-warmers, those who waited alone for hours and those who were relieved by members of their family. It was becoming increasingly obvious that the Government would have to institute a system of meat-rationing before long, but meanwhile the population was left to shift for itself.

As for other foodstuffs, bread was still quite plentiful, but fish, vegetables, eggs and butter were all scarce and commanded exorbitant prices. In expectation of a worsening of the food situation, the Academy of Sciences had turned its attention to the problem and produced a whole series of recommendations. The virtues of green tea were lauded, candles were suggested as a substitute for butter, the qualities of the blood and bones of sheep and oxen were gravely discussed, and Parisian housewives were given the recipe for a supposedly delicious dish composed of tallow-fat mixed with pulped corn, seasoned with salt and flavoured with a fried onion. The men of science concluded their advice by informing the population that if they felt hungry this did not necessarily·mean that they needed food. "Mere hunger", they said,

is a very bad guide. A common method of allaying its pangs is to press the stomach tightly. It is quite certain that one physical sensation will get rid of another, such as hunger, which, moreover, may be dissipated by having recourse to inert substances like sand, which assuredly contain no sort of nourishment.

40

In the meantime the French troops had been getting ready to make a sortie in which their commanders hoped to retrieve the humiliating defeat they had suffered at Châtillon. The sortie finally took place on 30 September and took the form of a combined action on both banks of the Seine to discover the strength of the enemy forces in the villages of Choisy-le-Roi and Chevilly. In their mood of ludicrous optimism the people of Paris naturally magnified what rumours they heard of this engagement into news of a great victory and a junction with the Army of the Loire. A brief dispatch issued by General Trochu in the evening of the 30th reduced matters to their proper proportions. "Our troops", he wrote,

> successively occupied Chevilly and L'Hay, and advanced as far as Thiais and Choisy-le-Roi. All these positions were strongly occupied, the latter with cannon. After a sharp artillery and musketry engagement our troops fell back to their positions with remarkable order and calm. The Garde Mobile were very firm. All in all, a very honourable day. Our losses have been heavy, the enemy's losses probably no less heavy.

The French losses were in fact very considerable, and included General Guilhem, who was killed at Chevilly. The day after the engagement the French Chief of Staff, General Schmitz, went in person to the Prussian advanced posts to ask for General Guilhem's body. Maurice d'Hérisson, who accompanied him, has left us a vivid account of their mission. "We were followed", he wrote,

> by a convoy of ambulance waggons with doctors and litter-bearers, so that we might rescue and bring back all the wounded we could find between the two armies. The Prussian sentries mounted guard in pairs, each man being posted only a few paces from the next. While one of them went in search of the officer appointed to confer with us, I got off my horse and started searching the neighbouring fields.
> We were to the right of where the hottest part of the battle had been fought. There was not a tree that had not been hit. The French *mitrailleuses* had mowed long lanes in the vines, cutting down plant and pole alike. Nothing had been changed; nothing had been touched as yet on the battlefield; and in certain places a sickening moisture marked the pools of blood with which the ground was reeking. Here there were helmets, there guns, further on pouches, képis, sword-bayonets, belts, account-books, all sorts of soldiers' effects, and above all a large number of cartridge-boxes.

41

As I passed through the vines I startled a couple of thrushes which were quietly picking the forgotten grapes. Close to the place where they had risen I discovered a poor little infantryman, barely twenty-two, who had had both legs smashed at the ankle-joint by the bursting of a shell. One of his feet had been completely torn away; the other, the bones of which were absolutely crushed, was still hanging by the sinews and a strip of flesh. The poor fellow had dragged himself to where his foot was, about three paces from where he had fallen, had seized hold of it in its pool of clotted blood, and was pressing it close to him. There was still a gleam of intelligence in his dull, glazed eyes, and when he recognized my French uniform he mustered up enough strength to say in a low voice, like a sick child: "Something to drink."

I leaned over him, took hold of both his arms, passed them round my neck, and turning sharply, so as to put him on my back, I carried him towards our waggons. He moaned slightly, and behind me I felt his remaining foot swinging to and fro, knocking against my legs. I laid him on a litter and gave him a large glass of water with some rum in it. He drank and died.

During the first part of the engagement our wounded were, as a rule, hit in the legs, between the feet and the knees. As the day wore on the enemy adjusted his aim. In the evening all the wounds were either in the head or full in the breast.

General Guilhem's body, pierced by ten bullets, was handed over to us. The Prussians gave it up with all the solemnity possible under the circumstances. Eight soldiers carried the bier, covered with flowers and foliage, on Uhlan lances; and, as they passed by, the various guards and isolated sentries presented arms, the officers saluting with their swords. It was a more impressive sight, in the midst of that ravaged and desolate countryside, than the most splendid funeral procession that ever approached the gate of the Invalides.

The following day another blow was dealt to the morale of the Parisians, with the news that Strasbourg and Toul had fallen. Yet this blow did not make the impact it would have made only a week before. "This evening", Edmond de Goncourt wrote in his *Journal*, "I did not notice in Paris the effect I had expected from this sad news. I think I found more indifference than exasperation." For the Parisians were now firmly convinced that, however many provincial fortresses might fall to the enemy, their own city was impregnable. And had not Hugo assured them that "if Paris has crowned the statue of Strasbourg with flowers, history will crown Paris with stars"?

Demonstrations

The first intimation that Edmond de Goncourt had of the capitulation of Strasbourg was a voice in the darkness of the boulevard saying: "Now they'll be on top of us!" The speaker had obviously grasped a fact which occurred to most Parisians only after a few hours of reflection: that the fall of Strasbourg and Toul had set free another German army and a considerable amount of siege artillery which could now be used against the fortifications of Paris. The Government, too, realized the growing danger of a bombardment of the capital and started issuing instructions to the population about precautions to be taken against this eventuality. Thus the holders of spirits stored in the great warehouse at Bercy were ordered to bury them under sand for the duration of the siege; municipal reservoirs, generally consisting of huge iron cylinders full of water, were installed all over Paris; and householders were urged to have stocks of sand and water in readiness in every courtyard and on every floor. The Oxford Graduate, noticing two diminutive cans of water on his staircase, and asking his concierge, the meaning of this warlike preparation, received the comforting reply: "Ah, Monsieur, the Government has told us to put sand in the courtyard and pails of water on the landing, and there they are, and we are quite safe now."

Not all Parisians were as complacent about their safety or as satisfied with the Government's policy; and there were constant protests about the injustices or inadequacies of living conditions in Paris and of the city's defence system. Accusations of cowardice were freely levelled at the vast number of *petits crevés* – gilded youths whom one correspondent qualified as best described by the English expression "nice young men for a small tea-party" – who had avoided military service by joining amateur ambulance brigades. Complaints were made about the old ladies who went about begging for money for the "wounded", and who generally, if not always, kept the proceeds for themselves. There was even a remonstrance addressed to the British Embassy from the inhabitants of the Rue de Chaillot, where the famous English courtesan Cora Pearl lived, pointing out that the so-called "Pearl from Plymouth" had a Union Jack flying above her house, and asking the "Ambassador of England, a country the purity and decency of whose manners is well known", to have this scandalous piece of bunting hauled down.

The greatest outcry, however, came from the people of the working-class district of Belleville, and was directed against the Government's "masterly inacitivity". The leader of this agitation was Gustave Flourens, the commander of the Belleville battalions of the National Guard and the so-called "Major of the Rampart". An old comrade in conspiracy of Henri Rochefort's, he regarded the latter's acceptance of a seat in the Government and his ironical nomination as "Organizer of the Barricades" as a betrayal of the revolutionary cause, and he had now decided to disregard Rochefort's appeals for unity and stir up the suburbs against the Government. He was not unnaturally represented by the conservative press as a bloodthirsty demagogue, ambitious to secure the post of Commander-in-Chief for himself; but there can be little doubt that both he and his battalions were genuinely eager to defeat the Germans and infuriated by the poor spirit shown by Trochu and his Government.

On 5 October some 5,000 or 6,000 National Guards from Belleville, led by Flourens, marched to the Hôtel de Ville to present the Government with such demands as a *levée en masse* of the entire nation, the dismissal of all civil servants suspected of disloyalty to the Republic, and the immediate election of a Municipal Commune. After Trochu and General Tamisier, the Commander of the National Guard, had arrived at the Hôtel de Ville, to be greeted with hisses from the Belleville battalions, Flourens and a deputation of officers were received by the Government. "I was simple enough", wrote Maurice d'Hérisson,

to believe that violent hands would be laid on the Major of the Rampart, and that he would be cast into the deepest of dungeons until the end of the siege. The General preferred treating him in a parental sort of way, called him by his full title of *Monsieur le Major*, and asked him why he had abandoned his post on the rampart. Under any other circumstances his irony would have been charming. Flourens did not understand it. "I demand ten thousand *chassepots* and a sortie", he said, and finally flung his resignation in the face of the Government. The most extraordinary thing is that the Government appeared to be alarmed by this, and General Trochu replied: "Then I will resign too." Flourens took his departure and when he appeared again before his men their cheers made the windows shake. Then it rained, and everybody went to dinner.

During the next two days the people of Paris almost forgot Flourens in their speculations about the activities of two other personalities: General Burnside and Gambetta. General Burnside was an American officer who had arrived in Paris from Versailles at the beginning of the week. He explained to General Trochu that he had come to Europe "attracted by the grandeur of the military events which were taking place in France", and asked permission to visit Paris as he had already visited the Prussian lines outside the capital. He wished, he said flatteringly,

after having studied the mechanism of the most colossal investment ever undertaken, to make himself equally well acquainted with the means of defence, and to contemplate the spectacle, so consoling to humanity, of a patriotism capable of giving birth to such mighty efforts.

This curiosity was not in itself suspicious, and indeed it was typical of the attitude of many of the American residents in Paris. One American lady, for example, who had been under fire during the Civil War, stated to the *Daily News* correspondent: "I regard a bombardment as the finest and most interesting effort of pyrotechnical skill, and I want to see if you Europeans have developed this art as fully as we have, which I doubt." But Trochu suspected that Burnside might have been sent by Bismarck, and was determined, even if this was not the case, to turn his visit to good account. He accordingly instructed Maurice d'Hérisson to show the American general the most strongly fortified parts of the defence system, in the hope that Burnside would be so impressed that he would urge Bismarck to offer an armistice on reasonable conditions.

After a tour of the ramparts and a conversation with Jules Favre on the subject of an armistice, Burnside did in fact make what he called "an urgent representation to Bismarck in favour of the French". However, the conditions which he brought back with him from Versailles on the 6th proved just as unacceptable as those laid down at Ferrières; and he confided to Hérisson that Bismarck clearly had no intention of granting an armistice, being convinced that internal divisions in Paris would complete the work of his master's armies. Paris, knowing nothing of these new secret negotiations, concluded that General Burnside had visited the city simply to discuss the fate of the Americans who were still there, shrugged her shoulders, and turned her attention to the more interesting matter of Gambetta's flight to the provinces.

It had been decided that Gambetta, who at this time was a fiery, energetic 32, should leave for the provinces, to reinforce the three very old men who had been sent from Paris before the siege began to form what was known as the Delegation of Tours. Jules Favre had previously been urged to join the Delegation, but had refused to trust himself to a balloon, so Gambetta had been chosen instead. His departure, originally fixed for 5 October, had to be delayed, ostensibly because there was not enough wind, but according to malicious gossip because Gambetta was afraid to risk his life in the air. Finally, however, the great man set off on his journey, leaving the Place Saint-Pierre at Montmartre, on 7 October in the *Armand Barbès*, together with his secretary Spuller, a vast number of letters and a basket of homing pigeons. Victor Hugo recorded the incident in his diary as follows:

> This morning, strolling along the Boulevard de Clichy, I saw a balloon at the end of a street leading to Montmartre. In this space three balloons were being inflated, a large one, a medium-sized one, and a small one. The large one was yellow, the medium one white, and the small one striped yellow and red. In the crowd it was whispered that Gambetta was leaving. Sure enough, I saw him in a group near the yellow balloon, wearing a heavy over-coat and a sealskin cap. He sat down on a paving-stone and pulled on a pair of fur-lined boots. A leather bag was slung over

his shoulder. He took it off and climbed into the car of the balloon, and a young man, the aeronaut, tied the bag to the cords above Gambetta's head.

It was half-past ten. The weather was fine, with a light southerly breeze and a gentle autumn sun. All at once the yellow balloon rose, with three men in it, including Gambetta. Then the white balloon went up with three men, one of whom waved a tricolour flag. Under Gambetta's balloon there hung a long tricolour streamer. "Long live the Republic!" shouted the crowd.

The white balloon was the *George Sand*, which carried two Americans called May and Reynolds who were to negotiate the purchase of arms for the French Government from the United States. May later told the Bordeaux correspondent of the *Daily News* that he had enjoyed the journey immensely, the only drawbacks being the Prussian bullets whistling round the car and the faint smell of gas, "which betrayed the poor quality of the varnish used by Nadar in the manufacture of his cotton balloons". He was also impressed by the fact that he and Reynolds were able to converse with Gambetta and Spuller at an incredible distance while floating over Creil. Gambetta's impressions were entirely different. He was, to quote his own words, "almost stunned by the overpowering idea of Nature's strength and man's weakness", and he thanked heaven when he touched earth again and "returned to a sphere where man has a *point de résistance* in struggling against the tyranny of Creation". Meanwhile, back in Paris, the population prayed for his safety, admired his courage, and pored over his *Proclamation to the French People*, of which he had thoughtfully left a copy behind. "You who have already given us your sons", this document concluded, in the best Hugolian style,

> you who have sent us the valiant Garde Mobile, whose ardour and exploits are daily signalized, rise in a mass and come to us. Alone, we shall know how to save our honour; but with you and through you we swear to save France.

The following day, Saturday the 8th, the people of Paris, whose thoughts were still with the handsome balloon-minister, were literally brought down to earth with another huge demonstration before the Hôtel de Ville. This demonstration, which was unarmed, was organized by the Central Republican Committee with the object of forcing the Government to agree to the immediate election of a Municipal Commune, an institution which was beginning to have an almost magical attraction for the poorer classes. Several thousand people assembled outside the Hôtel de Ville, where a few members of the Government were working, and set up a shout of: "Long Live the Commune!" The only response to this shout was the display of an armed battalion of bourgeois National Guards drawn up in line in front of the building, behind which Gardes Mobiles with fixed bayonets were posted. Eventually a delegation was admitted, only to be told by Jules Ferry that their demands could not be granted. By this time the crowd had grown to enormous proportions, and it was now that General Trochu made his appearance. Maurice d'Hérisson later wrote in his memoirs:

We received word at the Louvre that the Place de l'Hôtel de Ville was black with people, that there was a great deal of noise and shouting, and much calling for Trochu. The Governor simply shrugged his shoulders and said:

"Those buffoons are determined to give me no peace." He then called for his horse and rode off.

Commandant Bibesco and I followed him. He had no escort. We entered the Place de l'Hôtel de Ville from the Rue de Rivoli. Heads, nothing but heads. It was like a huge tub covered with corks floating on the disturbed water. The compact mass, a very ill-disposed one, began to hiss us vigorously. We made our way into it. In a few minutes Bibesco and I were separated from the Governor, and very soon I was separated from Bibesco. I saw him ten paces from me; some men had rushed to his horse's head and had seized the animal by the bridle, heaping insults and abuse on him at the same time. Some others honoured me with similar attentions, and I then heard shouts of "Down with the capitulators! Down with the traitors!" I should have preferred being anywhere else. Far away, above the crowd, I saw the shining cranium of the General, who was saluting right and left, and, at a standstill like ourselves, was towering over the swarm of human ants from the top of his horse.

We were three lost men in the midst of that crowd of ten thousand. An impatient gesture, a movement of our horses, an imprudent word, or a moment's forgetfulness of the discipline which imposed silence on us, might have destroyed us, or caused us to be cut down, massacred, and torn to shreds. We had to be careful, too, not to fall, for once on the ground there would have been an end of us. The crowd was like a mass of wild beasts, and keeping upright was our only hope.

It was, in fact, difficult to fall, for we were embedded in human flesh. I felt my horse trembling under me; the poor beast could not move. I had not room to stretch my legs, and I had to turn my toes inwards so as not to run my spurs into him. Hands were on my holsters, on the cantle of my saddle, on my saddle-cloth, on my thighs; if I had had to draw my sword there would not have been enough room for my left hand to get at the hilt and carry it across to my right. There was nothing for it but to wait, to remain motionless, and to stare at my horse's ears.

Finally a small opening in the crowd enabled the three of us to come together again in front of the Hôtel de Ville. A battalion of the National Guard was there. Jules Favre made a short speech, and spoke of the cannon which could be heard and which should teach us unity . . . .

From other reports of the incident it appears that Favre did not make his speech until the square had, to quote one observer, "been completely occupied by National Guards friendly to the Provisional Government and hostile to the election of the Commune". The Minister praised the bourgeois National Guards, the bourgeois National Guards cheered the Minister, and both parties went home convinced that right and victory were theirs. This conviction was shared by such conservative observers as Henry Vizetelly, the Paris correspondent of the *Illustrated London News*, who sent his readers a report studded with the words "demagogues" and "agitators".

"When the members of the Government appeared on the Place", he wrote,

they passed the National Guards drawn up in line in review. The warm reception they met with on the part of these citizen soldiers, and the great majority of the people massed around the three sides of the Place, furnished a convincing proof that these demonstrations got up by the more violent demagogues are entirely out of favour with nine-tenths of the Parisians. Shouts of "Long Live France!" "Long live the Republic!" "Long live the Government!" "No Commune!" arose on all sides, and were prolonged until the Government of National Defence retired in front of the entrance of the Hôtel de Ville, where Monsieur Jules Favre made an eloquent speech to the officers of the National Guard, congratulating them upon the attitude of their Corps and the union that was shown to prevail, and urging them not to harbour any feelings of animosity in reference to what had transpired that day. "We have no enemies," said he, "and I do not think we can even call them adversaries. They have been led astray, but let us bring them back by means of our patriotism." A heavy fall of rain eventually dispersed the assemblage most completely; but, in spite of continued showers, towards dusk fresh battalions of National Guards came to signify their entire adhesion to the Government and their unqualified approval of the decision they had come to, to postpone the municipal elections until after the termination of the siege.

The only neutral correspondent to express sympathy with the demonstrators was the outspoken Labouchère, who although admitting that "the leaders of the *ouvriers* talk a great deal of nonsense and are activated as much by personal ambition as by patriotism", declared that "the individual working man is the only reality in this population of corrupt and emasculated humbugs; everyone else is a windbag and a sham". Commenting on the demonstrations and counter-demonstrations of 8 October, he wrote:

No one seems to see any incongruity in the friends of the Government making an armed demonstration as a protest against armed and unarmed demonstrations in general. The question of the municipal elections will lie dormant for a few days, but I see no evidence that those who were in favour of it have altered their minds. As far as yesterday's proceedings were concerned, they only go to prove the fact, which no one ever doubted, that the bourgeoisie and their adherents are ready to support the Government, but they have also proved to my mind conclusively that the working men as a body have entirely lost all confidence in the men at the head of affairs. On the pure merits of the question, I think that the working men have reason on their side. They know clearly what they want – to make sorties and to endeavour to destroy the enemy's works; if this fails – to make provisions last as long as possible by a system of rationing – and then to destroy Paris rather than surrender it. The Government and their adherents are waiters on Providence, and except that they have some vague idea that the Army of the Loire will perform impossibilities, they are contented to live on from day to day, and to hope that something will happen to avert the inevitable catastrophe. I can understand a military dictatorship in a besieged capital, and I can understand a small elected council acting with revolutionary energy; but what I cannot understand is a military governor who fears to enforce military discipline, and a dozen respectable lawyers and orators whose sole idea of government is, as Blanqui truly says, to issue decrees and proclamations, and to make speeches.

A final glimpse of General Trochu that week, given to us by Henry Markheim, seems to confirm Labouchère's doubts. Walking out towards the Point-du-Jour by way of the Versailles road, the Oxford Graduate stopped to watch a company of Parisian Mobiles on their way to the front. "Next to me", he wrote,

a young Adonis of the Law Schools, with a pair of carefully-trimmed whiskers, dressed in the tight-fitting tunic of the Paris Mobile, was leaning against a *victoria* which contained two young ladies from the Latin Quarter, and seemed absorbed in his attentions to the charmers. He paused suddenly and stood aside, telling them: "I must salute" – pointing to a group of horsemen who were coming up from the bridge. In front of this group I recognized the well-known features of the Governor of Paris. His complexion was pale, and his eyes told of many sleepless nights; the face is energetic, but slightly wizened, the expression cold, as he raises his forefinger to his képi in acknowledgement of the military salutes of the Mobiles. The crowd was silent as he passed: his presence seems to inspire silence. He must be a man of great reserve and even shyness of manner and disposition. Poor Trochu! was the expression that rose to my lips as I marked his bent frame – a fine philosophical, religious head, full of calm and resigned courage – but not the physique of a coercer; no smiter, where a smiter is needed.

Monday, 10 October – Sunday, 16 October

The Amazons

None of the pigeons which Gambetta had taken with him in his balloon had returned over the weekend, and considerable anxiety was felt about the minister's safety. But late on the 10th a message arrived from Gambetta which, according to the Rothschild agent in Paris, a certain C. de B., announced that the provinces were rising as one man, especially Brittany. "It appears", C. de B. told his employer,

> that all the men between the ages of twenty and fifty are marching to our aid, accompanied by the doctors of each district and the priests of each parish. The rich landowners of Brittany and the local councils have imported Remington rifles from England. . . .

The text of Gambetta's message as published by the Government was rather less detailed but no less enthusiastic. It read as follows:

> Arrived after accident in forest at Épineuse, balloon collapsed. Leaving in an hour for Amiens, then by railway to Le Mans and Tours. Everywhere the people are rising *en masse*. The Government of National Defence is acclaimed everywhere.

The Government of National Defence must have reflected bitterly that it was not exactly being acclaimed in Paris, where the previous Saturday's demonstrations were still having repercussions. First the newspapers on Monday morning published a letter from Rochefort to his friend Flourens, apologizing, as a supporter of the Commune, for not having resigned his position as a member of the Government, and explaining that he had compromised with his convictions simply because he did not wish "the roar of the cannon on the ramparts to be mingled with the report of musketry in the streets". Then, during the afternoon, the Mayor of Belleville telegraphed to the Government that Flourens had ordered the *rappel* to be beaten with the intention of marching the men under his command upon the Hôtel de Ville. The *générale* was promptly beaten all over Paris, and National Guards crowded into the Place de l'Hôtel de Ville to defend the Government if necessary. But then a fresh telegram arrived from Belleville announcing that the five battalions under Flourens' command had refused to obey his orders, and the day passed off quietly.

The next day Jules Ferry visited Belleville at the invitation of the local National Guards, who greeted him with cries of "Vive la République!" and "Vive le Gouvernement!" and assured him of their loyalty. Flourens himself, who had first resigned his command and then resumed it on the pretext that he had been re-elected by his officers, was informed by the *Journal Officiel* that his re-election was illegal and that he was to be tried by a court martial for stirring up an insurrection. Various other commanders of the National Guard who had demonstrated in favour of the Commune were called upon by their men to resign, and one, a certain Sapia, was actually arrested by his own officers and taken to the Conciergerie to await trial. As a final consolation for right-thinking people, the commanders of the Mobile Guard battalions from Brittany – whose men had been seen to burst into tears at the sight of the scurrilous caricatures of the Pope displayed on the Paris bookstalls – informed General Trochu that as long as he remained at the head of the Government they would be responsible for peace in the capital. "The Communists of Belleville", C. de B. told Lionel de Rothschild with evident satisfaction, "would do well to take this into account."

Yet the Communist clubs continued to proliferate all over Paris, gathering together people who were violently hostile to the Government but no less patriotic than the Breton Mobiles. Even Edmond de Goncourt, when he visited a club just off the Boulevard de Clichy that week, had to admit, despite all his prejudices against the working class, that the audience's loyalty to their country was irreproachable. In one of the finest descriptions we possess of a revolutionary club during the Siege of Paris, he wrote:

At the end of a little passage, constricted and illuminated by a sort of gaslight sun, the door of the Salle de la Reine Blanche opens to the crowd slipping into it. A dance-hall decorated just like all the dance-halls on this boulevard; a hall with paintings of the sky framed in red paper pelmets, narrow mirrors fixed to the pillars, and zinc-and-glass chandeliers with only three jets lit for the occasion.

Where the mob dances in peaceful times, it legislates in times of revolution. The band-stand is the tribune, occupied by the grim members of the committee, all in black, and the evening's speakers; in front of them, on the wooden balustrade where the necks of the cellos rested yesterday, there stands the parliamentary decanter. In the blueish fog created by the pipes, sitting on the benches or face to face on the little tables, are National Guards, Mobiles, suburban philosophers, red from the insides of their hats to the uppers of their shoes, and workers in peaked caps and blue jackets. There are women of the people, prostitutes, girls in red hoods, and even women of the lower middle class with no idea where to spend an evening nowadays.

At last the bell is rung, that bell with which the common people, like children, love to play at the Chamber of Deputies. Tony Revillon stands up and announces the foundation of the Club de Montmartre, destined to establish liberty and hence, so he tells us, to destroy monarchy, the nobility and the clergy. Then he declares his intention of reading out the instalment of the *Journal de Rouen* published in this evening's *Vérité*. It is touching to see how easily these flocks of men are taken in by speech and print, how wonderfully devoid they are of any critical faculty. Sacrosanct democracy can concoct a catechism even richer in miraculous fibs than the old one, and these people are perfectly prepared to swallow it obediently.

And yet, underneath this stupidity, this unthinking acceptance of impossible things, there appears every now and then a warm emotion, a generous impulse, a fervent sense of brotherhood. Thus at this meeting, at the news that 12,300 of our men are prisoners in Germany, a cry which came from every breast died away in a murmur of pain, during which the whole audience looked at one another with inexpressible emotion.

When Tony Revillon had sat down, Citizen Quentin took the floor and demonstrated, with pathetic phrases and sentimental humbug, that none of our misfortunes since Sedan would have happened if a Commune had been appointed. And once the providential character of a Commune had been duly proved and established, everybody went out into the entrance-hall to sign a petition at the box-office for the immediate appointment of the aforesaid Commune.

In the meantime, the war was being waged at the same gentle pace which had provoked the recent Communist demonstrations. Most of the army's activities that week had a certain musical comedy quality about them. At the beginning of the week Rear-Admiral Saisset, angered by the sight of the Germans clearing the surrounding countryside of its food crops, sent out a detachment of street-urchins on the same mission; they came back with 150,000 francs' worth of vegetables, which were promptly taken to the Central Market to be sold. Then on Wednesday the 12th, a party of Mobiles returned from a sortie at Pierrefitte with a cask of wine which they had found in a deserted Prussian outpost. "The Prussians", they reported triumphantly, "had just broached it but had scarcely had time to taste it; at the very most they had drunk the stirrup-cup when the militia-men were seen approaching."

So far, judging by these light-hearted expeditions and the equally light-hearted disposal of the booty, there was little serious concern about the food and drink situation in Paris. Admittedly a rough-and-ready system of rationing was organized about this time in certain arrondissements, by which each person was entitled to 100 grammes of meat a day (50 grammes for a child), to be bought from his regular butcher. But well-to-do citizens could eat their fill in restaurants and if they bothered to collect their ration cards it was often in a spirit of amused condescension. Some, such as Edmond de Goncourt, were also interested in collecting visual and documentary evidence of the history they were making. "It seemed to me", Goncourt wrote after getting his card from the local Mairie,

> that I was looking at one of those queues in the great Revolution which my poor old cousin Cornélie used to describe to me, in that patient line of heterogeneous individuals, of ragged old women, of men in peaked caps, of small shopkeepers, cooped up in those improvised offices, those whitewashed rooms, where you recognized sitting round a table, omnipotent in their uniforms of officers of the National Guard and supreme dispensers of your food, your far from honest tradesmen. I came away with a piece of blue

paper, a typographical curiosity for future Goncourts and times to come, which entitles me and my housekeeper to buy every day two rations of raw meat or two portions of food cooked in the municipal canteens. There are coupons up to 14 November: a good many things may happen between now and then . . . .

On Thursday, 13 October, General Vinoy's troops carried out what was called "a reconnaissance on a grand scale" on the plateaux of Bagneux and Châtillon. It ended, as one disillusioned observer commented, "in the 'retreat in good order' which, to the disgust and discomfort of the Parisians, is now understood to be the necessary *finale* of all siege operations". The retreat was sounded at two o'clock in the afternoon, shortly after Trochu had made his appearance on the battlefield, and the Mobiles who had taken the village of Bagneux fell back to their original positions, applauded by a vast crowd of Parisians who had driven out on to the plain of Montrouge to watch the engagement as if it were a theatrical performance. Men and women clapped their hands and waved their hats as the Mobiles marched past carrying captured helmets on their bayonets, and the Bavarian wounded were loaded into cabs and private carriages drawn up behind the ramparts as on some gala night at the Poéra. About 100 German prisoners had been taken at Bagneux, and during the course of the afternoon they were brought into Paris and marched along the Boulevard Saint-Michel on their way to the Place Vendôme and the prison of La Roquette. "Most of them", Henry Vizetelly reported, "were very young men, and all were more or less haggard-looking."

Then, a good hour after the fighting had come to an end, Henri Rochefort and a few of his colleagues in the Government arrived at the Fort of Vanves to watch the battle, and came under fire from the enemy's field-guns – a circumstance which, according to the Paris newspapers, reflected great credit on the "President of the Barricades". And finally, in the evening, a shell from Mont Valérien set fire to the ex-Emperor's palace at Saint-Cloud, which after burning for several hours was reduced to a complete ruin. "Poor, beautiful Saint-Cloud", lamented Queen Victoria,

has been burnt and destroyed by the French which is too sad. How well I remembered the pleasant ten days spent there in '55 with the poor Emperor and Empress, our lovely rooms and the beautiful grounds – all, all, swept away!

But the people of Paris could scarcely be expected to share Victoria's sorrow and indignation, and altogether the 13th was generally considered to have been a good day.

Unfortunately it was followed by several days of elaborate self-congratulation, mourning and documentation. First Vinoy submitted a detailed report on the reconnaissance to Trochu, ending with the words:

> The aim which you had set yourself has been completely attained; we have forced the enemy to show his strength, to call up considerable reserves, and to come under the murderous fire of our fixed batteries and our excellent field-guns. He must have suffered heavy losses, whereas ours are only slight considering the results obtained.

Next, on Sunday the 16th, Trochu himself and most of Parisian high society attended a Requiem Mass at the Madeleine for the Comte Picot de Dampierre, the commanding officer of the Mobiles of the Aube, who had been killed at the head of his troops in the attack on Bagneux. And then, as if his officers had not enough to occupy their attention, the Governor of Paris ordered them to send him a list of "not more than forty names" of those soldiers who had distinguished themselves in the last three engagements. "Let your investigations be slow and sure", he wrote, "let them descend to the lowest ranks of the hierarchy, let them be scrupulously checked, and let this be an inquiry of honour conducted with all due care and circumspection." Trochu's intention – to break with the traditional practice of citing a string of names beginning with those of the generals and ending up with those of a few privates – was admirable, but his subordinates must have wondered whether they might not be more usefully employed.

The same curious obsession with the past was to be seen in other quarters in Paris, and nowhere more than at the Tuileries, where an official commission was engaged in examining the ex-Emperor's private papers. The indefatigable Edmond de Goncourt prevailed on his friend Philippe Burty, a member of the Commission, to do him the honours of the palace, and noted with aristocratic distaste some National Guards playing cards in the courtyard, a canteen set up under the peristyle, next to a pile of camp beds, and a paper bearing the words "Death to thieves" pinned to dust-sheets on the banisters. Describing the scene in his *Journal*, he went on:

Beneath those old ceilings blackened by the smoke of the receptions and suppers of the Empire, beneath that beautiful burnished gold which reminded me of the gold of the ceilings of Venice, in the midst of those bronzes and marbles in the process of being packed into crates, and in the glass of those splendid mirrors, could be seen ugly pen-pushers' faces, heads framed in long republican locks or crowned with greying red hair, the surly countenances of the pure and virtuous. Deal cupboards had been arranged along the walls and went up as far as the ceiling, packed with files and bundles of documents. There were trestle-tables sagging under untidy heaps of letters, papers, bills, and receipts. On the end of a nail that had been hammered into the gilt frame of a mirror hung the *Instructions regarding the examination of the Correspondence*. I felt as if I had entered the secret chamber of the Revolutionary Inquisition, and this odious unsealing of History had something about it which I found repugnant. . . . It is in the Salle Louis XIV that the members of the Commission hold their sittings. It is there that the final sorting is done. Among the papers that were there I picked up one at random: it was a bill showing that the extravagant Napoleon III used to have his socks darned at a cost of 25 centimes a hole. . . .

While the men of Paris busied themselves investigating the ex-Emperor's misdemeanours and their own merits, the women displayed a commendable eagerness to inflict defeat on the enemy. Already, on 7 October, a column of 150 women and girls, wearing Red Cross armlets, and headed by two drummers of the National Guard, had marched to the Hôtel de Ville and asked the Provisional Government to put women in charge of the ambulances, in order to release more men for service on the ramparts. Now, not content with serving as medical orderlies, they claimed the right to form a corps of Amazons and share the dangers of the battlefield with their husbands and brothers.

This was an idea which had been repeatedly discussed in recent weeks at the various women's clubs in Paris, notably at one in the Rue Pierre Levée presided over by Louise Michel, the schoolmistress who later played an important part in the Commune and was transported to New Caledonia, and at another in the Triat Gymnasium in the Avenue Montaigne, where the only man normally allowed to be present was the secretary, Jules Allix, an eccentric elderly survivor of the Revolution of 1848.

On Sunday, 9 October the members of this latter club,

being short of funds, decided to admit men to the audience at the modest charge of 4 sous a head. Ernest Vizetelly went along with his father and has left us this account of the stormy meeting they witnessed:

Citizen Jules Allix, while reading a report respecting the Club's progress, began to libel some of the Paris convents, whereupon a National Guard in the audience flatly called him a liar. A terrific hubbub arose, all the women gesticulating and protesting, whilst their *présidente* energetically rang her bell, and the interrupter strode towards the platform. He proved to be none other than the Duc de Fitz-James, a lineal descendant of our last Stuart King by Marlborough's sister, Arabella Churchill. He tried to speak, but the many loud screams prevented him from doing so. Some of the women threatened him with violence, whilst a few others thanked him for defending the Church. At last, however, he leapt on to the platform, and in doing so overturned both a long table covered with green baize, and the members of the committee who were seated behind it. Jules Allix thereupon sprang at the Duke's throat, they struggled and fell together from the platform, and rolled in the dust below it. It was long before order was restored, but this was finally effected by a good-looking young woman who, addressing the male portion of the audience, exclaimed: "Citizens! if you say another word we will fling what you have paid for admission in your faces, and order you out of doors!"

Business then began, the discussion turning chiefly upon two points, the first being that all women should be armed and do duty on the ramparts, and the second that the women should defend their honour from the attacks of the Germans by means of prussic acid. Allix remarked that it would be very appropriate to employ prussic acid in killing Prussians, and explained to us that this might be effected by means of little india-rubber thimbles which the women would place on their fingers, each thimble being topped with a small pointed tube containing some of the acid in question. If an amorous Prussian should venture too close to a fair Parisienne, the latter would merely have to hold out her hand and prick him. In another instant he would fall dead. "No matter how many of the enemy may assail her," added Allix enthusiastically, "she will simply have to prick them one by one, and we shall see her standing still pure and holy in the midst of a circle of corpses!" At these words many of the women in the audience were moved to tears, but the men laughed hilariously.

A few days later, on the pretext that disorderly scenes were taking place on his premises, the landlord of the Triat Gymnasium gave the club notice to quit, but in the meantime the women of Paris had found a new male champion. This was a certain Monsieur Félix Belly, a gentleman who had an unfortunate genius for hitting on original ideas long before public opinion was ready for them: thus before the war he had tried to start a Panama Canal Company which had been laughed out of court, and now he came forward with a detailed

Fig. 2 An Amazon of the Seine

'Let no Prussian trifle
With this maiden fair,
For she sports a rifle
And anything will dare.'

scheme for an armed corps of women which was clearly doomed to suffer the same fate. On Wednesday, 12 October, Paris awoke to find the walls placarded with green posters headed: "Amazons of the Seine" and announcing:

In accordance with the wishes expressed in numerous letters, and out of regard to the generous disposition of a considerable portion of the female population of Paris, there will be formed, as soon as resources are available for their equipment and organization, ten battalions of women, without distinction of social rank, and who will take the title of "Amazons of the Seine". These battalions are chiefly intended to defend the ramparts and barricades, together with the stationary National Guard, and to render to the combatants, in whose ranks it is proposed that they should be distributed by companies, all such domestic and fraternal services as are compatible with moral order and military discipline.

Belly had clearly given careful thought to every aspect of his Legion of Amazons. He explained that they would be armed with light guns with a range of 200 yards, and equipped with a uniform consisting of a black blouse with a cape, a black cap with an orange band, and black trousers with orange stripes down the outer seams. The officers would all be ladies, generally wives and daughters of serving officers, and apart from a team of doctors to attend to wounded Amazons there would also be a committee of ladies acting as the *conseil de famille* of the corps, to see to "its healthful condition, to the proper organization of the ambulances, and to providing against the incelemencies of the weather". Finally, to ensure a high moral standard, candidates who presented themselves at the recruiting office in the Rue Turbigo were instructed to bring a National Guard with them to act as guarantor.

The journalists who hurried round to the Rue Turbigo to interview Monsieur Belly, a wiry little man with a grey moustache and a military bearing, and to listen to him play on the piano the specially commissioned "Marseillaise of the Amazons of the Seine", found that he was laying down new and more stringent requirements. To be a guarantor, one had to be not only a National Guard, but also the recruit's father, brother, husband or employer, and the recruit herself had to furnish a certificate from her local Commissioner of Police testifying to her unexceptionable moral character. In spite of these precautions, a crowd of ribald males gathered outside the recruiting office and expressed doubts as to Monsieur Belly's own moral character, while the police for their part raided the Rue Turbigo premises and carried off all the papers they found there. They justified this summary action on the ground that General Trochu had forbidden the formation of any more free corps, and that Monsieur Belly had taken entrance fees from his recruits. The fact that no further action was taken suggests that there was no truth in this latter statement. But the raid itself was enough to kill Monsieur Belly's scheme, and his organization was disbanded.

He found some consolation in the composition of an elaborate history of the whole affair. "What", he asked indignantly in this document, "was so ridiculous about this idea of rescuing twenty or thirty thousand women from the evil counsels of idleness and hunger and plunging them in the healthy preoccupations of the common peril?" What indeed? But if Monsieur Belly and the would-be Amazons were disappointed, the cartoonists had a field-day depicting hordes of Germans surrendering to a handful of beauties. And Paris was hugely amused.

Guns, more guns, still more guns

The affection which, in the early days of the siege, the Parisians had devoted to the city of Strasbourg had now been transferred to the guns defending their own city. Everyone, from the gunners themselves to the smallest children, called the best-known guns by name – especially Big Joséphine on Mont Valérien – and regarded them with almost amorous tenderness. Thus in a battery of artillery rolling along the Rue de Rivoli an observer noticed "a gunner stroking the bronze of a cannon with a loving hand, which seemed to be fondling beloved flesh". Again, when Parisians complained that Mont Valérien remained silent for hours on end, the commander of the fort was transferred, and his successor, to quote one correspondent, "banged away at every Uhlan in sight", to keep the public happy. And on sunny afternoons the people's favourite amusement was now a visit to one of the batteries on the outskirts of Paris.

"The cannonade", wrote Edmond de Goncourt on 18 October,

attracted me to the Bois de Boulogne, to the Mortemart battery. There is something solemn about the serious gravity and the thoughtful slowness with which the men serving a gun carry out the loading operations. At last the gun is loaded. The gunners stand motionless at each side, some of them leaning, in beautiful sculptural attitudes, on the garnets with which they have set up

63

and adjusted the gun; one gunner in shirtsleeves, standing at the right, holds the string in his hand. There are a few moments of immobility, of silence, I might almost say of emotion. Then, at the pulling of the string, a clap of thunder, a flame, a cloud of smoke, in which the clump of trees masking the battery disappears. For a long time a snow-white cloud hangs over the scene, dissipating only very slowly and bringing out the yellow of the sand whipped up by the shot, the grey of the earth-bags, two or three of which have been torn open by the side-kick of the gun, the red of the gunners' caps, and the white of the shirt of the man who was holding the string.

This thing which kills at a distance is a real show for Paris, which, as in the heyday of the lake, has carriages and landaus standing around the butt and whose women mix with the Mobiles and press as close as possible to the tremendous din. Among the spectators are Pelletan, whose grey beard and ancient philosopher's head do not suit the képi, Jules Ferry and Rochefort, who talks, laughs and gesticulates like a man whose nervous system is affected by these convulsions of the air.

The cannon fires six shots; then the old commanding officer removes the little brass instrument for finding elevations from its tripod, puts it carefully into a deal box, stuffs it into his pocket, and goes off, while on the gun which has been put to rest there sits a young gunner, a fair-haired man with a feminine face, imprinted with that indefinable heroic quality which Gros gives his military figures, who, with his police cap askew on his head, a gaudily striped Algerian belt clasping his waist, and his cartridge pouch on his belly, a delightful picture in his picturesque untidiness, rests from the fatigue of this deadly exercise. The performance is over and the audience scatters.

They make off towards Boulogne, towards those milky-blue landscapes such as you find in Switzerland and the Tyrol, and which are manufactured here, today, by gunsmoke; or else they go back in the direction of the Auteuil rampart, which has begun firing today for the first time and whose shells pass over your head with a gasping whistle. Under the gun, poor drabs are calmly picking up droppings, street-urchins are fishing in the pool, with horse-sausage as bait, and young women, enjoying the vibration of the cannon and reluctant to go off, have to be pulled away by prudent husbands. ...

On 19 October the Mayor of Paris, Étienne Arago, decided to turn this passion for the artillery to good account, and issued a proclamation to the effect that the city needed 1,500 heavy guns for its defence and that he was opening a fund to cover the expense, which was estimated at nine million francs.

The next day bill-stickers were at work all over Paris putting up posters appealing for subscriptions to the fund, and soon all manner of societies were busy organizing concerts, readings or simple house-to-house collections to raise money for guns. Victor Hugo, who promptly gave his proceeds from the first Paris edition of *Les Châtiments* to the national cannon fund, described one of these collections in his diary on the 23rd.

> The 17th Battalion asked me to be the first subscriber of one sou to a fund for purchasing a cannon. They are going to collect 300,000 sous. This will make 15,000 francs, which will buy a 24-centimetre gun with a range of 8,500 metres – equal to the Krupp guns. Lieutenant Maréchal brought to collect my sou an Egyptian cup of onyx dating from the Pharaohs, engraved with the moon and the sun, the Great Bear and the Southern Cross, and with two cynocephalus demons as handles. The engraving of this cup represented the life-work of one man. I gave my sou. Alton-Shée, who was present, gave his, as did also Monsieur and Madame Meurice, and the two servants, Mariette and Clémence. The 17th Battalion wanted to call the gun the *Victor Hugo*. I told them to call it the *Strasbourg*. In this way the Prussians will go on receiving shots from that city.

As the public continued to clamour for "guns, more guns, still more guns", the collecting fever grew, and in all parts of Paris open-air stalls, presided over by local officials and protected by National Guards, were set up to receive subscriptions, not only in money but also in the form of jewellery and precious objects. General Trochu was said to have commented sardonically that he did not want guns so much as gunners, but his colleagues argued that the casting of cannon inspired the public with hope and confidence. Meanwhile, to reassure the population until their precious cannon had been cast, the Government announced that it had ordered from the private armaments-factories in Paris no fewer than 227 *mitrailleuses* with 312,000 cartridges, 50 mortars, half a million shells, and 300 breechloading guns of medium calibre. It wisely refrained from specifying what proportion of this order had so far been delivered, but even at the lowest estimate the city undoubtedly already boasted an impressive arsenal.

One of the things which most struck neutral observers in Paris during the siege was how little crime there was in the city, in view of the tremendous number of arms it contained and the darkness of the streets at night. Various explanations of this phenomenon were offered, of which, perhaps, the most plausible was that put forward by the Oxford Graduate. "Those who tell us", he wrote,

> that crime, lawlessness and anarchy have always flourished in besieged cities, forget that our lawlessness is organized, and that our anarchy is legal – therefore less dangerous in their immediate effects, so far as individual comfort and property are concerned, than in their possible and remote consequences to the state and society at large. With regard to crime, the usual incentive of misery is wanting: the "dangerous" classes, amongst whom the crises of labour determine crime, are at present cared for, clothed, fed, enrolled, and subsidized by the state. The siege, in fact, realizes the working-man's Utopia of Pay and No Work, to the amount of thirty sous a day. Vagabonds, professional thieves, etc., were expelled in great numbers before the investment; and the natural propensity for theft has found an outlet in marauding outside the city walls, so we purchase part of our safety at the expense of the furniture and valuables in our country homes. Never was Paris so free from crime as during the last six weeks, and that not in spite of, but by reason of the siege.

This happy state of affairs certainly owed nothing to the new police force which had been instituted in September. "I have been much exercized of late", an English correspondent had written at that time,

> respecting certain persons whom I have seen strolling about the streets, avoiding as much as possible their species. Whenever anyone looked at them they sneaked away with deprecating glances. They are dressed in a sort of pea-jacket with hoods, black trousers, and black caps, and their general appearance was a cross between a sailor and a monk. I have at length discovered with surprise that these retiring innocents are the new *sergents de ville* of Monsieur Kératry, who are daily denounced by the Ultras as ferocious wolves eager to rend and devour all honest citizens. If this be true, I can only say that they are well disguised in sheep's clothing.

Since then, the police had not grown any more venturesome, and their effectiveness as a means of enforcing law and order remained nil. Labouchère, in one of his most humorous reports, even went so far as to claim that his hat commanded greater respect than a policeman's uniform. "It is somewhat amusing", he wrote,

> to observe how justice is administered when any dispute arises in the streets. The *sergents de ville* immediately withdraw, in

order not to prejudice the question by their presence. A sort of informal jury is empanelled, each disputant states his case, and the one who is thought by the tribunal to be in fault is either taken off to prison or cuffed on the spot. I have bought myself a sugar-loaf hat of the First Republic, and am consequently regarded with deference. Today a man was bullying a child, and a crowd gathered round him; I happened just then to come up, room was immediately made for me and my hat, and I was asked to give my opinion as to what ought to be done with the culprit. I suggested kicking, and as I walked away, I saw him writhing under the boots of two sturdy executioners, amid the applause of the spectators. "The style is the man", said Buffon; had he lived here now he would rather have said: "The hat is the man." An English doctor who goes about in a regulation chimney-pot has already been arrested twenty-seven times; I, thanks to my revolutionary hat, have not been arrested once. I have only to glance from under its brim at any one for him to quail.

One of the few arrests made by the police during the siege took place on 15 October, when Portalis, the editor of *La Vérité*, was seized and committed to the Conciergerie prison. His offence had been to publish that morning, in the form of questions, a number of dispatches communicated to him by an American friend, and taken from a copy of the *Standard* which had found its way into Paris. "Is it true", he had asked, in large print and across several columns of his paper,

that the Army of the Loire has been worsted in several engagements? – that a Red Republic has been proclaimed at Lyons? – that an armistice, proposed by Count Bismarck, has been refused by the Government of National Defence?

The number of the *Vérité* containing these questions, or rather this information, had immediately sold out on the boulevards; and after ordering the arrest of the editor during the afternoon, the Government felt obliged to publish a long note in the *Journal Officiel* the next day, denying or evading Portalis's questions and denouncing the *Standard* as "a journal notoriously hostile to France". The effect of this note, as one writer put it, was

that the more intelligent classes have lost all confidence in the statements of the Government, and that the great majority, whom any official falsehood, however gross, will always lull to sleep, have felt even their confidence shaken by the severe measures taken against Monsieur Portalis.

The Paris newspapers almost without exception joined in a

protest at the arrest of an editor on such a flimsy pretext, hinting that it had something to do with a quarrel between Portalis and his former colleague Ernest Picard, who was now a Minister; and within a few days the unfortunate journalist was freed.

This affair did nothing to enhance General Trochu's reputation, which was under fire from all sides. On the 14th the Governor of Paris had replied to the growing clamour for a *sortie en masse* with a long address in which he had unwisely admitted that at the beginning of the war he had been far from sharing the general confidence in victory. "The will which I placed at that time", he had written, "in the hands of Maître Ducloux, the Paris solicitor, will bear witness one day to the painful and all too well-founded presentiments with which my soul was filled." He had gone on, even more unwisely, to announce that he had a plan:

> I declare here that, imbued with the deepest faith in the return of fortune which will be due to the great resistance exemplified by the Siege of Paris, I shall not give in to the pressure of public impatience. Drawing my inspiration from the duties which are common to us all, and from the responsibilities which no one shares with me, I shall follow to the end the plan I have worked out, without revealing it, and all I ask of the population of Paris, in exchange for my efforts, is the continuation of the confidence with which they have so far honoured me.

From now on, Trochu was subjected to a merciless bombardment of caustic references to his plan. Wags suggested asking Maître Ducloux to let them see it for a consideration; boasters claimed to know what it was; enemies inquired sarcastically after every reverse whether it had been allowed for in the famous plan. Even fair-minded, unbiased observers began to think he talked too much and acted too little. "Of General Trochu", wrote one,

> into whose hands, by the mere force of circumstances, all civil and military authority is concentrating, *bonum virum, facile dixeris, magnum libenter*. He is, I believe, a good general and a good administrator. Although he awakens no enthusiasm, confidence is felt by the majority in his good sense. It is thought, however, that he is wanting in that energy and audacity which are requisite in a leader, if victory is to be wrested from the Germans. He forgets that time is not his ally, and that merely to hold Paris until that surely inevitable hour arrives when the provisions are exhausted will neither save France nor her capital. He is a man

slow to form a plan, but obstinate in his adherence to it; unwilling to move until he has his forces perfectly under control, and until every administrative detail is perfected – better fitted, in fact, to defend Troy for ten years than Paris for a few months.

On the 21st, however, as if to confound the doubters, General Ducrot launched an attack across the Gennevilliers peninsula against the German front line between Saint-Cloud and Bougival. This attack, which was given the name of the Battle of La Jonchère, was intended only as a limited action to test both the German defences and the morale of the French troops; and indeed it could not reasonably have been expected to achieve anything more, since the Prussian defences were at their deepest where it took place. But although the Prussians soon realized that Ducrot's force was not strong enough to represent a serious threat – it numbered little more than 8,000 men – the French civilian population both in Paris and behind the German positions jumped to the conclusion that a serious attempt was being made to break out of Paris – with disastrous results in some instances.

On the battlefield itself the French troops fought well, occupying Buzenval without much trouble and holding their positions bravely under heavy fire before retiring in good order after four or five hours. Ducrot led every attack with fool-hardy courage, a conspicuous figure on a white horse, and earned the admiration both of his own men and of the Prussians. And the French had the minor but considerable satisfaction of killing an English sharpshooter who had become something of a legend among the besieged garrison.

"Near La Jonchère", writes Maurice d'Hérisson, describing this incident,

some soldiers who were rushing to the front called out as they passed me:

"The sergeant has killed the Black Bird. And about time, too."

A few paces farther on, I saw, writhing in agony, and for all the world like a circus clown walking on his knees, an individual very carefully dressed in a black velvet coat and knickerbockers, who had been hit full in the chest by a bullet fired, according to the soldiers, by their sergeant. One of them told me that for several days they had noticed this individual constantly on the watch for our sentries, and that he never missed an opportunity of sending them a bullet from his Snider carbine. He fired with extraordinary precision and rarely failed to hit his mark. They had nicknamed him the Black Bird. He was an Englishman; an eccentric fanatic who made war on his own account as an amateur and an ally of the Prussians. He was dispatched with a bayonet, and I am pretty sure that neither his watch nor his purse found their way to the British Embassy. At all events, I had no time to find out, having business elsewhere. . . .

Inside Paris there was considerable excitement as soon as news of the attack spread through the capital. The Oxford Graduate, considering that a battle was "the most uninteresting sight next to a grand review", found

more interest in watching its effects on this feverish crowd of spectators massed from the Arc de Triomphe down to the fortifications on the Avenue de Neuilly, and on this other crowd of amateurs who have smuggled themselves outside the walls in ambulance-carriages and by all manner of devices, to enjoy the fluctuating emotions of the fight. How keen their sight is to detect the smoke of imaginary French cannon behind the crests in the rear of the Prussian front, pounding the unconscious foe with shells that with a little observation and unprejudiced use of the glass you can see bursting in the ranks of the red trousers. "Surely," cries a gentle lady, flapping her parasol and clapping her delicately-gloved hands, "there is General Polhès, and now those hordes of savages are getting it in the rear. I know all about it, for a friend of mine who knows General Trochu told me that Monsieur Gambetta's dispatch contained no end of good news, which General Trochu did not publish for fear of letting the Prussians into the secret; but the general has told my friend all about it." We soon persuade ourselves that the Army of the Loire is advancing, and the success achieved by the first dash of the French troops at Montretout is certainly a satisfactory beginning.

But this elation was followed within a few hours by profound depression as news of the inevitable withdrawal arrived –

news that Montretout had been abandoned, that cannons had been lost, that the Mobiles of Ducrot's army had fled, with a whole chapter of accidents, in the commissariat and ambulance arrangements, and the usual story of "treason" and the "incapacity of our chiefs".

The same sequence of optimism and despair occurred behind the German lines, where the English correspondent W. H. Russell watched the battle from the heights of Saint-Germain. "My coachman", he wrote afterwards, unwillingly drove on, and, as we turned in towards Marles, there came in great streams men, women and children, along the road, why or wherefore I could not make out. They seemed in a state of joyous flight. Women, to be sure, crying and wringing their hands, but the men exulting, and snapping their fingers, and laughing, till they came to the place where the Prussians were drawn up, rigid as iron, along the road. I heard afterwards that these French people had been driven by the soldiery from the Terrace at Saint-Germain and the slopes of the hill, where they were supposed to be encouraging their countrymen, and they were seeking other points of observation for, as they hoped, a French victory. Saint-Germain at last. The Hôtel du Pavillon Henri IV was crowded with Prussians. Everybody in immense excitement. Yet, how odd it was, Monsieur Barbot's waiters were serving people in the gilded saloon, and groups of officers at their breakfast discussing what they saw through their fieldglasses as they ate their meals. The French population were swarming in the few places where they were allowed to congregate, whence they could get a glimpse of the battle. I could not but think how disheartening it must have been for the troops who were advancing from under the cover of Valérien to see before them nothing but a great belt of woods, fenced in with walls, from which came a spitting fire of musketry and the rush of those terrible Prussian shells, not a soul almost being visible, except when now and then a sunbeam lighted up the spike of a helmet or flashed off a bayonet. The cries of the people, their exclamations of joy, in which sometimes English words were heard from alien sympathizers, as the action seemed to go in favour of the French, and their low murmurs of grave disappointment as the onward progress of their friends was stayed, and at last a retrograde movement was commenced, were something quite new to me, for never before had I seen a multitude of civilians present as spectators of an actual combat.

At Bougival, some of these civilian spectators, taking a temporary Prussian withdrawal for a final retreat, brought out their old shot-guns which they had hidden and started firing at the German troops. The Prussian reprisals that evening were swift and brutal. Nineteen civilians were arrested, two were shot, the houses of all nineteen were razed to the ground, and a fine of 50,000 francs was imposed on the village. The Versailles correspondent of the *Standard*, reporting these reprisals, insisted that they were entirely legitimate as "the indispensable justice of war". "But, oh, the pity of it!" he added, almost despite himself. "Oh, the pity of it!"

THE SIXTH WEEK

Monday, 24 October – Sunday, 30 October

Disastrous News

In his *Journal* for 24 October Edmond de Goncourt noted:

> This evening, over the whole length of the Rue Saint-Lazare, above the white building of the railway station, a sky of blood, a cherry-coloured glow, dyeing the sky as far as the darkest blue of the night; a strange sight, in the nature of those prodigies which used to trouble ancient antiquity. Around me one voice says: "It's the Forest of Bondy burning." Another: "It's an experiment in lighting at Montmartre." A third: "It's an aurora borealis."

The third voice was right. The aurora borealis appeared about six o'clock and lasted for an hour. At half-past seven it reappeared with all its original brilliance, fading away gradually between eight and nine. According to one eye-witness,

> the centre was a greenish or bluish white, at the two ends in the east and west there were two bright gleams of a remarkable, almost currant red, which might have suggested a huge fire in the distance, if it had not been for the absence of any reflecting cloud, so that the stars remained visible through the colours. Now and then a bright ray, rather reminiscent of rays of electric light, rose from the horizon towards the zenith. This curious phenomenon had rarely appeared with such intensity at the latitude of Paris.

The very rarity of the sight convinced many Parisians that the aurora borealis was an omen, though opinion was divided as to whether good or evil. One of the most confirmed pessimists was the veteran Romantic, Théophile Gautier, now a

sad, embittered old man with only two years to live. Edmond
de Goncourt, who went to see him on the 26th, has left this
record of the disillusioned conversation they had:

"This revolution", he said, "has finished me off. At my age,
you can't start your life all over again. ... I've lost everything.
I've become a hack again, at my age. ... A wall, to smoke my
pipe in the sun, and soup twice a week, that's what I ask for. ...
The worst of it all is the hypocrisy I have to put in the things I
write: you understand, my descriptions have to be tricolour!

"Isn't it tragic, all this ironmongery!" he went on, as we passed
Chevet's window, where the marble shelves, decorated only
yesterday with all the solid succulences of the table, now hold
nothing but tinned vegetables. Then, after a few moments of
silence, during which his meditation leaned heavily on my arm,
he suddenly said: "What a disaster! And how complete, how
concrete! First, capitulation; today, famine; tomorrow, bombardment. How artistically this disaster is composed!"

He added: "But isn't it odd that courage, our native quality,
that thing which was such an essentially French product, wasn't
it? – everybody believed that we were born heroic – no longer
exists! Everybody runs as fast as he can. Did you see those soldiers whose tunics had been turned inside out, and whose faces
the population were invited to spit in? That's an official declaration of cowardice by the army if ever there was one!"

"My dear Théo," I said, taking leave of him, "my opinion is that
cynicism has killed all the heroic imbecility of old; and nations
which have lost that are doomed to die."

Another writer who took a gloomy view of the situation
was the Besieged Resident, who, after reporting that the
appeal for volunteers for the National Guard had been a failure and that those citizens who had answered the appeal
refused to venture outside the ramparts, commented:

It really does appear too monstrous that the able-bodied men of
this city should wear uniforms, learn the goose-step, and refuse to
take any part in the defence within shot of the enemy. I was
reading yesterday the account of a court-martial on one of these
heroes, who had fallen out with his commanding officer, and
threatened to pass his sword through his body. The culprit,
counsel urged, was a man of amiable, though excitable disposition; the father of two sons, had once saved a child from drown-
ing, and had presented several curiosities to a museum. Taking
these facts into consideration, the Court condemned him to six
days' imprisonment; his accuser apologized to him, and shook
hands with him. What is to be expected of troops when military

offences of the grossest kind are treated in this fashion? I know myself officers of the National Guard who, when they are on duty on the ramparts, quietly leave their men there, and come home to dinner. No one appears to consider this anything extra-ordinary. Well may General Trochu look up to the sky when it is overcast, and wish he were in Brittany shooting woodcocks.

On an expedition to Choisy-le-Roi, which the Paris papers reported was no longer occupied by the Prussians but which he found to his peril was, Labouchère discovered that the Breton Mobiles felt a similar contempt for the citizen soldiers inside the walls. "These Breton Mobiles", he wrote,

> are the idols of the hour. They are to the Republic what the Zouaves were to the Empire. They are very far, however, from reciprocating the admiration which the Republicans entertain for them. They are brave, devout, credulous peasants, care far more for Brittany than they do for Paris, and regard the individ-uals who rule by the grace of Paris with feelings the reverse of friendly. The army and the Mobiles, indeed, like being cooped up here less and less every day, and they cannot understand why the 300,000 National Guards who march and drill in safety inside the capital do not come outside and rough it like them.

What exasperated the Mobiles most of all was the fact that the rulers of Paris, instead of devoting their entire energy to the war, spent much of their time on measures which were often anticlerical in nature and always petty-minded. Thus the Mayor of the 23rd Arrondissement published an order for-bidding the teachers in his district to take the children in their charge to hear Mass on Sundays; and the Boulevard Prince Eugène was renamed the Boulevard Voltaire, the statue of the prince being replaced by the statue of the philosopher. The newspapers had also begun demanding that the Rue de Londres should be rebaptized on the ground that the name of London was hated even more than that of Berlin. "If Prussia", said one writer,

> wages against us a war of bandits and savages, it is England which, in the gloom of its sombre country houses, pays the Uhlans who oppress our peasants, rape our women, massacre our soldiers, and pillage our provinces. She rejoices over our sufferings. . . .

This recurrence of anti-British feeling was probably due to the fact that the departure of a party of British residents had been announced for the 26th. Some Americans and Russians were due to leave the city at the same time, but it was the

British who were singled out for condemnation as cowardly neutrals taking flight to avoid the dangers of bombardment. After a farewell dinner at Brébant's, where the Paris correspondent of the *Standard* noted with disappointment that "there is neither soup nor vegetables, that the only *entrée* is a sardine, the only *hors-d'oeuvre* a pickled onion, and that for dessert they throw you a cigar", the British party duly assembled at the Porte de Charenton early on the 26th. To their horror and indignation, however, they were told that while the Russians and the Americans would be allowed to pass the Prussian outposts, the list of the British had not reached Count Bismarck in time to enable them to leave at the same time. "The guard", wrote one of the English correspondents with them,

> had literally to be turned out to prevent them from endeavouring to force their way through the whole German army. I spoke this morning to an English butler who had made one of the party. This worthy man evidently was of opinion that the end of the world is near at hand, when a butler, and a most respectable person, is treated in this manner. "Pray, sir, may I ask," he said with bitter scorn, "whether Her Majesty is still on the throne in England?" I replied I believed that she was. "Then", he went on, "has this Count Bismarck, as they call him, driven the British nobles out of the House of Lords? Nothing which this feller does would surprise me now."

The people of Paris would undoubtedly have derived a malicious satisfaction from this incident if their attention had not been distracted by a sensational piece of news. On the morning of the 27th the Republican newspaper *Combat* appeared with a paragraph headed, "Bazaine's Plan" and enclosed in a deep mourning border, which read as follows:

> It is a fact, sure and certain, which the Government of National Defence is keeping to itself as a state secret and which we denounce to the indignation of France as high treason, that Marshal Bazaine has sent a colonel to the King of Prussia's camp, to treat for the surrender of Metz and for peace, in the name of His Majesty the Emperor Napoleon III.

This statement caused tremendous excitement all over Paris, for it was generally recognized that Metz was of paramount importance to the French cause. Bazaine's surrender would not only deliver a fine fortress and a huge army into the enemy's hands, but would release Prince Frederick Charles's army to march on Paris just when General d'Aurelle de Paladines

75

was thought to be hurrying to the relief of the capital with the Army of the Loire. Public opinion tended to discount *Combat*'s report as too fantastic to deserve belief, but in fact it was perfectly well founded. More interested in keeping his army intact to restore the Empire than in defending Metz, Bazaine had sent General Bourbaki to London to consult the Empress and General Boyer to Versailles to negotiate the surrender of the fortress. Both Eugénie and some of Bazaine's generals had shown a patriotic reluctance to approve of these negotiations, whereupon on the 27th, the very day *Combat* published its sensational statement, the Marshal simply surrendered Metz, all the munitions it contained, and its garrison of 4,000 officers and 150,000 men.

Refusing to believe that Bazaine could even contemplate what in fact he had already done, a number of Parisians stormed into the offices of *Combat*, and, finding that Pyat had fled, took his secretary with them to the Hôtel de Ville. There they were received by Jules Ferry and Henri Rochefort, who emphatically denied the truth of *Combat*'s statement, the latter also indulging in some sarcastic comments on Pyat's integrity and courage. Excited groups gathered on the boulevards all afternoon, and a few irate patriots suggested attacking the *Combat* offices and smashing the printing presses. In the end, however, the National Guards contented themselves by seizing all the copies of the paper they could find and burning them in the streets, in the midst of cheering crowds.

The next morning the *Journal Officiel* published an outright denial of the truth of Pyat's allegation, stigmatized *Combat* as a Prussian organ, and praised Bazaine as "the glorious soldier of Metz". This dogmatic attitude was sheer folly, for although the news of Bazaine's capitulation was not known to the Government until the 30th, when Thiers arrived in Paris with a safe-conduct to discuss an armistice, there had been reports that the Marshal's loyalty to the Republic was questionable, and Jules Ferry for one had heard from the Society for the Relief of the Wounded that Versailles was full of rumours of negotiation. But for the moment public confidence was restored, and the population's morale soared to new heights when news came that evening that Le Bourget had been captured from the Prussians by the *franc-tireurs* of the Press, under General Carré de Bellemare, supported by detachments of the line and the Garde Mobile.

Bellmare's success, oddly enough, was regarded by the Government as a considerable embarrassment. "This", Trochu was reported as saying, "is increasing the death-roll for no purpose whatever." His point was that Le Bourget formed no part of the general plan of defence, and that Belle-mare, by capturing the village without orders, had merely secured a useless position which it would be both difficult and futile for the French to hold. Yet, as Maurice d'Hérisson pointed out in his memoirs,

> while its capture could not compromise the situation of the in-vesting army, it compelled the Prussians to widen their circle and make a detour. It did not hurt them, but it inconvenienced them to a certain extent. It is undeniable that if the same action had been taken all round Paris, the German cordon would have been stretched to breaking point. As an isolated case, however, the attack and success were not of much account, and were not really worth the blood shed on them.

This was not, of course, the opinion of the people of Paris, who had been waiting for weeks for a French success and could now celebrate what they regarded as a splendid victory. If Trochu had been anything of a psychologist he would have realized the tonic effect this minor success had had on Paris, and, still more important, the disappointment which would follow if Le Bourget were recaptured by the enemy; but he was a text-book soldier, and he sternly ignored Bellemare's appeals for reinforcements. The Prussians, on the other hand, though doubtless attaching no more military importance to Le Bour-get than did the French, saw its value in the battle of morale, and set out to recover possession of the village. On the 29th, they brought up a battery of 21 heavy guns to bombard the Mobiles, who had only three cannon, and on the 30th, after an engagement lasting barely an hour, they put half the tired, demoralized defenders to flight and made the rest prisoners.

Meanwhile, inside Paris, anxiety and uneasiness had taken the place of the elation of the 28th. In the first place, rumours had reached the city of the plight of Bellmare's men, who were reported to be starving, underarmed, heavily bombarded, and in danger of being cut off by a large Prussian force. Then the affair of Bazaine's alleged capitulation was revived, with *Combat* stating that "it had the news of Metz from Flourens, who had it direct from Rochefort, a member of the Govern-ment". Finally, on the morning of the 30th, with the Government reeling under the blow of this revelation, Pyat published a brilliant ironical attack on "the Romans of the Hôtel de Ville" which laid the ground for the events of the following day.

"These men are Romans," he wrote;

in them alone are centred all the glories of the great Roman commonwealth, all the glories and all the titles. They have not with them, it is true, Fabius or Brutus; but Fabius is at the Louvre, where more than ever he deserves his surname of Cunctator; and as for Brutus, Brutus is departed – let us hope not for the plains of Philippi. Brutus is magnificent; every now and then he sends dispatches after this style: "All is well: we have been beaten at such a place; such and such a town has surrendered; such a general has capitulated; but all is going well, remarkably well." Perhaps you might fancy that thirty-eight million men, if they chose, would not allow themselves to be stamped out in handfuls of two thousand without stirring from the spot; and possibly the thought might occur that if we had guns, those guns would fire, and that if we were the strongest we should not always be the weakest; but Brutus affirms the contrary, and Brutus is, we know, an honourable man. Again, some might say that up to the present the only thing which has not failed is the defence of Paris, and since nothing has succeeded of what has been attempted, it is perhaps time to try our hands at something new; but Brutus affirms the contrary, and Brutus is, we know, an honourable man. ...

The news that Le Bourget had been retaken by the Prussians reached Paris in the late afternoon of the 30th, but was dismissed by most of those who heard it as an enemy rumour. It was confirmed the next morning in the *Journal Officiel,* which at the same time gave the people of Paris two other disastrous pieces of information. In terms which could scarcely have been more misleading, it announced that "Marshal Bazaine and his army have been obliged to surrender after heroic efforts, which the shortage of food and munitions prevented them from continuing any longer." It also stated that the veteran statesman Adolphe Thiers had returned to Paris the previous day after his tour of the European capitals, not, as had been hoped, with a promise of armed intervention by some friendly Power, but with proposals for an armistice nominally supported by Great Britain, Russia, Austria and Italy.

As Maurice d'Hérisson wrote later,

the most expert of stage-managers could not have more cleverly combined these three fateful incidents at one and the same point in a play – a defeat before Paris, the annihilation of our last and finest regular army, and the admission that our provincial forces had done nothing of any value, seeing that, as Tours as well as in Paris, there was an inclination to lay down arms.

The moment was ripe for insurrection.

Insurrection

The triple shock caused in Paris by the news that Le Bourget was lost, Metz had capitulated and negotiations for an armistice were being considered was followed by the suspicion – a suspicion which occurred swiftly and naturally to Parisian patriots at the slightest reverse – that Trochu's Plan and Bazaine's Plan were synonymous, and that Paris was being betrayed. Determined to discover whether there was any foundation for this suspicion, hundreds of National Guards of what were called "advanced opinions" made their way to the Place de l'Hôtel de Ville, where by midday a huge crowd had gathered. Deputations were admitted now and then to interview members of the Government, which was in council, being assured by Jules Ferry that the disasters France had suffered were not irreparable, and by Étienne Arago that the Prussians would never enter the Hôtel de Ville as long as he was alive. These assurances did not satisfy the crowd outside, which had grown to about 15,000, and was shouting: "Long live the Commune!" and "No armistice!" About 2.30 some 300 people managed to slip into the building by a side door, and after a brief, panic-stricken withdrawal when three or four shots were fired in the square, hundreds more forced their way inside.

The Government was meanwhile considering three proposals put to it by Ernest Picard as sops to offer the malcontents:

that municipal councillors should be elected, that the Government should submit itself to election by the citizens of Paris, and that no decision should be taken about an armistice without consulting the population. The Council promptly voted for announcing the municipal elections, though without indicating any date; but when Arago left the room to announce this decision, he found the mob smashing windows, tables and desks, and tendered his resignation in disgust. And the members of the Government were still debating whether to endanger their positions by submitting themselves for election when the doors of the council-room were forced open and a group of National Guard officers rushed in, demanding the election of the Commune, and the formation of a new Cabinet presided over by Dorian, the popular Minister of Public Works. Picard managed to slip out of the room and make his escape, but his colleagues stayed in their seats, to be harangued, threatened and spat at by a growing crowd of rioters.

This commotion was at its height when, at four o'clock, Gustave Flourens arrived at the Hôtel de Ville with his own free corps, the Belleville Sharpshooters, and took command of the situation. He proposed that the Commune should be nominated there and then by acclamation, and wrote his own name at the head of the list, but in response to shouts that Dorian should be made president he gave way.

Eventually the following names were agreed on – Dorian Flourens, Mottu, Victor Hugo, Louis Blanc, Delescluze, Blanqui, Avaial, Raspail, Ledru-Rollin, Félix Pyat, Ranvier and Rochefort – and scraps of paper containing the whole list, of simply the words: "Commune decreed – Dorian President" were thrown from the windows to the crowd in the square.

Out there Edmond de Goncourt was scrupulously registering everything he could see and hear for posterity. "There was a throng", he wrote that evening,

a multitude, a mêlée of people of all sorts and conditions, through which National Guards would force their way now and then, waving their rifles in the air and shouting: "The Commune for ever!" The building was in darkness, with time moving heedlessly round the illuminated clockface, the windows all wide open, and the workmen who had led the movement of 4 September sitting on the sills with their legs dangling outside. The square was a forest of rifle butts raised in the air, the metal plates gleaming in

81

in the rain. On every face could be seen distress at Bazaine's capitulation, a sort of fury over yesterday's reverse at Le Bourget, and at the same time an angry and rashly heroic determination not to make peace. Some workmen in bowler hats were writing in pencil, on greasy pocket-books, a list a gentleman was dictating to them. Among the names I heard those of Blanqui, Flourens, Ledru-Rollin, and Mottu. "Things are going to move now!" said one workman, in the midst of the eloquent silence of my neighbours; and I came across a group of women already talking fearfully of the division of property. It seemed, as I had guessed from the workmen's legs dangling from the windows of the Hôtel de Ville, that the Government had been overthrown and the Commune established, and that the list of gentleman in the square was due to be confirmed by universal suffrage within twenty-four hours. It was all over. Today one could write: *Finis Franciae!* .... Shouts of "The Commune for ever!" went up all over the square, and fresh battalions went rushing off down the Rue de Rivoli, followed by a screaming, gesticulating riff-raff. ... Poor France, to have fallen under the control of those stupid bayonets! Just then an old lady, seeing me buy the evening paper, asked me – oh, the irony of it! – whether the price of Government stock was quoted in my paper. ...

Henry Labouchère had a closer view of what was happening inside the Hôtel de Ville, for he had entered the building with the mob during the afternoon, but it could scarcely be said that he had any clearer idea of the situation. "For more than two hours", he wrote,

I remained there. The spectacle was a curious one – everybody was shouting, everybody was writing a list of a new Government and reading it aloud. In one corner a man incessantly blew a trumpet, in another a patriot beat a drum. At one end was a table, round which had been sitting, and from this vantage ground Félix Pyat and other virtuous citizens harangued, and, as I understood, proclaimed the Commune and themselves, for it was impossible to distinguish a word. The atmosphere was stifling, and at last I got out of a window on to the landing in the courtyard. Here citizens had established themselves everywhere. I had the pleasure to see the "venerable" Blanqui led up the steps by his admirers. This venerable man had, *horresco referens*, been pushed up in a corner, where certain citizens had kicked his venerable frame, and pulled his venerable white beard, before they recognized who he was. By this time it appeared to be understood that a Government had been constituted, consisting of Blanqui, Ledru-Rollin, Delescluze, Louis Blanc, Flourens, and others. Flourens, whom I now perceived for the first time, went through a corridor, with some armed men, and I and others followed him. We got into an antechamber, and then into a large room, where a great row was going on. I did not get farther than close to the door, and consequently could not well distinguish what was passing, but I saw Flourens standing on a table, and I heard that he was calling upon the members of the Government of National Defence, who were seated round it, to resign, and that Jules Favre was refusing to do so. After a scene of confusion, which lasted half an hour, I found myself, with those round me, pushed out of the room, and I heard that the old Government had been arrested, and that a consultation was to take place between it and the new one.

As darkness fell and the evening wore on, the scene in the council-chamber took on a fantastic, ghostly quality. "Round the council table", writes Maurice d'Hérisson,

behind the seated members of the Government, calm and silent, the men of the National Guard were packed close one against another, and were constantly being jammed closer together by the arrival of fresh reinforcements. Their leaders, Flourens, Millière, Delescluze, Blanqui, Pyat, Mottu, etc., had transformed the baize-covered table into a circus ring, and strode along it, treading on the paper and jotting-books, upsetting the inkstands and sand-boxes, and crushing pens and pencils beneath their feet. They all shouted alike, and, as their audience also shouted, nobody could hear them. Trochu, with his two officers still behind his chair, smoked his cigar, and watched the coming and going of these spurred or worn heels on a level with his chest.

Meanwhile Picard had been busy organizing a counter-attack. First he had gone to the Louvre to get help from the Army, but General Schmitz had received strict instructions from Trochu to take no action without orders from him, and he refused to send his troops against the Hôtel de Ville. At the staff offices of the National Guard, however, Picard met with a readier response, and orders were promptly given for the *rappel* to be sounded all over Paris. The indefatigable Picard also contrived to have the National Printing House garrisoned, to prohibit the insertion of any Communard decrees in the *Journal Officiel*, and to warn all the different ministries to get ready to defend themselves.

The Oxford Graduate, who was writing in bed when he heard "the long mournful blast of the *rappel*, calling the National Guard to arms", confessed that "if I were a National Guard, the trumpets would have to blow at least thrice before

I should turn out from under the warm coverlet, buckle on my military accoutrements, belt, cartridge-box, bayonet and *tabatière* rifle". A good many actual National Guards felt the same reluctance to turn out, and Goncourt records seeing an angry young officer running along the middle of the boulevard shouting at the top of his voice: "To arms! To arms, damn you!" Eventually, though, one bourgeois battalion, the 106th, was marched to the Hôtel de Ville, where its commander managed to release Trochu, Ferry and Arago. But then the insurgents, who had been taken off their guard, rallied; the other members of the Government were put in a bay window under armed guard; and the 106th battalion was driven out of the building. Even so, Flourens and his colleagues felt less sure of themselves, conscious of the opposition building up against them and depressed by the failure of all the measures they had so far tried to take. A detachment they had sent to seize the Ministry of Finance and the artillery park behind Notre-Dame had failed in its object; a lieutenant who had gone to the Treasury with an official demand for 600,000 francs had come back empty-handed; and a decree naming a provisional Municipal Council and summoning it for the next day had been rejected by the *Journal Officiel*. When, about 11.30, some fresh battalions of the National Guard, led by Jules Ferry and Edmond Adam, the Prefect of Police, arrived at the Hôtel de Ville, and it was reported that General Ducrot was approaching with 10,000 Mobiles, the insurgents decided that the time had come to parley.

Delescluze accordingly went out on to the square, explained to Ferry that he was acting as mediator in the interests of peace, and asked for a delay of half-an-hour while his colleagues discussed terms – a request which Ferry promptly granted. But Delescluze had scarcely finished persuading the other insurgents to agree on evacuation of the Hôtel de Ville, provided the Commune was elected the next day, when Flourens was informed that a whole battalion of Breton Mobiles had entered the building by an underground passage. The insurgents hurriedly approached Dorian, the Minister of Public Works, who had remained in the Hôtel de Ville all day, pathetically trying to reconcile his popularity and his duty, and obtained an agreement from him that no action should be taken against any of them for what had happened, that the municipal elections should take place the next day, and that the Government should submit itself to election two days later. By this time, however, Ferry had been let into the building by the Mobiles and was insisting on unconditional surrender. The ring-leaders of the insurrection barely had time to persuade their prisoners to ratify the agreement with Dorian before beating a retreat with as much dignity and calm as they could muster. General Trochu and General Ducrot then arrived from the Louvre to review the loyal bourgeois battalions of the National Guard in the Place de l'Hôtel de Ville, after which – at about three or four o'clock in the morning – everybody went home to bed.

Early the next morning the walls of Paris were found to be covered with notices signed by Dorian, Schoelcher and Arago, summoning the population to elect four municipal councillors for each arrondissement, and for a few hours Paris wondered which side had in fact triumphed the previous day. But when the Government met in council it decided to disavow these notices, and in the afternoon a fresh proclamation by Jules Favre was posted up, announcing that on the following Thursday the population would be called on to vote whether they wanted immediate governmental and municipal elections. The Government also considered the question of Dorian's agreement with the insurgents, and after a stormy discussion and a lengthy adjournment voted to prosecute the ring-leaders of the insurrection – whereupon the Prefect of Police, to his honour, resigned rather than break his word. He was replaced by a lawyer called Cresson, and within the next few days a number of the insurgents were arrested and committed to the Conciergerie. Flourens and Blanqui, however, had gone into hiding and could not be found, while several of their comrades who had been arrested were soon released, the magistrate in charge of the case deciding that they were being prosecuted simply on account of their political opinions.

On 2 November the Government issued the official form on on which a vote was to be taken the following day, and which read: "Does the population of Paris maintain, Yes or No, the powers of the Government of National Defence?" At the same time it was announced that on Saturday the 5th each of the 20 arrondissements was to elect a Mayor and four adjuncts, who were to replace those nominated by the Governments. The Republicans or Ultras promptly raised a tremendous outcry against these measures, protesting that the

Government was following in the steps of the Empire by taking refuge in the dishonest device of the plebiscite, traditionally defined by the French peasant as "a Latin word which, according to Monsieur le Curé, means *oui*." As for the elections to be held on the 5th, one shrewd but cynical writer observed that

> Monsieur Jules Favre has a double object in view; he wants to get rid of the mayors in office, and at the same time to keep, or appear to keep, his promise of municipal elections. The triumphant majority which he evidently expects on the vote of confidence will, in all probability, secure for him on Saturday the return of reactionary mayors, and these, instead of forming a united deliberative body, in fact a Commune – which the term "municipal" is understood to imply, will be isolated and confined to their respective mayoralties, where they will become mere clerks of the Central Government at the Hôtel de Ville.

Labouchère's comments on the plebiscite were as penetrating and perceptive as ever. "Of course the Government will today have a large majority", he wrote on the 3rd.

> Were it to be in a minority the population would simply assert that it wishes to live under no government. This plebiscite is in itself an absurdity. The real object, however, is to strengthen the hands of the depositories of power, and to enable them to conclude an armistice, which would result in a Constituent Assembly, and would free them from the responsibility of concluding peace on terms rather than accept which they proudly asserted a few weeks ago they would all die. The fact is that the great mass of the Parisians wish for peace at any price. Under the circumstances I do not blame them. No town is obliged to imitate the example of Moscow. If, however, it intends, after submitting to a blockade, to capitulate on terms which it scouted at first, before any of its citizens have been even under fire, and before its provisions are exhausted, it would have done well not to have called upon the world to witness its sublimity.

The tradesmen and well-to-do classes in Paris undoubtedly both wanted peace and felt confident that they would soon have it. "Not a soul you meet", wrote Henry Markheim,

> questions the conclusion of the armistice, which is "as good as signed: Bismarck will of course make objections *pour la forme*, but they won't hold in the presence of the moral support of Europe." All is going on well, and there seems to be an implicit understanding between the conservative voters and the Govern-

ment that the latter will, in acknowledgement of their support, make things easy and smooth all further difficulties which lie in the way of peace: Monsieur Jules Favre will forget his inch and his stone – that was a mere *façon de parler*, and besides Alsace and Lorraine are not to be annexed to Germany, but "mediatized". Few people know what is meant by "mediatizing" a province, but that is just the point of the expression. What would be the use of diplomacy if it called things by their names? The shop windows begin to fill with unknown plenty; articles which had reached fabulous prices, such as butter, eggs, etc., are offered, in consequence of the armistice, at what we have learnt to consider "a very reasonable rate". A friend has just purchased an entire ham, a real *jambon d'York*, of a grocer who discovered it this morning by the merest chance in his back-shop upon reading his *Petit Journal*. I went into the same shop with the most *couleur-de-rose* print I could lay hold of, and the obliging *épicier* was tempted by a paragraph in the *Électeur Libre* to discover a second edition of the armistice-jambon. I wish there could be an armistice every day: we might make up for all the time lost before and since the beginning of the siege, when we neglected to lay in a store of provisions. ...

The result of the plebiscite, which was a foregone conclusion, was announced by torchlight in the Place de l'Hôtel de Ville shortly before midnight, to wildly cheering crowds. The next day the Government published the actual voting figures, which were 321,373 ayes against 53,585 noes; taking into account the army's votes, the overall figures were 557,996 for the Government and 63,638 against, or roughly a proportion of 9 to 1 in favour of the established order. This massive vote of confidence was naturally acclaimed by the Government's supporters as a splendid victory, but it did not succeed in allaying all anxieties. "The vote of Thursday", wrote one neutral observer,

> has somewhat surprised the bourgeoisie. That one-seventh of the population should have registered their deliberate opinion that they prefer no government to that under which they are living is by no means a reassuring fact, more particularly when this seventh consists of "men of action", armed with muskets and provided with ammunition.

Moreover, widespread surprise was expressed at the size of the army vote, and not a little scepticism as to the fairness of the plebiscite as a whole. "Many complaints are made", wrote Labouchère, about the mode in which the vote was taken on Thursday; some of them appear to me to be just. The fact is, that Frenchmen have not the most elementary notion of fair play in an election. No matter what body of men are in power, they conceive that they have a perfect right to use that power to obtain a verdict in their favour from their fellow-citizens. Tried by our electioneering code, every French election which I ever witnessed would be annulled on the ground of "intimidation" and "undue influence".

The mayoral elections of 5 November, which were more difficult to falsify than a plebiscite, resulted in the return of extreme Republicans or Ultras for three of the 20 arrondissements. This was a blow for the Government, even though Favre had publicly stated that the election of mayors was "the negation of a Commune", for if the Government lost its popularity the council of mayors, as the only legally elected body in Paris, could and would become a commune. But the result of these municipal elections was of far less interest to the people of Paris than the all-important question of the armistice which Thiers had been negotiating with Bismarck since 1 November.

The old statesman had left Paris in the afternoon of 31 October, aware that there was considerable agitation in the city, but completely ignorant of the insurrection. To begin with, his negotiations with Bismarck went well. The Chancellor agreed not only to the armistice but also to the re-victualling of Paris, which was a vital condition since without it an armistice would be a voluntary blockade offering no danger to the besieger and no hope to the besieged. Bismarck still refused to agree to legislative elections for Alsace and Lorraine, but he consented to the nomination of notabilities to represent the population of those two provinces.

Things had reached this point when, on Wednesday night or early on Thursday morning, news of the events of 31 October reached the Prussian Headquarters, first from the reports of the advanced posts and soon afterwards from the Paris newspapers. Moltke immediately insisted on continuing the siege rather than negotiate with a Government incapable even of controlling its own citizens; the King of Prussia readily accepted this view; and Bismarck himself, though readier to adopt a conciliatory attitude, could scarcely maintain it in these new circumstances. Thiers was accordingly informed, first, that revolution had broken out in Paris, and then that the Prussians' terms had had to be modified to meet the situation. An armistice could be granted to enable a National Assembly to be called, but the revictualling of Paris would not be allowed unless one or possibly two forts were surrendered as a guarantee.

There was nothing left for Thiers to do but return to Paris to confer with the Government. In the event, Trochu decided that it was unsafe as yet either for Thiers to enter the city or for himself to leave it, and he therefore sent Ducrot and Favre to represent him at a meeting with Thiers at the foot of the ruined Pont de Sèvres. An eyewitness described this fateful meeting as follows:

> This morning, about nine o'clock, General Ducrot and Monsieur Jules Favre arrived at the Pont de Sèvres; a few moments before, on the Sèvres bank, a bugle had sounded, and a rider had hoisted a white flag; on our side a similar flag had been hoisted. At a quarter to ten a little green boat left the bank occupied by the Prussians and brought across a figure dressed in a black macfarlane, holding a paper packet in one hand and a hawthorn stick in the other; this was Monsieur Thiers, whom General Ducrot and Monsieur Jules Favre came forward to meet. Their conversation started immediately, the three men walking along the bank while the boat returned towards Sèvres, and after a quarter of an hour or half an hour two Germans got into it and came to join Messieurs Favre and Thiers. After a few moments' conversation, General Ducrot beckoned a courier, who took an envelope and made off in the direction of Paris. The five men continued their walk along the bank, sometimes all together, sometimes in pairs, with General Ducrot often remaining behind.

It was Ducrot, in fact, who in the course of this conversation rejected the Prussian terms, insisting that honour and common sense called for a continuance of the struggle. Favre, who was understandably reluctant to provoke another insurrection, supported him; and it was in vain that Thiers urged the acceptance of the German conditions, pointing out that Bismarck had told him that while peace at the moment meant the cession of Alsace and an indemnity of three milliard francs, after the fall of Paris it would mean the cession of both Alsace and Lorraine and the payment of five milliard francs.

At a meeting in Paris that evening the Government confirmed the attitude adopted by Ducrot and Favre, and at noon on Sunday an envoy left Paris for Versailles to inform the Prussians of the rejection of their conditions. The same day the *Journal Officiel* told the people of Paris the unwelcome news in the following terms:

> The four great neutral powers, Great Britain, Russia, Austria and Italy, had taken the intiative in proposing an armistice to allow the election of a National Assembly. The Government of National Defence made known its conditions, which were the revictualling of Paris and the voting for the National Assembly by the whole French population. Prussia had expressly refused the revictualling of the capital, and only admitted the voting of Alsace and Lorraine with certain restrictions. The Government of National Defence has unanimously decided that the armistice, thus understood, must be rejected.

"The news that the armistice had been rejected", reported Labouchère,

> fell like a thunderclap upon the population. I never remember to have witnessed a day of such general gloom since the commencement of the siege. The feeling of despair is, I hear, still stronger in the army. Were the real conditions of things outside known, I am certain that the Government would be forced to conclude an armistice on no matter what terms.

But the people of Paris knew nothing of the situation in the provinces; and by the plebiscite of 3 November they had placed themselves in the power of a Government which was now committed to a policy of war to the end, of *une résistance à outrance.*

Monday, 7 November – Sunday, 13 November

Paris in November

For the people of Paris, the beginning of the eighth week of the siege was overshadowed by the bitter realization that all hope of an armistice had to be abandoned. For many of the English residents, on the other hand, it was marked by joyful preparations for imminent release. Some 60 or 70 of them, together with about 50 Austrians and Swiss, had at long last obtained permission to pass through the German lines, and arrangements had been made for them to leave Paris early on 8 November. A great many more British citizens would have joined the party if they had known that there was a chance of getting away; but the Embassy had done nothing to inform them of this possibility apart from putting up a notice in the Consular Office where hardly anybody was likely to see it. Among the keen-sighted residents who did spot the notice, a good many had been discouraged by a characteristic proviso, that "the Embassy *could not* charge itself" – the italics were its own – "with the expense of assisting British subjects to leave Paris". The result was that the 60 or 70 Britons who eventually left were either sufficiently well-to-do to pay their own passage or sufficiently humble to have admitted their poverty and applied to the British Charitable Fund for a grant of money.

The closer the hour of release approached, the louder the British grew in their complaints against the Embassy for having, as they put it, "humbugged" them for so long. In fact, the long delay was not the Embassy's fault: it was due, first, to the difficulty of communicating with Versailles, and secondly to the fact that since the British Government had not recognized the Republic, Trochu could not be approached officially. In the end it was thanks to the American Minister, Washburne, that the necessary permission was obtained. "I need hardly observe", wrote an English journalist,

> that the Foreign Office has done its best to render the question more complicated. It has sent orders to Mr. Wodehouse to provide for the transport of British subjects, without sending funds, and having told Lord Lyons to take the archives with him, it perpetually refers to instructions contained in dispatches which it well knows are at Tours.

At seven o'clock in the morning of 8 November the British party left Paris by the Porte de Charenton, accompanied by the Chief Secretary of the Embassy and the Vice-Consul. About half the members of the party had provided themselves with vehicles of their own, while the rest travelled in cabs and buses as far as Le Petit Créteil, a village some two miles outside the walls. From Le Petit Créteil everybody had to make his way on foot through the French advanced posts to the Prussian lines. As the refugees also included Austrian and Swiss subjects, and all three groups were accompanied by friends and embassy officials, it was a large cavalcade which advanced towards the Prussians, preceded by a trumpeter and the indispensable white flag. The inspection of passports and the filling in of safe-conducts took another couple of hours, after which the refugees took leave of their friends. Or, as one correspondent put it,

> one section of the assemblage went hopefully forward into promised lands, overflowing with milk and honey, while the other retraced their steps to the beleaguered city, to famish on their ounce and a half of meat a day.

The beleagured city was now at last beginning to look and feel the part. Most of the artistic and architectural treasures of Paris had disappeared from sight. The famous horses of Marly at the entrance of the Champs-Élysées had been boxed in timber and buried under sandbags, as had the groups of the Arc de Triomphe. Jean Goujon's bas-reliefs at the Louvre had been coated with plaster, all the entrances of the museum walled up, and most of the pictures and statues consigned to the cellars. The valuable books and manuscripts in the Bibliothèque Nationale and the Bibliothèque Mazarine had similarly gone underground, like the precious instruments of the Observatory. Again, at the Sainte-Chapelle, Pinaigrier's windows were completely hidden behind piles of sandbags and turf; and while nothing appeared to have been done to protect the roof, the old encaustic tiles with which the chapel was paved had all been taken up, so that any shell falling on the building would bury itself in the soft earth.

The streets themselves had changed beyond recognition. In the thousand or two unfinished houses in the "Haussmannized" districts of Paris all work had been abandoned, and the same was true of the new Hôtel-Dieu, which had been under construction when war had broken out. The crowds of smartly dressed strollers had disappeared from the boulevards, the *flâneur* having been transformed into a soldier and the *Parisienne* into a nurse. Sombre dress had become the rule and any elegantly dressed woman would have run the risk of being mobbed. As for the shops, a good many – notably the *crémeries* and *rôtissieries* – had closed down for want of anything to sell, but most offered some more or less unusual form of merchandise. "The chandlers and picture-dealers", noted Edmond de Goncourt,

> are selling oilcloth képi-covers. The bookmakers' establishments, at present deprived of business, have becme siege bazaars; in their windows you see revolvers, telescopes, knives, covers for bastions, sheepskin beds, cartridge-extractors for rifles, filter-cups, etc. The milliners tempt the military collector with the classic Prussian helmet with its spread-eagle lightning-conductor, or with a Bavarian's chocolate-coloured helmet "picked up at Châtillon".

The number of German helmets on sale in Paris was indeed something of a mystery until, early in November, a factory was discovered in the city where enemy helmets and sabres were being made. When arrested, the owner protested that he was merely trying to meet the demand for trophies from the battlefield. He was certainly both industrious and ingenious: one room of his house was littered with forged letters in German purporting to be from mothers, sisters and brides to their loved ones in the besieging army; these, he explained, he had been going to sell as guaranteed from the pockets of German corpses.

Not all the trade in Paris, of course, was conducted over shop-counters. The kerbs of the main boulevards were lined with hawkers, invariably sporting the képi and sometimes the full uniform of the National Guard, who sold everything from breastplates to brandy-flasks and from canteens to sword-sticks. They did a lively trade in caricatures and photographs, which a disapproving English journalist described as "frequently being of a most indecent description". Caricatures of Napoleon III and his Empress were fewer than they had been presumably because even the most rabid Republicans had grown tired of flogging those dead horses, but the Pope was still a popular butt. On several occasions, indeed, vendors of caricatures of the Pope were pursued and illtreated by irate Bretons, the most devout of all the capital's defenders. It was safer, they found, to confine themselves to the sale of patriotic caricatures which could not easily cause offence: caricatures of "Butcher William", for example; or of Bismarck in seven-league boots, making ineffectual attempts to stride from Versailles to Paris; or again of a regiment of mice dressed as Prussian soldiers marching into a mousetrap labelled France in which Paris was the cheese.

Similar cartoons were to be found in the Paris newspapers, some of them – such as the Daumier drawing of Death thanking Bismarck for his generous provision of victims – impressive works of art. There were also mildly humorous stories of the sort from which people in danger or hardship have always derived comfort. That of the National Guard, for instance, who complained that his captain was a traitor, "because every time he orders us to march forward, we meet the enemy"; that of the citizen who felt ill after dinner and complained that he had always thought himself a better *horseman*; or that of the man who, wanting to create a sensation, had gone into a café and called for a railway timetable.

The newspapers did not, of course, rely solely on caricatures and cartoons in their efforts to keep up the spirits of the besieged population. Some launched blood-thirsty schemes such as the subscription opened by *Combat* for the manufacture of a "rifle of honour" to be presented to the man who shot the King of Prussia: no fewer than 6,000 citizens offered money to pay for this weapon, which was to have the words "Liberty, Equality, Fraternity" engraved on it and bear the somewhat incongrous name of "the Pacificator". Another journal, not to be outdone, formed a society with the object of capturing Bismarck dead or alive, with the privilege, if the latter were achieved, of exhibiting the Iron Chancellor in an iron cage. And all the Paris papers, without exception, published accounts of the heroic achievements of Sergeant Hoff, a legendary and, according to some sceptics, non-existent warrior who contrived single-handed to kill vast numbers of Germans almost every day. (At a later stage of the siege Sergeant Hoff was reported to have disappeared and was officially branded as a traitor, which seemed to confirm the sceptics' suspicions; but after the war he reappeared and was rehabilitated.)

Public amusements in Paris were hard to find, and not particularly gay when found. In the early days of the siege any form of entertainment had been frowned on, but the authorities had gradually realized that amusements were essential, if only to draw people away from the revolutionary clubs, at that time the only places of resort. Permission had accordingly been granted for various musical recitals, dramatic performances, and lectures or readings, which were given two or three afternoons a week in such theatres as had not been converted into hospitals. The lectures were generally concerned with the character and psychology of the enemy; and probably the most successful of all these conferences was that given by the critic Lapommeraye, who established an elaborate comparison between Molière's Tartuffe and Bismarck – the former the Tartuffe of religion, the latter the Tartuffe of politics. At the little Bouffes, where Hortense Schneider had sung to a deliriously enthusiastic public under the Second Empire, the audience now listened in grave approval to recitations of Hugo's *Châtiments*. At the Théâtre-Français, the sometime "Comedians of the Emperor" presented plays from their usual classical repertory, but in everyday dress. And at the Ambigu, although the melodrama still held sway, the play presented was a topical offering called *Les Paysans Lorrains*.

The changes in songs, plays and costumes on the stage were reflected in the auditorium. Gas being too precious to waste on amusements, the theatres were lighted either with petroleum lamps, which filled the air with smoke and smell, or else with candles, which, as one correspondent observed, "gave a soft and pleasant light enough, but left a bitter graveyard chill in every corner of the house". As for the audience, it usually sat huddled in furs and wraps, for the theatres were heated inadequately or not at all for their matinée performances. At the Opera in the Rue Lepelletier, however, evening performances were given in a reasonably heated house, and there the audience discarded its coats and cloaks to display an almost unbroken succession of uniforms and sable dresses. The usual order of things was in fact completely reversed. It was the men, normally confined to black evening dress, who supplied the only touches of colour, with the facings and galloons of their uniforms, while the women were invariably dressed in black. "The belles of Paris", an English writer reported, "are in mourning for the misfortunes of France".

Most of the theatres, of course, had been wholly or partly transformed into ambulances. Such was the case with the Porte-Saint-Martin, which Victor Hugo visited on 12 November to attend a rehearsal of a reading of *Les Châtiments*.

"After the rehearsal", he wrote in his notebook that day,

the wounded of the Porte-Saint-Martin ambulance asked me, through Madame Laurent, to go and see them. I said: "With all my heart," and I went.

They are installed in several rooms, chief of which is the old green-room of the theatre with its big round mirrors, where in 1831 I read *Marion de Lorme* to the actors.

On entering, I said to the wounded men: "You see in me a man who envies you. I desire nothing more on earth than one of your wounds. I salute you, children of France, favourite sons of the Republic, elect who suffer for the Fatherland."

They seemed to be greatly moved. I shook hands with them all. One held out his amputated wrist. Another had lost his nose. One had undergone a painful operation that very morning. A very young man had been decorated with the military medal a few hours before. A convalescent said to me: "I am a Franc-Comtois." "Like myself," I said. And I embraced him. The nurses in their white aprons, who are the actresses of the theatre, burst into tears.

While the largest ambulances were those installed in theatres such as the Porte-Saint-Martin and hotels such as the Grand, they were by no means the only ones. By mid-November there were 243 ambulances in Paris, most of them in private houses whose owners' motives varied between genuine charity, snobbery and avarice.

"The wounded soldier is in favour", reported Edmond de Goncourt.

> Going along the Boulevard Montmorency, I saw a lady taking a wounded man in a grey coat and a police cap for a ride in her open carriage. She was all eyes for him, and kept pulling the fur up over his legs; the hands of a wife and mother were constantly moving over his body. For some, the wounded soldier has become a fashionable object. For others he has become a useful object, a lightning-conductor. He defends your apartment house from the invasion of the suburban populations; he saves you in the future from fire, looting, and Prussian requisitioning. Somebody told me that an acquaintance of his had installed an ambulance in his house. Eight beds, two nurses, lint, bandages – nothing was lacking. In spite of all that, not a single wounded man came into sight. The owner of the ambulance was full of anxiety about his house. What did he do? He went to an ambulance blessed with wounded soldiers and paid out 3,000 francs – yes, 3,000 francs – to have one handed over to him.

Another writer reported without comment how a lady had called at her Mairie to ask for a wounded soldier to look after. She had been offered a swarthy Zouave. "No", she said, "I want a blond, being a brunette myself."

Fortunately for the honour of the fair sex, this lady and the lady whom Goncourt had seen on the Boulevard Montmorency were not typical of the women of Paris. There were countless women of all classes who worked without stint to feed and nurse their menfolk. But one thing ladies of leisure and hard-working nurses had in common: they almost invariably showed no interest in the subject of war or peace. "One of the most curious phases in this remarkable siege", wrote Labouchère,

> is that the women seem to consider the whole question a political one, which in no way regards them – they neither urge their men to resist, nor clamour for peace. *Tros Tyriusque* seems much the same to them; a few hundred have dressed themselves up as vivandières; the others appear to regret the rise in the price of provisions, but to trouble their heads about nothing else. If they thought that the cession of Alsace and Lorraine would reduce the price of butcher's meat, they would in a sort of apathetic way be in favour of the cession, but they are so utterly ignorant of anything except matters connected with their toilettes and Monsieur

Paul de Kock's novels, that they confine themselves to shruggin their shoulders and hoping for the best, and they support all th privations to which they are exposed owing to the siege withou complaint and without enthusiasm. The word armistice bein beyond the range of their vocabulary, they call it "l'amnistie" an imagine that the question is whether or not King William i ready to grant Paris an amnesty. As Aeneas and Dido took refug in a cave to avoid a shower, so I for the same reason found mysel with a young lady this morning under a porte cochère. Dido wa a lively and intelligent young person, but I discovered in th course of our chance conversation that she was under the im pression that the Russians as well as the Prussians were outsid Paris, and that both were waging war for the King of Spain Sedan, I also learnt, was in the neighbourhood of Berlin.

The men of Paris might be better informed than th women as to the nationality of the besiegers and the where abouts of Sedan, and they might be more interested in th question of war or peace, but even Labouchère could no pretend that they were at all consistent in their attitude to th problem. Only a week before, they had been determined to fight to the end. By Friday the 4th, they were waiting impati ently for news of an armistice. Now, in the eighth week of the siege, there was violent controversy between those who advo cated continued resistance and those who called for im mediate capitulation.

On Tuesday the 8th the *Journal Officiel* published Jules Favre's circular to the French diplomatic agents abroad, explaining the negotiations between Thiers and Bismarck. In this document the French Foreign Minister maintained that the war was being continued solely to satisfy the ambition of the King of Prussia and placed the responsibility for the failure of the negotiations on Bismarck and William. "By refusing our demand to be allowed to revictual Paris", he declared, "Prussia rejected the armistice. It is not only the French army but the French nation which she seeks to annihilate when she proposes to reduce Paris by the horrors of famine." He concluded by stating that in default of an honourable peace, the Government of National Defence would fight on. "The whole of Paris", he announced, "rises in arms to show the country and the world what a great people can do when it is defending its honour, its home, and the independence of the Fatherland."

These brave words were flatly contradicted that very same

evening by Edmond About, who in the *Soir* insisted that the Government should have agreed to an armistice even without a revictualment. He maintained that it was impossible for Paris to hold out any longer, and that for his part he was grateful to Count Bismarck for not agreeing to an armistice and thereby giving the Parisians a chance of further prolonging their futile resistance.

The morning papers on Wednesday the 9th nearly all echoed About's sentiments. Jules Favre, who only a few weeks before had been praised to the skies for his famous speech refusing to yield one inch of territory or one stone of a fortress, was now generally abused for compromising the chances of peace by his mania for oratory. And in the *Figaro*, to quote an English correspondent,

> Villemessant blundered through three columns over being again disappointed in his expectations of embracing his wife, and plaintively told William that, though he might not be anxious to see his Augusta, this was no reason why he, Villemessant, should not be absolutely wild to see Madame. A more utter and complete collapse of all "heroism" I never did witness. ...

As the week wore on, the clamour for peace at any price grew louder. The *Figaro*, in an article entitled "Are we Lost?", openly stated its conviction that Paris could not work out its own deliverance and compel the investing army to raise the siege. "Let the Government", it said,

> be explicit on two points. For how long are we victualled? Is an army of succour really expected, and within what time? If the answer to these questions is satisfactory, we can struggle on, and will struggle with courage and perseverance. On the opposite supposition, why should Paris be sacrificed for the rest of France, watching it die with folded arms?

As if to put the final touch to the collapse of the city's morale, Trochu issued what was perhaps his most dismal proclamation to date, on the morning of the 14th. After informing the Parisians that it was their riotous behaviour on 31 October which had prevented the armistice, he told them that now all that remained for them to do was to "close their ranks and lift up their hearts". "If we triumph", he wrote,

> we shall have given our country a great example; if we succumb, we shall have left to Prussia an inheritance which will outdo the First Empire in the sanguinary annals of conquest and violence;

an inheritance of hatred and maledictions which will eventually prove her ruin.

The effect of this depressing proclamation would probably have been to extinguish the last spark of hope in the defenders' hearts. But fortunately, in the very afternoon of the 14th, news reached Paris which suggested that victory was still a possibility and thus transformed the situation.

THE NINTH WEEK

Monday, 14 November – Sunday, 20 November

Pigeons and Balloons

"We have passed", wrote the Besieged Resident on 15 November,

> from the lowest depths of despair to the wildest confidence.
> Yesterday afternoon a pigeon arrived covered with blood, bearing
> on its tail a dispatch from Gambetta, of the 11th, announcing
> that the Prussians had been driven out of Orleans after two days'
> fighting, that 1,000 prisoners, two cannon, and many munition
> waggons had been taken, and that the pursuit was still continu-
> ing. The dispatch was read at the Maires to large crowds, and in
> the cafés by enthusiasts, who got upon the tables. I was in a shop
> when a person came in with it. Shopkeeper, assistants and cus-
> tomers immediately performed a war dance round a stove; one
> would have supposed that the war was over and that the veracity
> of Gambetta is unimpeachable. But as though this success were
> not enough in itself, all the newspapers this morning tell us that
> Chartres has also been retaken, that the army of Kératry has
> effected a junction with that of the Loire, and that in the north
> Bourbaki has forced the Prussians to raise the siege of Amiens.
> Edmond About, in the *Soir*, eats dirt for having a few days ago
> suggested an armistice.

The victory of Coulmiers – the village outside Orleans
where the French under Aurelle de Paladines had defeated
the Germans on the 9th – certainly put Paris in a jubilee
mood. "For the first time", wrote one correspondent,

the flame of patriotism burnt bright and fierce in the beleaguered
city. Our heated imaginations took fire; we saw Kératry marching
with his Bretons from the west, Aurelle de Paladines pressing
onwards with his Algerian warriors from the south, and as
several days had elapsed since the fight of Coulmiers, we were
already straining our ears to catch the first sound of their cannon.

And when it was revealed that one of the private messages
just arrived by pigeon post mentioned "the Army of the
South", the press proclaimed triumphantly: "This means that
we now have: the Army of the Loire, the Army of Lyons, the
Army of the South, the Army of Brittany and the Army of
Normandy. Let the Prussians beware!"

There was no more talk of an armistice to be heard, and
newspapers which only a few days earlier had been hinting
at the advisability of suing for peace now confidently prophesied victory. Was it not at Orleans, they asked, that, four
and a half centuries before, Joan of Arc had won a victory
which had struck the first blow at the English dominion in
France? And might not the same city now have given the
signal for the expulsion of the hated Germans from French
soil? But not content with waiting for relief to come from
outside, several papers insisted that Paris should make a
supreme effort to break through the enemy's lines and go to
meet the victorious Army of the Loire. "Is this war never
to have an end?" asked the *Constitutionnel*.

> Can we spend our lives buying rifles, organizing armies and free
> corps, and daily contemplating the appearance of some new
> uniform? A battle must be fought, and the affair concluded.

Ironically enough, the clamour made by press and public
for a sortie to meet the Army of the Loire actually delayed the
attempted break-out and resulted in the abandonment of
Trochu's famous plan. That plan, for which the Governor
later gave the credit to Ducrot, was to strike at the enemy at
the point where he least expected an attack – according to
Trochu "on the line from Paris to Le Havre by way of
Rouen". In the evidence which he gave to the National
Assembly in 1871, Trochu explained:

> The enemy's forces did not exist beyond Pontoise, and in one
> day's march his lines might have been passed, and the French
> might have reached first Rouen, and then the coast. That was the
> reason for the building of numerous redoubts on the peninsula of
> Gennevilliers, and for the construction of eight bridges of boats.

For the execution of the plan 50,000 troops were to march through Paris with a great show and launch an attack from the eastern forts, threatening Bondy, while at the same time 50,000 picked men were to concentrate secretly on the peninsula of Gennevilliers, cross the Seine, proceed by way of Corneil-en-Parisis, cross the Oise, and thus arrive at Rouen. Linked with this plan was a project for re-victualling Paris from the Lower Seine, and for that purpose the Government had ordered the formation of a flotilla of small vessels, and the storing up of a quantity of provisions to be held in readiness in the ports.

On 22 October Trochu had communicated this plan to the assembled Council, and on the following day he had sent a dispatch to Gambetta informing him of his intentions. A few days later, on the 27th, he had made the pompous pronouncement that "Paris may now have confidence in its strength: it is not France which will save Paris, but Paris which will save France!" And on 10 November – even though he knew of the surrender of Metz and most have guessed that the German troops freed by Bazaine's capitulation had been used to reinforce the valley of the Lower Seine – he had sent Gambetta a message urging him to advance in the direction previously indicated between the 15th and the 18th of the month. Everything in fact was ready for the launching of the offensive when the news of the victory of Coulmiers reached Paris. "This victory", Trochu declared later, "upset all my arrangements, for Paris, elated with the hope of receiving help from outside, saw in this success, not a fortunate accident but an assurance of coming victories." When the Government in Paris and the Delegation in Tours joined the press and the public in calling for a sortie in the direction of the Army of the Loire, Trochu had no option but to give way – with the result that the rest of November was devoted to the arduous task of transferring all the preparations for a break-out from the west of Paris to the east.

In the meantime, while Paris waited for the decisive battle which would give France complete victory, the Post Office was indefatigably sending balloons and pigeons to the outside world. During the second fortnight of October, eight balloons had left the capital, seven of which had landed safely. The exception was the *Vauban*, which set off in the afternoon of 27 October and was fired at by some Uhlans when it was drifting over Verdun at a height of only 250 feet. The aeronauts were apparently too inexperienced to be able to rise out of range and allowed the balloon to drop to the ground, where three of them threw themselves out and were promptly taken prisoners by the Germans; the fourth very sensibly remained in the car of the balloon, which shot up in the air and carried him away to safety. Among the prisoners was a young Englishman called Worth, a relative of the famous couturier of the Rue de la Paix; he had paid a high price for his passage, only to be ignominiously captured, deported to Germany, and interned in a fortress there until the end of the war.

The fate of the *Vauban*, and the other balloons which left Paris in late October and early November, remained unknown to the Parisians for some time, since between 25 October and 13 November not a single carrier pigeon arrived in the capital. Pessimists maintained that the pigeons were physically unable to do their duty in cold weather, and the people of Paris began resigning themselves to a complete absence of news until the spring. But then, on 13 November, a pigeon which had been taken out in the *Ville de Châteaudun* balloon on the 6th flew back into Paris. It had taken a week to return home, and the news it brought was that the enemy was in possession of Orleans and Chartres, but it was none the less welcome for that. Even more welcome, of course, was the pigeon which arrived the following day, the 14th, for the dispatch it carried was Gambetta's announcement of the recapture of Orleans by the Army of the Loire.

In the meantime three more balloons had left Paris: the *Gironde*, which landed safety at Gondreville in the Eure, and the *Niepce* and the *Daguerre*, which both fell inside the German lines. The travellers by these last balloons managed to evade capture, luckily for them – and luckily for the Prussians too, for the *Niepce* carried plans and apparatus for a new system of communication between the capital and the provinces, and most of this material was saved.

Ever since the beginning of the siege, it had been possible to get letters out of Paris without much difficulty, thanks to the balloon service, but obtaining news from outside was a different matter. All sorts of methods were proposed to the Post Office, the most practical-looking and least eccentric being a plan for a dirigible balloon submitted by Henri Dupuy de Lôme, the former Chief Constructor to the French Navy.

The Academy of Sciences approved the design of his "aerial apparatus", which, as might have been expected of a former Chief Constructor to the French Navy, included such maritime features as a sail and screw; and the Government gave him a large grant of money for the making of the balloon. But when the balloon was completed Dupuy de Lôme refused to take it up, and the aeronauts of the balloon corps not unnaturally showed no enthusiasm to try out a machine which its own inventor did not trust. The dirigible nobody wanted was put on show for a while to the public, who inspected it with considerable interest and not a little sarcasm. Then it was quietly removed, presumably to be stripped of its sail and its screw and converted for use as a humble non-dirigible on the one-way route from Paris to the provinces.

In no way discouraged by this incident, other inventors came forward with plans for dirigible balloons with screws worked by gas or steam-engines, to which, as one correspondent put it, "the danger from fire was very justly objected." The same objection could not be levelled at an imaginative scheme put up by a bird-lover who suggested harnessing eagles from the Jardin des Plantes to balloons; but the Post Office doubtless felt that the idea presented other practical difficulties. Nor did the authorities give any encouragement to a certain Dr. Guérin's project for maintaining telegraphic communication with the provinces by means of a wire paid out from a captive balloon to a free one and kept up in the air by a succession of smaller balloons.

In the end the Parisians had to fall back on the use of carrier pigeons. To begin with, pigeons had been used to carry only official dispatches, which were written by hand on very thin paper, on one side only and in as many copies as were thought necessary. Then in mid-October, a chemist called Barreswil who happened to be at Tours put forward the idea of reducing the dispatches by photography, so that they could be multiplied as required without any fear of error. Under the supervision of the Postal Delegate in the Provinces, Steenackers, and his assistant Lafollye, who fancied himself as an expert on photography, the dispatches were accordingly copied in large letters on to sheets of cardboard which in turn were fastened to wooden panels and photographed. Little by little, the system was improved: first, impressed by the quality of the reproduction of extracts from the *Moniteur* sent with the

105

early dispatches, Steenackers and Lafollye decided to have all the messages set up in type and printed before being photographed; and then, using fine albumenized paper, heavily salted, they succeeded in printing proofs on both sides of the paper. By early November the process was so well in hand that on the 10th the Government issued a decree inviting the inhabitants of the provinces to send to the Postal Delegate messages for transmission by pigeon post to Paris.

Two types of private message were authorized. The first, which cost 1 franc, consisted of the sender's and recipient's name and address and the answers "Yes" or "No" to four questions such as "Are you well?" and "Do you want money?" which had been asked in letters sent out of Paris by balloon. Though it possessed the virtues of simplicity and brevity, it was limited in its usefulness and gave rise to serious misunderstandings when sender or recipient confused affirmatives and negatives. The public therefore resorted increasingly to the second form of dispatch, which was more expensive (50 centimes a word) but more satisfactory. This was an ordinary message of not more than 20 words, including names and addresses, and containing no public or military information. As many as possible of these messages were set up in 9-point type on a form divided into columns like a newspaper, and which, when reduced by photography, measured only one and a half inches by one and a quarter inches. Arrangements were also made by which money orders to the value of 300 francs each could be sent to Paris in a similar manner.

The first day that an office was opened at Tours to receive messages for transmission to Paris, it was besieged by a far bigger crowd than could be served; and during the following weeks Steenacker's staff were hard put to it to cope with the flood of dispatches which came pouring in. Their task was made more difficult by the fact that the local printing-house which prepared the dispatch forms for the photographers was understaffed on account of the war, and overburdened by the printing of the *Moniteur* and other newspapers which had taken refuge at Tours, as well as of the Government's circulars and decrees. Even so, between 10 November and 11 December, the date when the Tours Delegation moved to Bordeaux, Steenackers sent off 64 sheets of private dispatches, containing 9,800 messages of an average of 16 words each.

Meanwhile, on 27 November, the passengers from the ill-fated *Niepce* arrived at Tours after being fired at and pursued by the Germans and greeted with undisguised suspicion by the French peasants with whom they had sought refuge. They were Dagron, the famous photographer, Fernique, his chief assistant, and Poisot, his son-in-law; and they had been sent from Paris to organize at Clermont-Ferrand a microscopic-photography service which was to take over the work then being done by Steenackers and Lafollye. The Post Office officials at Tours were understandably annoyed at the intrusion of these arrogant Parisians, whom the Government apparently rated more highly than loyal civil servants – for Dagron brought with him a contract guaranteeing him 25,000 francs danger money for his flight and generous payment for his work – and it is clear that for some time they did little or nothing to help the great photographer. It was not until all the government services moved to Bordeaux that Dagron was able to begin carrying out his contract.

The advantage of the process he used – the reproduction of the dispatches on films of collodion – was that the reduction achieved was 15 times greater than before, while the collodion films were 10 times thinner and lighter than the paper on which the dispatches had previously been printed. When the films were smooth and firm, 12 to 15 of them could be sent by one pigeon, each film containing an average of 2,500 dispatches. The first film would be rolled to the size of a pin, and then served as the axis of a cylinder of films rolled successively one round another. This cylinder was inserted in a quill two inches long, which was fastened with a waxed silk thread to one of the larger feathers of a carrier pigeon's tail.

When the pigeon arrived in Paris, the quill containing the dispatches was split open with a penknife by no less a person than Mercadier, the Director-General of the Telegraphic Service. To unroll the films, they were placed in water containing a little ammonia, and then dried and enclosed between two plates of glass, ready to be deciphered with a microscope. This method of reading was soon found to be too slow and was abandoned in favour of the Duboscq megascope, an electric apparatus which projected the collodion films on to a large screen, so that four transcribers could work at once on different parts of the dispatch sheet. This method in turn was improved on when somebody hit on the happy idea of re-photographing the dispatches and enlarging the proofs to the size of the original printed matter; the collodion film was then transferred to a sheet of waxed cloth dressed with gum arabic, so that dispatches could be separated from each other with scissors and sent to their destination.

The first of these photographic dispatch sheets arrived in Paris on 14 November, containing 226 private messages which were said to concern over a thousand families in the capital. The pigeon carrying it arrived about four o'clock in the afternoon, and by eleven that evening all the messages had been enlarged, copied and sent by telegraph to the people to whom they were addressed. A second batch of messages arrived on the 17th, and over 500 on the 25th. In the meantime Gambetta's dispatches about the victory of Coulmiers and the occupation of Orleans had also arrived; but the brief messages from relatives and friends did far more to raise people's spirits than any official communications, however optimistic. From now on, the people of Paris watched impatiently for the arrival of some pigeon which might bring them news of their families. Very few of the birds released in the provinces got through to Paris: out of a total of 363, only four homed in September, 18 in October, 17 in November, 12 in December, three in January and three latecomers in February. Yet because each photographic dispatch sheet was reproduced 30 or 40 times and sent off by as many birds, no fewer than 60,000 of the 95,000 dispatches entrusted to pigeon post during the Siege of Paris reached home.

For the Parisians, the pigeon not unnaturally became a sacred bird, to whom poets and artists paid lavish tribute. Puvis de Chavannes, for one, produced a lithograph showing a young woman on the terrace in front of a church, pressing a carrier pigeon to her heart. And Paul de Saint-Victor expressed the general feeling on the subject in this eloquent eulogy:

In all history there will never have been a more beautiful or more touching legend than that of these saviour birds, bringing back to Paris the promises of distant France, the love and memories of so many separated families. They are the doves of this huge ark battered by waves of blood and fire. The delicate spiral of their flight draws in the air the rainbow which predicts the end of the storm. The soul of our country palpitates beneath their little wings.

How many tears and kisses, how many consolations and hopes

fall from their feathers moistened by the snow or torn by birds of prey! Returning to their nest, they bring back to thousands of human nests hope, encouragement and life. Today more than ever, and in the fullest meaning of the world, they are birds of love. Like the storks of northern cities and the pigeons of Venice, they deserve to become in like manner sacred birds

Paris ought to take the progeny of their dovecots and shelter and feed them beneath the roofs of one of her temples. Their race would be the poetic tradition of this great siege, unique in history. their flights in our streets and gardens would remind future generations that there was a day when every heart in this great city hung on the wings of a pigeon.

The fulsome respect paid to the carrier pigeons of Paris was not undeserved, for the birds had to face countless difficulties and dangers: wind, rain, the sportsman's gun, the poacher's trap, and, later on, cold weather and snow. What is more, the Germans imported a number of hawks from Saxony in the hope of intercepting some of the pigeons – a measure which, when it came to the Parisians' notice, evoked a storm of indignant if rather illogical protests at the enemy's barbarity and cruelty.

It was, of course, perfectly natural for the Germans to try to stop the pigeons entering Paris, just as it was natural for them to try to cut that other remaining link between the capital and the provinces: the balloon service. With this latter end in view, the German troops were ordered to fire on any balloon which came within range, and many a balloon was pursued for miles by German cavalry until it succeeded in rising out of reach of their bullets. Another device used against the balloons was a primitive ancestor of the anti-aircraft gun, invented and manufactured by Herr Krupp. According to an English correspondent, this weapon, known as the balloon-cannon,

comprised a platform resting on four wheels, movable in all directions, and from the centre of which an iron cylinder rose obliquely. In the upper part of this fixed cylinder there was inserted a tolerably short gun, having a range said to exceed five hundred yards, and movable like the platform: the arrangement was indeed not unsimilar to that of some large stationary telescopes.

But despite its four wheels, the balloon-cannon was anything but mobile, and if French balloons occasionally fell into the enemy's hands, this was due, not to Krupp's ingenuity, but to some technical fault or the inexperience of the aeronauts.

The loss of the *Vauban*, the *Galilée* and the *Daguerre* convinced the authorities that in future all balloons should be dispatched under cover of darkness. From 12 to 21 November there were no departures, on account of contrary winds, but shortly before midnight on the 21st the *Général Uhrich* left the Gare du Nord, hidden not only by darkness but also by a thick fog. A French journalist who was present has left us this vivid description of the scene:

In the middle of a vast yard at the Gare du Nord is the balloon, almost completely inflated. An enormous balloon made of yellow taffeta. The locomotives' reflector-lamps shed a strange light over it, making it look transparent. Huge shadows run along the net. Silence is maintained all around. Only Monsieur Dartois's whistle, giving the signal for the manoeuvres, can be heard at regular intervals.

The post office waggon has just arrived, bringing mailbags and copies of the *Officiel*. How many letters those bags must hold saying: *I love you and I hope we shall see each other again soon!* I defy the most fanatical statistician to make that calculation.

On the right are the letters from Paris to the provinces. On the left, the means for bringing back letters from the provinces to Paris. There are five basket-cages containing thirty-six pigeons, adorable pigeons, black, white, golden, puffing themselves out as if they were aware of the importance which events have just given them; pigeons which bear conquerors' names: *Gladiator*, *Vermouth*, *Daughter of the Air*.

Those who are interested in these intelligent messengers – and who is not? – will be happy to learn that Paris still contains about 1,400 of them, all perfectly trained. Enough to bring us news until the end of the siege. On one of the baskets I read the words: *Pigeons to be sent immediately to Orleans or Tours*. The owner of the pigeons declares that he has fifty young ones at home which he would be glad to sell to those who prefer pigeons to peas and horse. His hearers utter a cry of horror. Does anybody eat pigeons nowadays? There is an extenuating circumstance: these young pigeons are unsuitable as yet to act as messengers.

Monsieur Rampont is there rubbing his hands. This time the Prussians will see nothing but fog. The wind will drive the travellers towards Orleans. And the director of the post office casts a satisfied look at the pigeons and the mailbags.

The aeronaut is called Lemoine. He is a veteran of the air. The clouds know him and the sun doffs its hat to him. He is taking with him a pigeon-breeder and two persons who wish to remain incognito.

At half-past ten an aide-de-camp arrives, panting for breath.

"A dispatch from the Governor!"

The dispatch is carefully put on one side. The car is attached. The whistle blows ... I beg your pardon – there is a shout of "Cast off!" and slowly, majestically, the balloon rises, disappearing into the darkness. It has scarcely passed the glass roof of the station before we have lost sight of it. The darkness has closed over it. We can still hear the shouts of the brave passengers, bidding us farewell, but we can see nothing. The balloon has melted into the fog.

This time our letters will arrive safely, unless the balloon collides with a star on the way.

In the event, the *Général Uhrich* met with no accidents on its journey, and alighted safely at Luzarches in Seine-et-Oise early the next morning. Its successors during the rest of November travelled much farther afield, with frightening or tragic consequences. The *Archimède*, the next balloon to leave Paris, eventually landed at Castelze in Holland, while the *Ville d'Orléans*, which left on the 24th in the direction of Tours, was carried all the way to the mountain of Lidfjild in Norway, a distance of 840 miles which it covered in just over 15 hours. The worst moment for the aeronauts on this journey came on the 25th, when they heard what sounded like a number of locomotives, and found to their horror that they were drifting over the sea. The *Jacquard*, which left Paris during the night of the 25th, was also carried out to sea, but failed to make land like its predecessor: it was last seen five or six miles south of Eddystone lighthouse.

The same fate nearly overtook the *Jules Favre* (the second balloon of that name), which started from Paris on 30 November. The aeronauts' instruments got out of order during the night, so they could not tell which way they were drifting. Seeing water below them, they took it for the Loire, but soon, catching sight of a lighthouse and ships, they realized that they were above the island of Belle-Île and heading for the Atlantic. One of the two men climbed up the ropes and opened the escape valve, with the result that the balloon dropped so swiftly that both men lost consciousness. The *Jules Favre* tore off the roof of a house, broke down a wall, and was flung against an old church, but the aeronauts somehow survived this crash-landing. By a fantastic coincidence, the house whose

111

roof was torn off belonged to Trochu's brother Armand, and the General's 84-year-old mother was living there at the time. She declared to all and sundry that she had been praying all night for a sign from heaven that her son would save France, and that when the rafters collapsed about her she called out to her granddaughter: "The Providence of the King of Prussia is not going to win: this is proof of that!"

Paris, of course, could not know about this happy omen, but she had her own prophets. One of these had circularized all the newspapers with the following letter:

Sir: On the night of the aurora borealis, in the presence of a great many witnesses, I prophesied a victory, the *dawn* of France's victories. I prophesied that victory for the 110th day of the war. If you calculate from 19 July you will see that on the 110th day of the war we won the Battle of Orleans. It was only last night that we thought of doing the sum.

If I were more superstitious than I am, I would believe that I had *second sight*, for I am a *Scot* and the *seventh* son of a *seventh* son, the necessary condition in the Highlands of Scotland for supernatural sight.

Well, Sir, although I am not a superstitious man, I believe in *instinctive feelings* which *reveal* things, and I *feel* that France will triumph in the long run. Just as I *felt* that the aurora borealis, rising at an angle of 110 degrees to the horizon, suggested a hope which has been fulfilled.

I declare that I have not the *slightest doubt* that the French will triumph; I have *felt* this for a long time.

Your obedient servant, C. STUART MAC DOWALL, Assistant Adjutant to the War Companies of the National Guard.

Whatever other people thought of this prophecy, the Scottish colony at least was mightily cheered.

Monday, 21 November – Sunday, 27 November

The Lull Before the Storm

After the jubilation over the victory of Coulmiers had died down, Paris looked impatiently for signs of a great military effort by the Government. To the population's disappointment, there was scarcely any sign of such an effort, and indeed very little military activity at all. Some newspapers declared that the city's state of lethargy was equivalent to an armistice, and that a Constituent Assembly should have been elected to decide whether to sue for peace or prolong the war. Others, however, insisted that since the recapture of Orleans the Parisians had become strenuously opposed to the idea of resuming negotiations for peace. "Unquestionably", wrote one correspondent,

> great enthusiasm prevails among the marching companies of the National Guard; and I believe that if the Government were to hint of again treating respecting an armistice, it would be instantly overthrown.

Enthusiasm was certainly shown in plenty by the National Guard, but whether it was for fighting was another matter. The marching battalions had just been issued with a new *capote de campagne*, which was supposed to be a sky-blue colour; but because of a shortage of cloth, odds and ends of every conceivable shade had been pressed into service. Thus, next to a sky-blue battalion, there was one dressed in "billiard green", while a third, nicknamed the Devinck battalion after

113

a famous chocolate manufacturer, wore dark brown. "Benjamin Constant", observed the Besieged Resident,

> said of his countrymen that their heads could never contain more than one idea at once. Today the marching battalions of the National Guard have new coats, and we can talk or think of nothing else. The effect as yet of these marching battalions has been to disorganize the existing battalions. Every day some new decree has been issued altering their mode of formation. Perhaps the new coats will settle everything, and convert them into excellent soldiers. Let us hope so.

Other observers felt the same scepticism about the National Guard's enthusiasm and fitness for war. Thus the Rothschild agent C. de B. reported that its new commander, General Clément Thomas, had ordered a volunteer battalion from Menilmontant to be disbanded, as it consisted of youths under 18, most of whom were suffering from rickets and malnutrition; and that he had told the National Guards of Belleville, who had complained of married men being called up, that after clamouring so loudly for rifles they must use them against the enemy. Similarly, after witnessing one of several grand reviews of the National Guard on the Champs-Élysées, the Oxford Graduate wrote:

> These reviews are the most striking feature of our besieged life since the news from Orleans, which brought us out again from our nooks and corners into the public walks and boulevards. We crowd in great numbers to watch the manoeuvres of the war battalions, and admire them as they move past at a quick step, proudly conscious of their military appearance, each man taking a side-look at his comrade in the ranks, and now and then stealing a glance at his own toes. "See how wonderfully they drill!" says an old man. "Ah! Frenchmen are born soldiers; you see we have a love for glory and liberty. These are men who but a few weeks ago hardly knew a *chassepot* from an elephant; now they drill like old troops, and what is better still, they keep admirably steady under fire, and against odds." I see them merely marching down the Avenue of the Champs-Élysées, against no odds and under no fire, save that of the glances of admiring belles, who have come to see Alphonse at drill; but then, I suppose I was not born for *la gloire*. Clément Thomas was on horseback, amidst a numerous staff of young dandies, lounging gracefully in their saddles, and apparently unable to understand their General's orders. The General gesticulated and grew fidgety with repeating his commands, the aides-de-camp caracoled in the wrong direction,

and companies moved up and down in confusion until the band came opportunely to their relief by striking up the *Marseillaise*, and all our heroes marched off to its invigorating sounds. . . .

Meanwhile, virtually the only fighting which took place was some polite verbal warfare between Jules Favre and Bismarck. Favre had written to the Prussian Chancellor protesting at the arrest at Versailles of a local magistrate called Monsieur de Raynal, who had been charged with communicating with the enemy (the French maintain that he had simply written to his relatives in Paris to say that he was well) and had been sent to Germany. Bismarck replied in a letter to the American Minister that papers found in Raynal's house proved that he had been transmitting information to "the enemy" and, still on the subject of communication, added:

> I take this opportunity of informing you that several balloons sent out of Paris have fallen into our hands and that the persons travelling in them will likewise be tried by a court martial. I beg you to bring this fact to the French Government's notice, adding that any person using this means of transport to cross our lines without permission, or to engage in correspondence to the detriment of our troops, will be subjected, if they fall into our power, to the same treatment, to which they are just as liable as anyone making similar attempts by ordinary means of transport.

A more welcome and encouraging letter arrived by pigeon-post from Gambetta, who wrote that "perfect order reigns in every part of the country and our military resources are taking a thoroughly satisfactory turn". He assured the Government that the French success at Orleans had "excited the nation's patriotic sentiments to the highest degree", that France's position in the diplomatic world had greatly improved, and that by the beginning of December the provinces would have a new army of 100,000 men, "perfectly organized and equipped with everything they need". Sceptics remembered earlier assurances that the French army was "ready down to the last gaiter-button"; and one correspondent declared that

> such is the universal distrust felt now for any intelligence which emanates from an official source that if Gambetta were to send us in an account of a new victory tomorrow, and if all his colleagues were to swear to its truth, we should be in a wild state of enthusiasm for a few hours, and then disbelieve the whole story.

But there were many Parisians who were genuinely cheered by Gambetta's optimistic platitudes, and the clamour in the capital against the Government's temporizing grew louder every day.

The most common explanation of the lack of energy shown by the Government was that it was a government of legal men. "Burke," wrote an English correspondent,

> in his work on the French Revolution, augered ill of the future of a country the greater number of whose legislators were lawyers. What would he have said of a Government composed almost exclusively of these objects of his political distrust? When history recounts the follies of the French Republic of 1870, I trust that it will not forget to mention that all the members of the Government, with the exception of one – six ministers, 13 under-secretaries of State, the Prefect of Police, 24 prefects and commissaries sent into the provinces, and 36 other high functionaries – belonged to the legal profession. The natural consequence of this is that we cannot get out of "Nisi prius". Our rulers are unable to take a large statesmanlike view of the situation; they live from hand to mouth, and never rise above the expedients and temporizing policy of advocates; they are perpetually engaged in appealing against the stern logic of facts to some imaginary tribunal, from which they hope to gain a verdict in favour of their clients.

The solitary non-lawyer in the Government was of course Trochu, but he was generally regarded as even more of a lawyer by nature than if he had been trained to the trade. "His colleagues", declared one writer,

> own in despair that he is their master in strength of lungs, and that when they split straws into two he splits them into four. In vain they fall back on their pens and indite letters and proclamations – their President out-letters and out-proclaims them.

Army officers complained that Trochu had lived in an atmosphere of lawyers for so long that he had become one himself, and a sarcastic sub-lieutenant told Henry Markheim: "He has dipped his pen in his scabbard and his sword in his inkstand, and when he finally attempts to draw the sword, he'll only unsheath a penholder."

As for the famous Trochu plan, it was revealed by those who had known the Governor in Brittany that long before he had become a celebrity *le plan de Trochu* had been a standing joke throughout the province. It appeared that the General had always been fond of piquet; he used to sit down to play saying: "I have a plan", and when he got up after losing the game, as usually happened, he went off muttering: "All the same, it was a good plan." The odd thing, as onlookers at these games had remarked, was that nobody had ever been able to detect any sign of a system in his play; and more than one commentator began to wonder openly whether the present *plan de Trochu* was also non-existent. "At the commencement of the siege", wrote Labouchère,

General Trochu announced that he not only had a "plan", but that he had inscribed it in his will, which was deposited with his notary. An ordinary man would have made use of the materials at his command, and, without pledging himself to success, would have endeavoured to give the provinces time to organize an army of succour by harassing the Prussians, and thus preventing them from detaching troops in all directions. Instead of this, with the exception of some two or three harmless sorties, they have been allowed slowly to enclose us in a net of circumvallations. Our provisions are each day growing more scarce, and nothing is done except to heap up defensive works to prevent the town being carried by assault, which there is no probability that the besiegers mean to attempt. Châtillon and Meudon were ill guarded, but ditches were cut along the Avenue de l'Impératrice. The young unmarried men in Paris were not incorporated until the 50th day of the siege, but two or three times a week they were lectured on their duties as citizens by their leader. If there is really to be a sortie, everything is ready, but now the General hesitates – hints that he is not seconded, that the soldiers will not fight, and almost seems to regret at last his own theoretical presumption. "He trusted," said one of his generals to me, "first to the neutrals, then to the provinces, and now he is afraid to trust to himself. . . ."

Provisions inside the besieged city were indeed growing rapidly scarcer, and it was obvious that if the promised sortie failed to relieve the capital, Paris would soon be desperately short of food. Erudite journalists complacently reminded their readers of the dreadful straits to which Paris had been reduced in 1590, when Henri IV was besieging the capital with an army of Huguenots: in those days, they reported, Parisians forgot what meat was like, and ate nothing but oatmeal gruel, which was cooked in huge saucepans at street corners, while the Spanish Ambassador suggested grinding skeletons from the graveyard into a kind of flour, a proposal which was adopted

117

with disastrous results. Although the Parisians of 1870 never imagined that they would be reduced to such extremities, they began to feel apprehensive when, during the month of November, the daily ration of beef and mutton was reduced first to 50, then to 35 grammes ($1\frac{1}{6}$ oz.) for an adult, and to half that quantity for a child. Four thousand milch cows and a few hundred oxen were kept in reserve until the end of the siege; but early in November cattle and sheep belonging to private citizens had been requisitioned, and except for cows which had adequate stocks of forage to feed them, they had all found their way to the slaughter-house. By mid-November most Parisians had had to fall back on horseflesh as a daily article of diet, and on the 15th a uniform tariff for horse, ass and mule was fixed by the Government. At the same time a census was taken of all the horses, mules and donkeys in Paris and its suburbs, and the owners were forbidden to sell their animals without official permission.

It was estimated by the Horseflesh Committee that on 13 November there were 70,000 horses in Paris, of which 30,000 would be required for military purposes, leaving 40,000 to be slaughtered for food. By rationing horseflesh at the rate of 50 grammes a head per diem, it was calculated that there would be enough to feed the city for 100 days. Some valuable animals were inevitably included in the slaughter, and one butcher advertised "Thoroughbred horses from the Stables of the Comte de Lagrange"; but gourmets maintained that a slice of cab-horse was preferable to the finest cut from a pampered race-horse. The latter's flesh, they said, was invariably hard, while the cab-horse was deliciously tender – as was only to be expected, seeing that it had been beaten for years. And just as later in the siege Parisians were fond of telling about dog-eaters who answered to the names of the animals they had digested, so in November people who had never tasted horse-flesh before made self-conscious jokes about their new diet. The favourite anecdote concerned the mistress of a household who, while speaking to her cook, heard the sound of a bouillon boiling over in the kitchen. "Josephine", she exclaimed, "go and see what's the matter, your pot-au-feu is running away!" To which the cook replied: "I'm not surprised, Madame. The butcher told me the meat was race-horse."

The scarcity of beef, mutton and fish naturally resulted in

a transformation of the great Central Market in Paris. "The immense pavilion," wrote one correspondent,

which used to present such an animated scene on the arrival of the railway fish-trucks, was now devoted to the sale of *viande de cheval*, with, perhaps, an auction going on in one corner, at which a few Seine eels or gudgeons would fetch their weight in silver. In the meat pavilion, where one used formerly to pass in front of miles of sides of beef and legs of mutton, only some sheep and bullocks' lights, and a few bullocks' heels, were exposed for sale; all the rest being *viande de cheval*. In the butter and cheese pavilions, dripping and other kinds of melting fat, as substitutes for butter for culinary purposes, were displayed, together with honey and *saucissons de cheval – encore du cheval* and *toujours du cheval*. One could promenade in fact, for half a mile or more, in front of joints of horseflesh, growing small by degrees and beautifully less, from the entire side to the diminutive fillet. . . .

Few dogs had so far gone the way of the horse, but cats in plenty, invitingly set off with paper frills and coloured ribbons, were displayed for sale under the name of "gutter rabbits". Boiled and seasoned with pistachio nuts, olives, gherkins and pimento, they were said to make a tasty dish; and people were recommended to take sick friends a dead cat as a welcome substitute for flowers and sweets. There was even a rat-market on the Place de l'Hôtel de Ville, poorly patronized as yet but plentifully supplied with raw material by a whole team of rat-catchers, who obtained admission to the sewers and baited their traps with glucose, to which the rats of Paris proved extremely partial. *Paris-Journal* reported that

as the rats are shut up in a big cage, one has to choose the animal one wants out of the crowd. With a little stick the dealer makes it go into a smaller cage, where it is alone, and then a bulldog is brought along. The little cage is shaken and the rat escapes; but it is promptly seized by the formidable teeth of the dog which breaks its back and drops it delicately at the purchaser's feet.

Every conceivable source of food within the city was soon being tapped. One evening, crossing the Luxembourg gardens, Edmond de Goncourt noticed a cart full of barrels standing beside a pool, and a crowd of people leaning over the water. "Some men on their knees", he tells us,

were pulling at a huge net whose corks kept touching the swans, which rose from the water in frightened flurries and angry beatings of wings. They were fishing the pool in order to feed Paris; and soon, at the bottom of the net, on the surface of the rippling water, there appeared some carp and some enormous goldfish, which were put in the barrels in the cart.

The next day, Goncourt himself was reduced to killing one of his own chickens, which he characteristically executed with a Japanese sword. A fortnight later, he would be seriously considering killing sparrows in his garden for lunch.

Hoarders, or "forestallers" as they were called, had of course guarded against finding themselves in any such predicament, but they found it difficult to decide when it would be most profitable and least dangerous to get rid of their illegal stocks. Towards the end of the last week in November, seeing indisputable signs that a sortie was going to be made, many of them decided to unload their provisions on to the market; and foodstuffs which nobody had seen or tasted for weeks were suddenly put on display. When bad news came of the initial results of the offensive, the same foodstuffs naturally disappeared just as rapidly – but not quickly enough to save a good many tradesmen from suspicion and imprisonment.

It was on the 24th that Trochu decided that his forces were nearly ready to launch an offensive. On the same day he wrote to Gambetta informing him of his plans: the balloon carrying the letter drifted across to Norway, and Gambetta did not receive Trochu's message until the 30th, but the delay did not in fact affect the course of the war. In his letter Trochu declared:

What you call my persistent inactivity is the inevitable result of the enormous and complicated efforts I have had to make. I have had to organize 100,000 men, provide them with artillery, remove them from the fifteen leagues of positions which they occupied, and replace them with untrained troops and soldiers from the National Guard. And these wellnigh incredible efforts have had to be made in contradiction of a plan already being executed, which consisted of breaking out towards the west, in the direction of Rouen. The news from the Army of the Loire naturally decided me to break out towards the south and go to meet it whatever the cost. On Monday the 28th I shall have finished my preparations which are going on day and night. On Tuesday the 29th the outer army, under the command of General Ducrot, the most energetic of them all, will attack the enemy's positions, and, if it carries them, will push on towards the Loire, probably in the direction of Gien.

By the end of the week it was obvious to the whole of Paris that an offensive was imminent. As if the movement of whole battalions and the preparation of armour-plated railway waggons were not enough, a proclamation was issued to the effect that from Sunday the 27th until further notice the outer gates of the capital would be closed to all except military traffic. Edmond de Goncourt, who went out into the Bois de Boulogne on the 26th in company with hundreds of other Parisians, has left us this description of his last excursion before the great offensive:

There I was, this morning, walking along the winding road, dominated by the man with the telescope, who shouted: "Who wants to see the Prussians? You can see them very well. Just have a look, gentlemen!" I walked across the clearing, stopping at piles of sand, with smoke rising from them – charcoal stoves – and at empty soldiers' huts, marvels of industry and ingenuity, with their doors made of branches swinging open on creeper hinges.

Every now and then I had to jump over big ditches, embankments buttressed with fascines, barricades forming defence lines. Finally, I reached the top of that twisting road by which the carriages used to arrive at the races, and before me I had Saint-Cloud as if it were just below the road, Saint-Cloud with its blackened houses and its streets licked by flames.

The gate of the Pré Catalan was open. Cannon were lined up on its lawn and gunners motioned to people to keep clear. From the Pré Catalan I went on to the Jardin d'Acclimatation by way of that pretty path which runs alongside a stream, under green trees. There, a band of men, women and children were breaking those poor trees, which they left with white wounded branches hanging down to the ground, spirals of tortured wood – revolting havoc which reveals the Parisian population's love of destruction. An old countryman who was passing by and who loved the trees raised his eyes heavenwards in pain.

Coming back, I was somewhat mollified by the sight of the big island, preserved by the water surrounding it, and which, in the midst of the general devastation, had kept intact and unscathed its green trees, its shrubs, its English neatness. Along the shore of the lake, that shore which was once so popular, a tall, thin priest was walking by himself, reading from his breviary.

I hurried along to be back by five o'clock. The lawn stretching from the Butte Mortemart to the Porte de Boulogne was covered with Mobiles, who are going to camp there tonight. It was charming, that blueish crowd, and all those little white tents, soldiers and tents shading off into the distance to become tiny men and microscopic squares of canvas, in the midst of smoke rising from the canteens, which formed a real cloud on the horizon. The tall trees on each side stood out like trees and flats in the wings of a theatre, and right at the back a glimpse of the church of Saint-Denis could be seen, blurred like a stage building when the curtain is falling.

Five o'clock struck. Everybody was hurrying and jostling. There was a line of ammunition waggons which made it difficult to pass. A poor old man beside me took fright on the drawbridge and fell. I saw him being carried in on the shoulders of four men, inert, his head dangling. He had broken his back ...

Monday, 28 November – Sunday, 4 December

The Great Sortie

During the night of Sunday, 27 November the forts around Paris opened up a brisk cannonade, and many Parisians took this as an indication that the long-awaited offensive was about to be launched. Edmond de Goncourt, for one, was awoken by the sound of gunfire and went up to an attic room to look out over Paris. "In the starless sky," he wrote,

> cut by the branches of the tall trees, from the Fort of Bicêtre to the Fort of Issy, across the whole range of this wide hemicycle, there was a succession of little dots of fire which lit up like gas jets, followed by loud explosions. These great voices of death in the midst of the silence of the night moved me. After a little while, the howling of dogs joined the sound of the thundering bronze; the frightened voices of people roused from sleep started whispering; cocks sang out their shrill notes. Then guns, dogs, cocks, men and women, all fell silent once more and my ear, straining to catch every sound from outside, could hear nothing except, in the distance, in the far distance, a burst of gunfire which sounded like the dull noise made by an oar touching the wood of a boat.

In the morning the guns remained silent but there was considerable activity in the city, with columns of troops and batteries of the newly cast heavy artillery moving along the boulevards. All day Paris waited and wondered. Then, in the course of the evening, the walls were suddenly placarded with three proclamations. One was from Trochu, and called upon

Paris to make a supreme effort, throwing "the entire responsibility for the blood about to be shed upon those whose detestable ambition tramples underfoot the principles of justice and modern civilization". A second proclamation, signed by the remaining members of the Government, asked the population to keep calm during the coming battle; while a third was issued by Ducrot, who addressed his soldiers in the following terms:

> Courage and confidence! Remember that in this supreme struggle we shall fight for our honour, our liberty, the salvation of our dear and unhappy country; and if this motive does not suffice to inflame your hearts, think of your devastated fields, your ruined families, your sisters, wives, and mothers, who are desolate! May this thought imbue you with the thirst for vengeance, the uncontrollable rage which animates me, and inspire you with contempt for danger! For myself, I am resolved, I swear this before you – before the entire nation. I will only re-enter Paris Dead or Victorious! You may see me fall, but you shall not see me retreat. Then do not falter, but avenge me. Forward then! Forward! And may God protect us!

This last proclamation had an electrifying effect on both the population and the army, and the words "dead or victorious" were soon on everybody's lips. In fact, like the key words in so many momentous documents, this famous phrase was not the work of its supposed author. As Hérisson reveals in his memoirs, Ducrot was dining at a restaurant in the Rue de Mironesnil with Ferdinand de Lesseps when he received the proofs of his proclamation from the Imprimerie Nationale, and it was the great engineer who suggested: "You ought to add: 'As far as I am concerned, I am resolved that I will only return dead or victorious.' " It was a bold, inspiring phrase, but a rash promise which the unfortunate Ducrot, alive and defeated, would bitterly regret. Even when it was first published, there were some who detected a note of hysteria in the General's style. "He evidently feels", wrote one commentator,

> that he had to do with raw, inexperienced troops whose discipline is not firm enough to lead them into the brunt of battle up to those terrible loop-holed walls, and his language is a desperate appeal to their courage.

About midnight the forts all round Paris opened fire, supported by the advanced redoubts and the gunboats on the Seine, and this fire was kept up almost without a break until dawn, when the field-guns joined in. "This is the first time", wrote the Oxford Graduate,

> that the cannonading round Paris has kept me awake. At first I heard a rumbling sound like thunder in the distance. Gradually, as I awoke, I saw, from my bed, the dark sky lighted up with flashes in every quarter. I muffled myself up and went upstairs on the roof, which commands a splendid view of the whole range of heights between Mont Valérien on my right and the Seine towards Ivry on my left. Red tongues of flame were darting from the cannon's mouth towards Bagneux, and the great booming of distant guns came up from the east. The night is pitch dark as I write, and the roar of cannon is incessant. This is no doubt some terrible artillery duel, preparing the way for a desperate rush of infantry. ...

Trochu's plan was for 150,000 men, supported by 400 heavy guns, and placed under Ducrot's command, to cross the Marne near Joinville-le-Pont and occupy the enemy's positions at Champigny, while Vinoy created a diversion to the south of Paris and feint attacks were made in the direction of Aubervilliers, Gennevilliers and Buzenval. It was hoped that if this initial attack was successful it would be possible to continue across the plateau of Villiers and Coeuilly and eventually link up with the Army of the Loire. With this end in view, everything had been done to make Ducrot's force as mobile as possible: the clumsy baggage-train had been eliminated, the troops carried their own rations with them, and they were even ordered to leave their blankets behind to lighten their load. Hérisson later cited this last detail as proof that there had never been any intention of attempting a break-through; and he sneered at the National Guards' belief that the army had been trying to get out of Paris, expressing regret that

> nobody dared to say to them: "My good friends, your duty is to hold out as long as you can, and, by continued battles, to do as much harm as you can to the enemy, whom you force to remain around you, and from whom you thus set free the rest of France. But do not imagine for a moment that you can after any useful fashion pierce those investing lines – in other words, do not imagine that you can get out and join hands with the provincial armies."

But this is in complete contradiction with all that we know of Trochu's plans, and also with Hérisson's earlier statement about the sortie: that to meet the provincial armies and unite them to an army issuing out of Paris, to sew the Parisian strip, detached and cut off by the German army, on to the rest of the territory somehow or other was unquestionably the most reasonable course of action.

Unfortunately all hope of taking the Germans by surprise had to be abandoned. As one commentator wrote on the 28th:

Last Friday's formal notice about the closing of the gates must have given unfortunate publicity to the intentions of our generals. Besides, we knew this afternoon the hour at which the attack will be made tomorrow, and there is no reason why the Prussians should not possess the same knowledge, if they are willing to pay for it.

What is more, although on the 28th Admiral Saisset and his Marines occupied the plateau of Avron commanding the stretch of the Marne where Ducrot intended to cross, the army's plans started to go awry that night. The level of the Marne suddenly rose, the pontoons which had been brought across Paris in readiness for the crossing were found to be too short, and the operation consequently had to be deferred for 24 hours.

News of this postponement reached Vinoy only after eight o'clock in the morning of the 29th, and since dawn he had been engaged in what was now a futile diversion towards Choisy-le-Roi and L'Hay in which 1,000 of his men were killed or wounded and 300 taken prisoners. "The officers and soldiers", wrote Labouchère that evening,

who had not yet learnt that General Ducrot had failed to cross the Marne, were in a very bad humour at having been ordered to withdraw at the very moment when they were carrying everything before them. They represented the Prussians as having fought like devils, and declared that they appeared to take a fiendish pleasure in killing even the wounded. Within the town the excitement to know what had passed is intense. The Government has posted up a notice saying that everything is happening as General Trochu wished it. Not a word is said about Ducrot's failure. The *Liberté*, which gave a guarded account of what really took place, has been torn to pieces on the Boulevards. I have just been talking with an officer on the headquarters staff. He tells me that Trochu is still outside, very much cast down, but determined to make a desperate effort to retrieve matters tomorrow.

That "desperate effort" was accordingly made at dawn on the 30th, with diversions to the north and south of Paris drawing the German reserves away from the main attack across the Marne. This time the pontoons were adequate to their task, and the French crossed the river under cover of artillery fire, quickly capturing the villages of Champigny and Brie. But they could go no further, exposed as they were to murderous fire from the strongly entrenched Württembergers in the villages of Villiers and Coeuilly, which dominated the plateau. Flank attacks, by the left wing from Neuilly on Villiers, and by the right wing from Champigny on Coeuilly, proved no more successful than frontal assaults; and by sunset the French were simply hanging on to the villages of Champigny and Brie which they had occupied that morning. French losses had been heavy, especially among the officers, who had had to expose themselves recklessly in order to encourage their inexperienced troops. Two generals were among those who were mortally wounded: Renault, the commander of Ducrot's second corps, whose thigh was smashed while he was trying to rally the disheartened Normandy Mobiles between Brie and Villiers; and Ladreyt de la Charrière, who fell when the Württemburgers were forcing the French out of Mont-Mesly and back on Créteil. "The Mobiles, who were decimated", wrote an eye-witness of this last engagement,

> started to waver, and dragged with them the troops of the Line. From the spot where we were posted behind the Governor, we saw the heads of the columns hesitate, then waver, and finally recoil before the Germans, who were really magnificent in battle, coming on in dark masses, and, at the moment of taking skirmishing order, raising their rifles above their heads as one man with deafening cheers, the result being that their battalions, like the grotesque figures in a circus, seemed to increase in size. The Mobiles, who had never seen anything like it, took fright. Ladreyt de la Charrière galloped towards them, and with the idea of drawing them on, he put his képi on the tip of his sword and shouted: "Forward!" He was certainly not more than fifty yards from the Prussians. Suddenly the képi and the sword fell together – a bullet had smashed the General's wrist. Three minutes afterwards he himself fell with a bullet through his thigh. He was carried to the rear. . . .

That evening, Ducrot decided not to order a further advance the next day, as his troops were exhausted and demoralized. The French therefore spent the first day in December strengthening their newly won positions and burying their dead, with German burial parties joining them in their macabre work as the day wore on. Now that there was little or no prospect of a swift break-out, it was decided to send blankets out to the linesmen and Mobiles who had spent two nights sleeping out in the open. "It is questionable", wrote one observer with justifiable scepticism,

> whether all these stores will reach the troops in time to be distributed this evening; and a few more such nights of exposure to this bitter cold without proper covering would result in the utter demoralization of the army under General Ducrot's command.

At dawn the next morning the Germans launched a massive counter-attack on the French positions, which were nearly taken. But the Mobiles recovered quickly from the shock of surprise and held their ground well. For over eight hours the battle raged with undiminished fury, both sides fighting doggedly and suffering heavy losses. Perhaps the best account we have of the day's fighting is that given us by Hérisson. He had been left behind at the Louvre with the Chief of Staff, General Schmitz, who suddenly sent for him and instructed him to go to the Governor with an important message which had just arrived by carrier pigeon: a message from Gambetta saying that the Army of the Loire was on the move and hoped to be encamped in the Forest of Fontainebleau on 6 December. Describing the approach to Champigny, Hérisson writes in his memoirs:

> On the right, in the fields, a sort of encampment of ambulance men and stretcher-bearers had been formed. It looked like a lot of bee-hives. They were continually leaving empty and returning laden. Some went out to bring back the wounded; others carried them to the river, where they were taken on board little boats flying the white flag with the red cross. For hundreds of yards the melancholy convoys followed one after another, and some of them were converted suddenly into funeral processions. The bearers in that case halted, laid the corpse on the ground, left it there, and went further afield to find another wounded man who might in his turn soon become a corpse. Do not imagine that the detachments of the National Guard entrusted with this melancholy duty had a sorrowful air. In almost no time they became accustomed to it, and talked, laughed and joked among the dead and the wounded. There were also to be seen, making their way

128

through the indescribable and bloody mass, many brave women of Paris belonging to every social class, and some of them to the very highest. All were dressed in black with white aprons and the Geneva armlet. They had with them portable stoves similar to those used by the proprietors of coffee stalls outside the markets in the early morning. Most of them were bareheaded and their sleeves rolled up, and they came and went, active, gentle, devoted, tender, and lovely as ministering angels, carrying in their two two hands cups of warm soup or steaming chocolate. . . .

A little farther on, the road was crowded with soldiers, and I was obliged to slacken speed for fear of riding over some of them. I asked where I had the best chance of finding the Governor. A captain of the Mobiles, slightly wounded in the left shoulder, told me that the General was in Champigny. I rode on and reached the first houses of the village. At this spot there was such a crowd of troops that it would have been impossible for me to have got through it if the non-commissioned officers, recognizing my duties by my epaulets, had not ordered their soldiers to fall back to let me pass. I was obliged to walk my horse, and it was a good quarter of an hour before I reached the last houses of Champigny.

I emerged at last right on to the field of battle. Never in all my life, not in any of the battles at which I have been present, have I heard such a fearful uproar. Shot followed shot without a second's pause. Guns by hundreds, rifles by thousands, *mitrailleuses* by scores hurled and vomited lead and steel. It was impossible to hear oneself speak.

On this battlefield, which a short time before had been covered with living men, and where now the dead and dying seemed so numerous that they might have been taken for whole regiments lying down at the halt – alas, for most of them it was their great, their last halt – there was only one able-bodied man, and that was a priest of the Foreign Missions. When I saw him he was on his knees, in his loose black robe, bending over a Mobile, whose pale, beardless face, wrinkled by suffering, gave him the appearance of a boy of twelve. The priest had placed his right arm under his head, and, with his ear to the soldier's mouth, he was hearing his confession. As I approached, he looked up, gently laid the soldier's head on the ground, and came up to me.

"Have you seen the Governor?"

"Yes," he replied. "He is over there, five or six hundred yards from here."

A few moments later I found him; placing my horse close to his I repeated in his ear, word for word, General Schmitz's message. It seemed to me that a flash of joy, springing from his eyes, illuminated his grave, stern face for a moment.

"You are certain about the names?" he said.

I was all the more certain because I was reading them from my cuff.

"Good," he said. "You have had a long ride. Stay beside me."

We went from one point to another, wherever fighting was going on and he considered that his presence might encourage the troops. At one moment two or three hundred Mobiles fell back in disorder upon us, all of them running with their backs to the enemy. The Staff deployed before them like a squadron of gendarmerie, and they halted, pitiful enough, at the sight of the Governor, who at once adressed them. That devil of a man, even under fire, know how to string together charming, persuasive, noble and correct phrases. He got the men together and said a few kindly, affectionate words to them.

"Follow me," were his final words.

Then, marching straight against the German sharpshooters, he never stopped until the enemy's bullets whistled round us with that little strident noise one so quickly learns to know, and which indicates that the projectile is travelling at its full speed. The gallant little Mobiles, thus encouraged, took up their position again and fired away manfully.

We then turned to the left and rode up a little hill, from the top of which one of our batteries, placed in a hollow, was doing wonders. It was doing so well that the enemy seemed to have only one idea – to silence it. Not a moment passed without a shell falling, now on the right, now on the left. Fortunately only a few of them burst.

The General seemed to have chosen the exact spot where all these fearful projectiles had appointed to meet. We all remained motionless under this iron hail, while the Governor quietly looked through his glasses at the enemy's positions, which were perfectly distinguishable by the naked eye. If we could see the Prussians moving, we were equally visible to them, and all the more so because we formed a compact and fairly brilliant mass. Very soon we became the target of the German marksmen, and the number of shells redoubled around us.

The persistence shown by the General in remaining at this particular spot, without any special reason for staying there, began to seem odd to us junior officers; and I heard the following conversation going on around me:

"Don't you think the General seems bent on being killed?"

"Just what I was thinking myself."

"Well, that is his look-out. But I don't see why he should have us killed too."

"I agree," said Ducrot's orderly officer, who was with us. "You should see Ducrot. He is absolutely mad. All day he has been riding a snow-white horse, and he keeps on galloping in front of the Prussians. I should like to have as many francs as he has had shots, from rifles and ordnance, fired straight at him today. Would you believe it, he charged the Saxons single-handed. He cut one down with his small sword as if he had a regulation weapon in his hand. He is perfectly mad."

And a young captain who was resting his elbows on his holsters droned out the famous words: "Dead or victorious."

What was General Trochu's intention? Was he so accustomed to danger and did he despise it so much that he paid no attention to it; and had he taken up his position in that particular place just as he would have done anywhere else? Possibly. But I confess that for several moments I firmly believed that he was seeking death.

However, a shell having fallen under his horse's nose, there could be no doubt that to remain there any longer would have been suicidal. The Governor quieted his horse and slowly returned in the direction of Champigny. The part of the battlefield which we were crossing was literally paved with the killed and wounded, and over it were scattered a dozen priests, who were simply and heroically doing their duty. The General saluted them as he passed, and each large black hat was raised for an instant.

An infantry soldier, lying on the ground, whose left shoulder and arm had been smashed by a shell, raised himself on his right arm and shouted:

"Are you General Trochu? Well, *Vive la France!*"

The Governor, without stopping, returned the salute and replied:

"And we will save her, with God's help. . . ."

Meanwhile, back in Paris, the people watched and waited. At the Pont d'Austerlitz a great crowd had gathered to see the landing of the wounded. "Steamers with the white flag", wrote the Oxford Graduate,

were hurrying up and down the river to unload their cargo of mangled human flesh, or to fetch another. Cabs went on to the embankment as far as the edge of the water to receive the more slightly wounded, who could support this mode of conveyance. *Chassepots* and knapsacks lay piled up on the wharf in heaps that gave a dismal impression of the number of victims. The Nationals, who lined the parapet, looked silently towards the river, and many a face amongst them turned pale at the sight; their officer remarked it, and made them turn at once to the right-about. Every now and then, four carriers brought in a wounded man on a stretcher. The crowd pressed round them, like children half-scared, half-attracted by some horrible sight. Most of the sufferers lay motionless as corpses on their stretchers. One of these I shall never forget, as he lay with both arms twisted behind his neck, leaning his head in the hollow of his clenched hands, with a glassy film over his eyes, an expression of silent Laocoon-like agony on his face, looking before him without seeing, stunned as it were and deafened by the din of the fight. . . .

There were even greater crowds along the Avenue du Trône, where Edmond de Goncourt had the impression that the whole of Paris was standing there, in the grip of deep emotion, waiting for news. "On both sides of the road", he wrote,

kept clear by National Guards, as far as the gate with its columns turning blue in a ray of winter sunshine, there were two crowds standing in tiers and forming here and there, on piles of stones, mounds of men and women. The roadway was full of the coming and going of ambulances, shell-carriers, cartridge and artillery waggons, carriages of all sorts, which were held up and pushed together every quarter of an hour, in a noisy tangle of iron, by the closing of the level-crossing gate. And every eye was fixed on the far end of the avenue, where the returning ambulances appeared, every eye looking for a priest's hat on the box, a nun's white headdress in the bench, peering into the black holes beside the driver, where in the shadows a wounded man could be seen lying. Everybody displayed a horrified pity mingled with a greedy curiosity about those pale patches, those livid gleams, those bloodstains, those ragged uniforms, the suppressed agony of those wounded men who knew that they were being inspected and made an effort to rise to the level of the occasion.

There were wounded sitting at the backs of carts, their legs hanging dead and limp, pale-faced, with vague smiles which made you want to cry. There were wounded who bore on their faces a horrible anxiety about their wounds, ignorance as to whether they were going to be amputated, ignorance as to whether they were going to live or die. There were wounded who posed in theatrical attitudes on a bale of straw, perched on the top of a carriage, and shouting to the public: "There's plenty of Prussian meat back there!" A fat Saxon with a beaming face and a good-natured smile was smoking a cigar in the middle of the French wounded. One man was fiercely hugging his rifle, the broken bayonet of which was no longer than an iron thumb. In the depths of little carriages wounded officers could be glimpsed with gold-braided sleeves and soft hands resting on the pommels of their swords; and through the misty panes of omnibuses, rows of bent backs, of wounded soldiers kept passing before us.

And our eyes followed the wounded, the couriers, the aides-de-camp, everything that came galloping from over there. "Look, there's Ricord!" cried somebody, seeing the surgeon go by in a carriage. A National Guard yelled from his horse: "A mile past Chennevières and it's bayonet attacks now. ...." And we went on waiting, asking, making everybody say: *All's well*, that *All's well* which every rider had to repeat in order to be allowed past. We had no definite news, but everybody had the impression that things were going well. And then a sort of feverish joy filled all our frozen faces; and men and women, infected with a sort of childish gaiety, ran to meet the galloping horses, trying to elicit from the couriers, with laughs, jokes, compliments and gentle threats, the news they did not bear.

When at last it came, the news was bad. After three nights in the open, and two days of fighting which had cost them 12,000 officers and men, the French were exhausted and demoralized; and Ducrot decided to abandon the plateau and recross the Marne. The operation was carried out without loss on 3 December, under cover of thick fog; and on the following day Ducrot issued a proclamation informing his men that he had brought them back across the Marne because he was convinced that any further efforts in that direction would be fruitless. If he had persisted, he would have sacrificed thousands of brave men to no purpose. "Far from furthering the task of deliverance", he declared, "I would have seriously compromised it, and at the same time I would have led you to an irreparable catastrophe."

That evening Paris learnt that the great sortie from which so much had been expected had been a disastrous failure. The news, ironically enough, arrived just as the orchestra at the Opera was about to strike up the triumphal march of Wagner's *Tannhäuser*.

Aftermath of Defeat

In the evening of 6 December, Edmond de Goncourt noted in his *Journal:* "In the open air this evening, in every gleam, every glow of improvised lights, dismayed faces were bent over newspapers. It was the announcement of the defeat of the Army of the Loire and the recapture of Orleans."

The news had been given to the Government the previous evening in this sardonically courteous letter from Moltke to Trochu:

> It might interest Your Excellency to be informed that the Army of the Loire was defeated yesterday near Orleans and that that city had been reoccupied by German troops.
>
> Should, however, Your Excellency deem it expedient to obtain confirmation of this news through one of his officers, I will not fail to provide him with a safe-conduct there and back.
>
> Pray accept, General, the assurance of the high regard with which I have the honour to be your most humble and obedient servant.
>
> Count von Moltke, Chief of Staff.

Trochu had replied to this letter with a no less courteous message stating that he did not consider it necessary to verify the information by the means Moltke suggested; while the Government, in publishing the correspondence, added that even if the Prussian claims were true, that did not deprive Paris of her right to count on "the great movement of France rushing to our aid".

134

Most Parisians, however, refused to believe Moltke's information, or, if they had accepted it at first, soon changed their minds. They were encouraged in their scepticism by an incident which occurred later in the week. In the afternoon of 9 December, two pigeons arrived in Paris bearing dispatches supposedly sent from Rouen and Tours. The text of the first dispatch was as follows:

> Rouen, 7 December. Government, Paris. Rouen occupied by Prussians who are marching on Cherbourg. Rural population acclaims them: ponder this well. Orleans retaken by those devils. Bourges and Tours threatened. Army of the Loire completely routed. Resistance no longer offers any hope of deliverance. A. Lavertujon.

The second dispatch, which bore an illegible signature something like the Compte de Pujol or de Puget, was just as heavily disheartening:

> Tours, 8 December. Editor, *Figaro*, Paris. What disasters! Orleans retaken. Prussians five miles from Tours and Bourges. Gambetta gone to Bordeaux. Rouen surrendered. Cherbourg threatened. Army of Loire non-existent, fugitives, looters, Rural population gone, hand-in-glove with Prussians. Everybody has had enough. Country laid waste. Brigandage flourishing. Shortage of horses, cattle. Hunger, mourning everywhere. No hope. Make it clear to Parisians that Paris is not France. People wish to have their say.

Publishing these two dispatches, the Government gave its reasons for thinking that they were apocryphal: first, the owner of the pigeons had recognized them as having been sent up with the *Daguerre* balloon, which had left Paris on 12 November and had fallen into the enemy's hands; secondly, the dispatches had been fastened to the birds in a different way from that which had always been used; thirdly, "both the language and the penmanship of the dispatches betrayed a German origin"; and fourthly, the first dispatch was signed with the name of a Government secretary who was still in Paris. Even so, there were some Parisians who treated the Government's detective work with sceptical reserve and maintained that the pigeons were *canards*. The Oxford Graduate, for one, wrote of the dispatches:

> We have examined them, as Rabelais has it, *à grand renfort de besicles*, and have failed to detect the slightest trace of "Germanism", except, perhaps, in the epithet of "those devils" applied to

135

the Prussians; and even this is not German in idiom, though somewhat un-French in sentiment at such a crisis.

He admitted that the clerks at the Telegraph Office had identified the pigeons as those which had been sent out of Paris with the ill-fated *Daguerre*, but added: "Be that as it may, the news they bring must be substantially correct." As indeed it was.

The population as a whole, however, preferred to regard the pigeons as another ruse of war, albeit a clumsy one, used by an enemy they were beginning to regard as cunning and deceitful. "Saint-Victor," wrote Goncourt,

> in his article yesterday, said in a striking fashion that France had to rid herself of the idea which she had entertained until now of Germany, of that country which she had been accustomed to consider, on the strength of its poetry, as the land of innocence and good nature, as the sentimental nest of platonic love. He recalled that the ideal, fictional world of Werther and Charlotte, of Hermann and Dorothea, had produced the toughest of soldiers, the wiliest of diplomats, the craftiest of bankers. He might have added the most mercenary of courtesans. We must be on our guard against that race, which arouses in us the idea of childlike innocence: their fair hair is the equivalent of the hypocrisy and sly determination of the Slav races.

The Press, as eager as the public to find some plausible explanation for the recent French defeat other than French incompetence, naturally seized on this idea of German deceit and trickery, and every newspaper published details of some ungentlemanly stratagem employed by the enemy. One paper, for example, declared that

> among all the iniquitious tricks used by the Prussians since the beginning of the war, everybody has been struck by our enemies' persistence in raising the butts of their rifles in the air, in token of surrender, when they found themselves surrounded by our troops, whom they never failed to shoot at point-blank range when the latter went forward to make them prisoners.

Several instances of this trick were cited, including one occasion when the victims, a raiding-party of Zouaves, were swiftly avenged:

> The fusillade had attracted another party of Zouaves, and all the Prussians in the post were cut up, chopped up and hacked to pieces down to the last man.

And the newspaper drew the comforting moral that

when our generous soldiers find savages in front of them, it is as savages that they will treat them.

Some Parisians took these stories of German treachery as dispensing them from the necessity to observe the rules of war, as four Prussian officers discovered that week. These four officers had been taken prisoners during the recent sortie, and liberated on parole, after being

presented with money to enable them to provide themselves with private clothes in which they might go about Paris at their ease and judge for themselves of the food supply and of the determined spirit of resistance which animates all classes of the population.

After a few days, however, it was thought desirable to exchange them for four French officers in the enemy's hands, for while dining in a boulevard restaurant the Prussians had been subjected to what the Press called "grave insults on the part of some of the company present". True, the *Illustrated London News* reported that the insults in question were "very generally said to have been provoked by the loud and hilarious conversation in which, with questionable taste, they thought it becoming to indulge", but the more responsible Paris papers deplored the incident.

Foreigners from neutral countries were also treated as scapegoats for the failure of the great sortie, particularly by what one correspondent called "a scum who lived from hand to mouth during the Empire, and which infests the restaurants and the public places". Henri Labouchére, describing how he underwent an experience similar to that of the Prussian officers wrote on 7 December:

I was peaceably dining last night in a restaurant; a friend with whom I had been talking English had left me, and I found myself alone with four worthies who were dining at a table near me. For my especial benefit they informed each other that all strangers here were outlaws from their own country, and that the Americans and Italians who have established ambulances were in all probability Prussian spies. As I took no notice of these startling generalities, one of them turned to me and said: "You may look at me, sir, but I assert before you that Dr. Evans, the ex-dentist of the Emperor, was a spy." I quietly remarked that, not having the honour to know Dr. Evans, and being myself an Englishman, whilst the Doctor is an American, I was not responsible for him. "You are a Greek," observed another: "I heard you talk Greek just now." I mildly suggested that his knowledge of languages was, perhaps, somewhat limited. "Well, if you are not a Greek," he said, "I saw you the other morning near the Ambulance of the Press, to which I belong, and so you must be a spy." "If you are an Englishman," cried his friend, "why do you not go back to your own country, and fight Russia?" I replied that the idea was an excellent one, but it might, perhaps, be difficult to pass through the Prussian lines. "The English ambassador is a friend of mine, and he will give you a pass at my request," answered the gentleman who had mistaken English for Greek. I thanked him, and assured him that I should esteem it a favour if he would obtain from his friend Lord Lyons this pass for me. He said he would do so, as it would be well to rid Paris of such vermin as myself and my countrymen. He has not yet, however, fulfilled his promise. Scenes such as this are of frequent occurrence at restaurants; bully and coward are generally synonymous terms; any scamp may insult a foreigner now with perfect impunity, for if the foreigner replies he has only to denounce him as a spy, when a crowd will assemble, and either set on him or bear him off to prison. While, as I have already said, nothing can be more courteous than the conduct of French officers, French gentlemen, and, unless they are excited, the French poorer classes, nothing can be more insolent than that of the third-class dandies who reserve their valour for the interior of the town, or who, if ever they venture outside of its fortifications, take care to skulk beneath the protection of the cross of Geneva.

If some Parisians laid the recent defeat at the door of "foreign spies", others blamed the National Guard for demoralizing the army. Nearly all the newspapers and diaries of the time, expecially when written for and by the well-to-do, referred slightingly to the citizen soldiery of Paris. Edmond de Goncourt, for example, wrote in his *Journal*:

The crapulence of the National Guard surpasses anything the imagination of a well-bred man could invent. Today, I was in a railway compartment with three National Guards, whose every drunken gesture was practically a blow for their neighbours, whose every phrase had to be accompanied by the word *merde*. One represented imbecile drunkenness; another mocking, vicious drunkenness; the last, brutal drunkenness. In, the course of the journey, vicious drunkenness told brutal drunkenness that the guard had given orders for him to be arrested when he got off the train, on account of the din he had made getting on. I saw the man take his knife out, open it, and put it back in his pocket like that. I got out at the first station, having no desire to be present at my neighbours' arrival. . . .

In similar vein, the *Revue des Deux Mondes* castigated the conduct of the National Guards in this account of their habits when on duty behind the fortifications:

On the arrival of a battalion, the chief of the post arranges the hours during which each man is to be on active duty. After this, the men occupy themselves as they please. Some play at interminable games of *bouchon*; others, notwithstanding orders to the contrary, turn their attention to écarté and piquet; others gossip about the news of the day with the artillerymen, who are mounting guard over their cannon. Some go away on leave, or disappear without leave; they go on excursions beyond the ramparts, or shut themselves up in the billiard-room of some café. Many, during the course of the day, pay frequent visits to the innumerable canteens which follow one after another almost without interruption along the Rue des Remparts. Here old women have lit a few sticks under a pot, and sell, for a penny a glass, a horrible brew called *petit noir*, composed of sugar, brandy and coffee grains, boiled up together. Behind there is a line of cook-shops, whose proprietors announce that they have been commissioned to provide food. These speculators offer for sale greasy soup, slices of horse, and every species of alcoholic drink. Each company has, too, its *cantinière*, and round her cart there is always a crowd. It seldom happens that more than half the men in the battalion are sober. Fortunately, the night air sobers them. Between eight and nine in the evening there is a gathering in the tent. A circle is formed in it round a single candle, and while the flasks go round, story follows song, and song story, until at length all fall asleep, and are only interrupted in their slumbers by the corporal, who, once an hour, enters and calls out the names of those who are to go on the watch. The abuse of strong drink makes shameful ravages in our ranks and is productive of serious disorder. Few nights pass without false alarms, without shots foolishly fired at imaginary enemies and without lamentable accidents. Every night there are quarrels, which often degenerate into fights, and then in the morning, when explanations take place, these very explanations are an excuse for starting drinking again. True, there are rules in plenty to prevent all this but the trouble is that they are never enforced. The indiscipline of the National Guard contrasts strangely with the patriotism of their words. Most of the insubordination may be ascribed to drunkenness, but the unruly behaviour which is so apparent in too many battalions is due also to many other causes. The primary organization of the National Guard was ill-conceived and ill-executed, and when the enrolments had been made, and the battalions formed, a fresh series of orders were promulgated day after day, so diffuse, so obscure, and so contradictory, that the officers, despairing of making head or tail of them, gave up any attempts to enforce them.

In these circumstances it was scarcely surprising that the attempt to form marching battalions out of these citizen soldiers, by obliging each sedentary battalion to provide 150 men, had not been particularly successful. Admittedly the marching battalions had been duly formed, but the Commander of the National Guard discovered that a system of substitutes had been practised on a large scale, married men with families having been bribed to take the place of well-to-do young bachelors. And military men as a whole were unanimously of the opinion that, for the honour of French arms, the marching battalions of the National Guard should be kept in reserve as long as possible.

All the prejudices held against the National Guard by the army, the aristocracy and the bourgeoisie were confirmed on 7 December, when the *Journal Officiel* published a decree dissolving the famous battalion of the Belleville Sharpshooters, which had played such a conspicuous part in the insurrection of 31 October. It is still impossible to establish the truth about the incident which led to the dissolution of the Sharpshooters, for Left and Right naturally gave totally different accounts of the affair. An English correspondent summarized the official version as follows:

> The battalion in question, after having repeatedly demanded to be sent against the enemy, had, with other troops, been dispatched to the front at Créteil, distant some 120 yards from the Prussian outposts. On the night of 28 November, the commander, having recommended to his men not to waste their ammunition uselessly, was startled shortly afterwards by a lively fusilade at the front, and still more startled by seeing a couple of companies quit the trenches and scamper off as fast as their legs would carry them. With great difficulty he prevailed upon them to return, and next day the entire battalion was withdrawn from the post of honour, and accorded cantonments under the guns of Fort Charenton. The men, on being subsequently ordered to return to the trenches, flatly refused, and the commander reported that his battalion, the effective strength of which was 457 men, had become reduced by sixty-one men, and this was not by casualties in face of the enemy. It further appeared that Citizen Flourens, although degraded some time since from his military rank, had rejoined the battalion in its cantonments and endeavoured to resume the command, for which proceeding his arrest and trial before a court-martial

has been decreed; while as regards the battalion of sharpshooters, its dissolution has been determined upon, and the sixty-one fugitives are to be brought before a council of war.

The Republican clubs, on the other hand, maintained that police spies had been introduced into the battalion by the authorities, with instructions to run away and thus bring discredit on the entire corps, so that the Government would have a pretext for disarming the Belleville patriots. This struck most Parisians as unlikely, to say the least, particularly as the commander of the Belleville Sharpshooters, a certain Lampérière, had described his battalion as "incompetent and unmanageable", concluding his report on its conduct in these pompous but unambiguous terms:

> I have the honour to tender my resignation of its command, finding it impossible as an honourable man, and a former non-commissioned officer in the regular army, to remain any longer at the head of such a troop. I intend to enter the National Guard, as a private, to purify myself from my over-long contact with the Belleville Sharpshooters.

But after the battalion had been disbanded, Lampérière withdrew his aspersions on its behaviour; and the Oxford Graduate, expressing the general puzzlement, wrote in his diary:

> The affair of the Belleville Sharpshooters does not seem quite so clear as it did at first: and the letter of apology which their ex-commandant Lampérière has just written to *Combat* only proves – if it proves anything – that there is not much to choose between him and his men. The sharpshooters, disarmed by Clément Thomas, held a meeting, and invited "Delegates" to attend from the other battalions, whose indirect testimony had been used against them by the authorities. The word "Delegates" looks very fine on paper, but there are enough rascals in every battalion of the National Guard to constitute an adequate representation of the whole for the purposes of Belleville. These degelates, summoned to give their opinion as to the honourable conduct of the Bellevillites in presence of the enemy, agreed all to sign a paper, which conferred on them plenary absolution. Arthur de Fonvielle, commander of the 147th battalion of La Villette, protested against the allegation reproduced in the general's report, and according to which his men had taken such a violent disgust to their Belleville comrades that they had insisted on being separated from them by barricades at the outposts. The sharpshooters summoned their own ex-commander to attend their meeting,

and this invitation having been followed up with threats by some of their party, the President recommended the assembly to receive the culprit with the calm that befitted brave men vindicating their honour. Apparently the commander objected to a "calm" reception, for he did not appear at the meeting, but wrote his letter to *Combat*, in which he retracted all the charges he had brought against his men. Lampérière is an old exile, and as such had been received by Flourens with open arms; the greatest harmony seemed to prevail between them for the last two days at the outposts. Obliged to absent himself from his post at Créteil, the major asked Flourens in a friendly manner to replace him for a while in his command, and, on taking leave, he threw on his shoulders, in presence of the men, his own military cloak, with the four silver stripes that indicate the rank of commandant; then rode off to headquarters with his report already prepared in which he denounced Flourens for having usurped the insignia of command. Flourens, with his usual gullibility, fell into the snare, and gave an excellent opportuntiy to the Government for carrying out its long-delayed purposes against him: his name is now associated with the discreditable conduct of the Belleville battalion, and his person is under the lock and key of Monsieur Jules Favre, in retaliation for 31 October.

Baffled by these contradictory reports, but content that some scapegoats had been found to bear responsibility for the army's failure, the people of Paris waited for the Government to give them a new lead. But the Government itself was divided. It was widely known in Paris that at the council held to discuss Moltke's proposal, Ernest Picard, the Finance Minister, had been in favour of accepting, and it was rumoured that he had been supported by Jules Favre and Jules Simon. "The newspapers", wrote Labouchère,

·   still announce every morning that victory is not far off. But their influence is gone. The belief that the evil day cannot be far off is gradually gaining ground, and those who are in a position to know more accurately the precise state of affairs, take a still more hopeless view of them than the masses. The programme of the Government seems to be this – to make a sortie in a few days, then to fall back beneath the forts; after this to hold out until the provisions are eaten up, and then, after having made a final sortie, to capitulate. Trochu is entirely in the hands of Ducrot, who, with the most enterprising of the officers, insists that the military honour of the French arms demands that there should be more fighting, even though success be not only improbable but impossible.

In the meantime the authorities tried to raise the population's spirits with a series of daily parades and ceremonies at which each arrondissement in turn took possession of the guns for which its inhabitants had subscribed, and handed them over to the army. When the turn of the Sixteenth Arrondissement came round, three guns were brought from the Conservatoire, ceremoniously presented to the army at the Arc de Triomphe, and dragged through Passy and Chaillot to the music of the *Marseillaise* and the *Chant du Départ*. "Admiral Fleuriot de Langle", wrote an observer,

> walked at the head of the procession with the Mayor, Monsieur Henry Martin, thus bearing witness to the close bond which, in this once so peaceful and now so warlike district of Paris, has constantly linked the military and the municipality in the work of national defence.

Speeches were made at the Trocadéro, and in the middle of the mayor's tirade Mont Valérien opened fire. "What use are words?" asked the quick-witted orator. "That voice says enough. It is for us to reply. We wanted guns: here they are! Let us fire them as quickly as possible at the enemy!"

For Edmond de Goncourt, the voice of Mont Valérien spoke differently. On the 12th he complained of

> sleepless nights produced by the continuous cannonade from Mont Valérien which, all of a sudden, fires a number of shots in rapid succession, which resembles the six revolver shots let off by a man taken by surprise.

Waiting for News

The middle of December was a waiting period for the Parisians, who from day to day and even hour to hour alternated between hope and despair, now looking forward to news of victory in the provinces, now dreading imminent famine or disaster. As one observer put it,

> there is nothing more painful than this state in which you do not know whether the provincial armies are at Corbeil or Bordeaux, or even whether they exist at all; nothing more cruel than living in the dark, in ignorance of the tragedy threatening you, surrounding you, gripping you. It really seems as if Monsieur de Bismarck had locked up the whole of Paris in a prison cell.

In the meantime, Monsieur de Bismarck's prisoners had no option but to go about their habitual occupations, keeping as far as possible to their former routines.

The intellectual life of the city was affected least of all by the siege. The children went to school as usual, for both the primary schools and the *lycées* had been opened early in the siege; public lectures continued to be given and were well attended; and the city showed its continued regard for science by sending off an astronomer in the *Volta* balloon with the mission of making observations in Algeria of the approaching total eclipse of the sun. Facilities for study were even increased during the siege, for the reading-rooms of the public libraries

144

were kept open for longer periods, while the artistic world was invited to consult the valuable library of the Louvre, which had been closed to the public ever since the beginning of the Second Empire.

It is unlikely, though, that many people took advantage of these reforms, for most Parisians were more preoccupied with obtaining food for the stomach than for the mind. On Sunday, 11 December, there was something of a panic when the bakers' shops ran out of bread and closed their doors early in the afternoon; and the next day the Government had to issue a proclamation to reassure the public. It denied that there was any truth in rumours that bread rationing was going to be introduced and declared that there was enough wheat in the city to provide bread until the beginning of March. In a further proclamation it added that as soon as the stock of white flour was exhausted, the bakers would be allowed to sell only brown bread, which it described as nourishing, wholesome, pleasant to the taste, and "universally eaten by the peasants, even in the more favoured departments". The supply of meat, derived largely from the daily slaughter of 500 horses, was also assured, the public was told: in other words, each Parisian was guaranteed a daily ration of half an ounce of fresh or preserved horse-meat, with an equal quantity of salt fish in addition. "The situation", the proclamation concluded, "is therefore satisfactory. One might even say that it is unexpectedly good, for the third month of a siege."

The situation was not in fact as good as the proclamation pretended, and there was considerable anxiety in the Government on the subject. Magnin, the Minister of Commerce, could guarantee a supply of bread only until 10 January, and he also thought that the supply of horseflesh would fail about the same time. "What surprises me", wrote one English observer,

is the facility with which people believe in "immense stores" of wheat, just as at the beginning of the siege they believed in immense stores of flour: one would have thought that the first belief having proved false would have carried away with it the second. But Paris hopes against hope, like a patient in the last stages of consumption. I know not of any phase of mind that so exactly corresponds to the present fretful, peevish, dejected and yet hopeful state, in which the Parisians have lived for the last few days.

Although the basic essentials of the Parisian diet, bread and meat, were available in small quantities, most people found it impossible to make do with the bare rations provided by the Government, and nearly everybody supplemented his diet with more or less unusual foods. "The consumption of dogs, cats and rats is considerable," reported one newspaper, "but only the first of these animals appears to be held in esteem by the genuine gourmets, although rats, in one form or another, generally occupy a place in the more varied menus." There was a shop in the Rue Blanche which sold all three types of meat; it had a great many customers, but most of them looked around cautiously to see that no acquaintances were near before they sneaked inside. A certain prejudice had arisen against rats, because the doctors had stated that their flesh was full of trichinae, and many Parisians – not to mention the pet-loving English colony – had qualms about eating dog. "I own for my part", wrote Labouchère,

> I have a guilty feeling when I eat dog, the friend of man. I had a slice of spaniel the other day; it was by no means bad, something like lamb, but I felt like a cannibal. Epicures in dog-flesh tell me that poodle is by far the best, and recommend me to avoid bull-dog, which is coarse and tasteless. I really think that dogs have some means of communicating with each other, and have discovered that their old friends want to devour them: the humblest of street curs growls when anyone looks at him. . . .

Some restaurants offered their customers more exotic fare, obtained at considerable cost from the Jardin d'Acclimatation, and ranging from buffalo to kangaroo. The director of the zoo kept a careful record of the animals which he sold to be slaughtered, together with the date of the sale, the name of the butcher, and the price paid. This grisly list read as follows:

18 October	M. Courtier	1 Dwarf Zebra	350 fr.
,,	,,	2 Buffaloes	300 fr.
23 October	M. Lacroix	2 Deer	500 fr.
,,	,,	12 Carp	150 fr.
24 October	M. Deboos	2 Yaks	390 fr.
25 October	M. Groszos	3 Geese	60 fr.
27 October	M. Lacroix	1 Small Zebra	400 fr.
28 October	M. Bignon	1 Lot of Fowls, Ducks, etc.	862 fr.
31 October	M. Deboos	1 Lot of Ducks	115 fr.
3 November	M. X	11 Rabbits	100 fr.
17 November	M. Deboos	2 Reindeer	800 fr.

21 November	,,	2 Nilghaus	1,000 fr.
22 November	M. Lacroix	1 Bengal Stag	300 fr.
26 November	M. Deboos	2 Wapitis	2,500 fr.
9 December	,,	1 Nilghau	650 fr.
15 December	,,	2 Camels	4,000 fr.
,,	,,	1 Yak Calf	200 fr.
20 December	,,	2 Camels	5,000 fr.
29 December	,,	2 Elephants	27,000 fr.

As food grew scarcer, it became an obsession with the whole population, and Edmond de Goncourt wrote in his *Journal*:

> People talk of nothing but what is eaten, can be eaten, or is there to be eaten. Conversation has come down to this:
> "You know, a fresh egg costs twenty-five sous!"
> "It appears there's a fellow who buys up all the candles he can find, adds some colouring, and produces that fat which sells at such a price."
> "Mind you don't buy any coconut butter: it stinks a house out for three days at least."
> "I've had some dog chops, and found them really very tasty: they look just like mutton chops."
> "Who was it who told me that he had eaten some kangaroo?"
> Hunger is beginning and starvation is on the horizon. Elegant Parisiennes have started turning their dressing-rooms into hen-coops. Everybody is counting and calculating and wondering whether, with all the leavings, all the scrapings, all the trimmings, there will be anything left to eat in a fortnight's time.

For the poor, starvation was often already a reality. Goncourt records that an acquaintance told him of hearing a woman behind him in the street say: "Monsieur, come up to my room." The invitation was repeated in a different tone of voice. The third time, it was a beseeching: "Monsieur, *please* come up to my room!" which "sounded like the trembling, tearful voice of hunger".

The Oxford Graduate made a similar observation. "I see", he wrote,

> that we are greatly pitied in England for eating *salamis* of rats; but this is a mere caricature of our real miseries. Cast a scrutinizing glance amongst the families whose modest habits revealed the dignity of poverty, and examine the death-lists – for only the death-lists know their secrets: hundreds die of "pneumonia" – so the doctors call it – who were ashamed to stand in a queue at a municipal *cantine*. Only today, Monsieur L— saw in a courtyard two ladies, thickly veiled, who sang from door to door for half-

pence. But the world will ignore all this quiet dying and suffering, and will stare at some fashionable menu of a rat-dinner which a Special Correspondent enjoyed in the company of some half-dozen celebrities.

If there was little to eat in Paris at this time, there was no lack of wine and spirits, and many people took to drinking heavily in order to conquer hunger or banish care. "It must be confessed", Labouchère told the readers of the *Daily News*,

> that one can now see in the streets of Paris – hitherto the most sober capital in Christendom – the unwonted spectacle of intoxication. The anxieties of the siege, the want of amusement, and the badness of the food, all lead a number of people to seek for support in strong drink. What stuff it is they drink! Wine is not enough for them, and they take to spirits. The spirit which they adore is rum. They buy it at two francs a bottle, and make it into punch. The National Guards especially are great in punch. One battalion invites another to what they call "a punch", and when the war-companies of a battalion are ordered out of Paris to the advanced posts, the comrades who remain behind treat them to what they call the "punch of adieu".

At this point, Labouchère must have realized that he was providing ammunition for those of his readers who regarded Paris as a place of sin and debauchery, the modern Babylon, for he abruptly concluded his report with a sharp reminder of the prevalence of drunkenness in London, which could not plead the excuse of a siege. "I am not going to defend drunkenness," he wrote,

> either in ordinary mortals or in National Guards. There have been some gross cases of drunkenness in the National Guards, of which one cannot speak too contemptuously; but do not let us make too much of the crime; and above all, let us make every allowance for the temptation to it. There is not half the drunkenness in Paris that there is in London, and it is marked here because it is so unwonted. If the London populace were in the condition of the Parisian populace – reduced to such straits – let us try to imagine how they would behave, and especially how they would soak themselves in beer and gin. . . .

For several days in mid-December, the people of Paris had little else but drink to keep up their spirits, in the total absence of news. But somehow the capital remained remarkably cheerful. "Spite of almost unvarying reverses", reported the Paris correspondent of the *Illustrated London News*,

everyone seems to continue hopeful, and to be impressed with
the belief that ere long fortune will certainly favour one or other
of the various armies advancing to the relief of Paris, and that
the Prussians will be ultimately forced to raise the siege.

True, as the Rothschild agent in Paris informed his employer,
the United States minister was less encouraging and hinted
that the relief armies were in a bad way. But even here C. de
B. found cause for optimism. "You will remember," he added,

> that Mr. Washburne promised Monsieur de Bismarck that he
> would not show us any newspapers from outside. He is so anxious
> not to break his word that, having to remain in bed with a chill,
> he tucks his newspapers under a pillow! If our relief armies are
> really in such a bad way as Mr. Washburne would like us to
> believe, why does Monsieur de Bismarck not let us see the news-
> papers? The Prussians do not often neglect their propaganda.

Alas, Washburne's pessimism was soon proved to have been
fully justified, for on the 14th two pigeons arrived with messages from Gambetta corroborating Moltke's news of the loss
of Orleans, and announcing that Rouen was about to fall to
the Prussians, that General Bourbaki was in retreat, and that
General Chanzy was fully occupied holding the army of
Prince Frederick Charles at bay between Josnes and Beaugency. Gambetta added, almost as an afterthought, that the
Government Delegation had fled to Bordeaux, or, as he put it,
"moved to Bordeaux to avoid impeding the strategic move-
ments of our armies". As if all this were not sufficiently disheartening, the *Journal Officiel* which published Gambetta's
dispatches threw in for good measure some extracts from a
Prussian newspaper which revealed that when the enemy had
captured Orleans he had taken no less than 10,000 prisoners,
77 cannon and four gun-boats.

Contrary to all expectations, this "disastrous intelligence",
as one correspondent called it, failed to discourage the Parisians. Perhaps, as Labouchère suggested, this was because of
Gambetta's style, which he described as "so grandiloquently
vague that we can make neither head nor tail of it". A more
probable explanation, put forward by Baron Lionel de
Rothschild's agent, was that the people of Paris preferred to
be told bad news than none at all. "Moreover", the incorrig-
ibly optimistic C. de B. went on,

> the fact that our provincial armies suffer occasional reverses
> proves that we are not fighting quite alone, and the fortunes of

149

war that are against us today may turn in our favour tomorrow. Our chief concern is for the Government to renew an offensive with the 250,000 stout-hearted, well-equipped troops now in the capital. If the provincial armies cannot come to the help of Paris, it is up to the Army of Paris to break out and join up with the provinces. . . .

There were signs that the Government was in fact planning a new offensive, for during the past few days every branch of the Army of Paris had been reorganized. The National Guard in particular had been subjected to more stringent disciplinary measures, and it was clear that General Clément Thomas, the Guard's new commander, was determined to stand no non-sense from his citizen soldiers. Scarcely a day went by without some officer of the National Guard being tried by court-martial for drunkenness or disobedience, and if a battalion mis-behaved itself, it was promptly pilloried in the order of the day. Thus on the 14th an order of the day was published dissolving the battalion known as the Volunteers of the 147th, which the day before had flatly refused to obey marching orders, on the excuse that the wives of the Volunteers had not been paid the 75 centimes per day to which they were entitled by Govern-ment decree when their husbands were called upon for active duty. There were some protests in the press at the publicity Clément Thomas gave to his men's misdemeanours. The newspapers accused him of forgetting that the National Guards were his children, and that dirty washing ought to be washed at home; and one complained: "If this goes on, posterity will say that we were little more than a mob of undisciplined drunkards". Most responsible observers, how-ever, approved of the General's methods, and only feared that he would not have time to carry out his reforms.

In the evening of the 16th a Council of War was held, with Trochu in the chair and all the generals commanding corps in the Army of Paris present. The next day, the *Moniteur de l'Armée* contained a long list of promotions, principally of officers who had taken part in recent engagements, giving the impression that the reorganization of the army was complete and that the new offensive everyone had been waiting for was imminent. The same impression was created by an address Trochu issued to the army, in which, in his usual grandilo-quent style, the Governor declared that "the Army of the Loire, like the Army of Paris, renews itself under fire at the price of heroic sacrifices in a struggle which amazes the enemy, who is appalled by the enormity of his losses and the indomitable energy of the resistance he encounters". Cynics also saw cause for optimism in a new decree awarding Generals Vinoy, d'Exéa and Frébault grand crosses of the Legion of Honour.

Meanwhile the Parisians possessed their souls in as much patience as they could muster. The dreary monotony of the average citizen's life at this stage of the siege is skilfully rendered in this account by the Besieged Resident of his activities during a typical day:

In the morning the boots comes to call me. He announces the number of deaths which have taken place in the hotel [which was used as a hospital for the wounded] during the night. If there are many he is pleased, as he considers it creditable to the establishment. He then relieves his feelings by shaking his fist in the direction of Versailles, and exit growling "Canaille de Bismarck". I get up, I have breakfast – horse, *café au lait* – the *lait* chalk and water – the portion of horse about two square inches of the noble quadruped. Then I buy a dozen newspapers, and after having read them, discover that they contain nothing new. This brings me to about eleven o'clock. Friends drop in, or I drop in on friends. We discuss how long it is to last – if friends are French we agree that we are sublime. At one o'clock get into the circular railroad, and go to one or other of the city gates. After a discussion with the National Guards on duty, pass through. Potter about for a couple of hours at the outposts; try with glass to make out Prussians; look at bombs bursting; creep along the trenches; and wade knee-deep in mud through the fields. The Prussians, who have grown of late malevolent even towards civilians, occasionally send a ball far over one's head. They always fire too high. French soldiers are generally cooking food. They are anxious for news, and know nothing about what is going on. As a rule they relate the episode of some *combat d'avant-poste* which took place the day before. The episodes never vary. 5 p.m. – Get back home; talk to doctors about interesting surgical operations; then drop in on some official to interview him about what he is doing. Official usually first mysterious, then communicative, not to say loquacious, and abuses most people except himself. 7 p.m. – Dinner at a restaurant; conversation general; almost everyone in uniform. Still the old subjects – How long will it last? Why does not Gambetta write more clearly? How sublime we are; what a fool everyone else is. Food scanty, but peculiar. At Voisin's today the bill of fare was ass, horse, and English wolf from the Zoological Garden. A

Scotchman informed me that this latter was a fox of his native land, and patriotically gorged himself with it. I tried it, and not being a Scotchman, found it horrible, and fell back upon the patient ass. After dinner, potter on the Boulevards under the dispiriting gloom of petroleum; go home and read a book. 12 p.m. – Bed. They nail up the coffins in the room just over mine every night, and the tap, tap, tap, as they drive in the nails, is the pleasing music which lulls me to sleep. How, I ask, after having endured this sort of thing day after day for three months, can I be expected to admire, Geist, Germany, or Mr. Matthew Arnold? I sigh for a revolution, for a bombardment, for an assault, for anything which would give us a day's excitement.

After waiting for news, Paris was now waiting for action.

Le Bourget

With Christmas a few days away and the siege apparently no nearer to its end, the Versailles correspondent of the *Daily News* wrote on 21 December:

> The shortest day of the year finds us where the bright afternoons in September found us, waiting before Paris. Three months ago yesterday the great army of the Germans circled around the city, and all communication was cut off, and all supplies were stopped. I shall be slow to forget the exciting impression of that first arrival on the heights of Meudon, and that first glance over the white houses, and domes, and towers of Paris. It then seemed certain that the Parisians would yield so soon as they realized their peril. They might be shelled. Was not that enough for them? Their daily newspapers would be deprived of news, their coffee would lose its flavour in the dullness of the time, and Paris would yield with tears of joy at being spared to fight some other day. Such were the prospects of 20 September – when the Crown Prince rode up to the Prefecture on the Avenue de Paris. What are the prospects on 21 December – when German uniforms have become as familiar to Versailles as the tall figures of the Life Guardsmen are to Knightsbridge? The answer is simple. Paris is more likely to hold out six weeks now than she seemed likely to hold out six days on 20 September. The Parisians have risen to some extent to the measure of their destiny. We are in presence of a population which begins to feel proud of what it has achieved, and there will only be a surrender when such is absolutely necessary.

153

Morale inside Paris was in fact very high; and, far from thinking of surrender, the people had for some days been clamouring for action. On the morning of Sunday the 18th, the *Journal Officiel* had published a message from Gambetta sent from Bourges on the 14th and stating:

> The Prussian retreat is a movement about which there can be no mistake. If we can only hold out – and we can if we have the will – we shall beat them. They have already suffered enormous losses, and are experiencing the greatest difficulty in obtaining supplies of food. But to triumph we must resign ourselves to supreme sacrifices without murmuring, and fight even unto death.

The newspapers, almost without exception, greeted this message with optimistic enthusiasm. The *Pays* declared that the invaders must soon see, if they did not see already, that the best thing they could do would be to return home while the road was still open to them; the *Liberté* maintained that the moment had come for Paris to act energetically and without regard for the sacrifices she might be called upon to make; and even the moderate *Opinion Nationale* attacked the Government for its inaction, asking why, with an army of 400,000 men and formidable artillery, 16 days had been allowed to pass without anything being done. "We neither try to pierce the lines", it complained,

> nor to raise the siege, nor even risk partial actions, in order to kill as many Prussians as possible. We are losing time; we are eating up our stores, and we are not pushing on the work of deliverance. This inaction is deplorable. It allows the enemy to detach 100,000 or even 200,000 men from Paris, and to send them into the provinces to the succour of Prince Frederick Charles. Why, we may ask, were the war battalions of the National Guard formed? Was it for precaution or action? Why are cannon being made by thousands and projectiles by hundreds of thousands? Was it to offer to the King of Prussia examples of Parisian industry on the day when hunger forces us to capitulate? Let Parisians die, but save Paris!

The *Journal Officiel* replied on the 19th to these reproaches with another long-winded declaration of the Government's "indomitable resolution to fight and to conquer". This time, however, there seemed to be some substance in the Government's assurances, for the same day the signs of preparations for a sortie began to appear: troops and National Guards on the march, cannon rolling, and ambulances driving through the streets. By the 20th, Paris was buzzing with rumours, both optimistic and pessimistic. Some people said that Bourbaki and Chanzy had joined up and hurled part of Prince Frederick Charles's army into the river; others that it was Chanzy's army which had broken up. Baron Lionel de Rothschild's agent in Paris reported that a huge crowd had gathered in the Rue de Rivoli, simply because a pigeon had perched on the roof of the Governor's office. "Parisians are so avid of news", he wrote,

> that they thought that the pigeon had just arrived from Tours with a sheaf of telegrams and they showed their impatience with a good-natured demonstration. In fact, the pigeon was one of those friendly Parisian birds that never fly more than a short distance from the heart of the city. It probably spends the major part of its quiet life on the top of the Louvre. ...

The night of the 20th saw the culmination of the preparations for the new sortie. At two o'clock in the morning of the 21st, bugles called the battalions which were to make the sortie, while drums summoned the companies of the Sedentary National Guard which were to accompany the marching battalions to the gates of Paris. The troops were marshalled together, then disposed in echelon from the Madeleine to the Château-d'Eau, and at half-past four the march began.

"This long procession", wrote J. d'Arsac the next day,

> had something solemn about it as it made its way through the darkness. From time to time the column, meeting other troops, would slow down and come to a halt: then, on the left of the road, it would see ambulance and transport waggons going past, a few staff officers, a few cavalry detachments. These all passed by like shadows, and it was impossible to make out either faces or uniforms.
>
> At every halt, other shadows came up to the marching battalions, and sometimes, by the light of lanterns which they lifted to the height of the soldiers' faces, they tried to recognize a son, a brother, a lover. These were the women's farewells. Along the whole of this long route, from the new Opera to the Place du Trône, the march took place in perfect order and an impressive silence.
>
> About six o'clock in the morning, the head of the column reached the barricade across the Avenue de Vincennes, in front of the two monuments at the old gate, and deployed along the Vincennes railway which cuts the road at that point.
>
> It was the moment of parting. The sedentary companies which

155

had formed up in good order and marched behind the combat troops, broke ranks and went to take leave of their comrades. There were handshakes, farewells and good wishes, but no shouting, singing, drinking or boasting. Everybody knew that a decisive moment had come.

In the meantime officers on horseback, riding up from the direction of Vincennes, announced that fresh detachments of troops were arriving. Ranks were formed again. Some of the troops crossed the barricade and went through the gates, while the others took the road back to Paris.

At dawn all the forts opened fire, and an attack was launched along the entire northern half of the perimeter of Paris, from Mont Valérien to Nogent. Trochu's intention was to link up with, or at least help, the Army of the North, under General Faidherbe, on which Paris had pinned her hopes since the defeat of the Army of the Loire. In the second week of December Faidherbe had set off from Lille, and after passing La Fère and Saint-Quentin, had suddenly retraced his steps and started advancing towards Paris. Trochu was determined to establish himself in the best position, either to join up with Faidherbe if he approached the German lines outside Paris, or to hold the troops of the investing army so that they could not assist Manteuffel against the Army of the North. Unfortunately the Germans were on their guard all round Paris: in the first place they had learnt to recognize the preliminary signs of a sortie, such as the closing of the city gates, and then a balloon fell within their lines, containing a dispatch from Trochu stating that a great sortie was to be made on the 20th. What is more, however good the morale of the French troops might be, their organization was inefficient. As Hérisson observed,

to mass inexperienced and young troops, such as the French were, a very long time was necessary. The extemporized officers did not know much. The extemporized soldiers knew nothing. They were never ready. An immense amount of time was lost in getting them into line, man by man. And when the whole lot had fallen in something like order, the columns got mixed up, the battalions overlapped, the convoys and batteries obstructed the route, and a fresh mess had to be disentangled.

The immediate aims of the sortie were to extend the line of investment towards the north-east; to take certain positions commanding the roads which the Germans used for their convoys, thus cutting their communications; and finally to make it possible to establish entrenchments beyond the plateau of Avron, so that the positions of Villiers and Coeuilly might eventually be turned. Accordingly Ducrot marched against Le Bourget and Vinoy against Ville-Évrard, while a diversion was made to the west of Paris, in the direction of Bougival, below the woods of La Celle-Saint-Cloud and Mont Valérien. The main attack, that on Le Bourget, was made in a pincer movement, with a mixed force of regular troops, Mobiles and Marines on the left and a force under Ducrot on the right. Six hundred Marines were flung into the initial assault on Le Bourget, storming the earthworks in thick mist with their axes in their hands; four officers lost their lives and 270 Marines were killed or wounded. The survivors fought with amazing courage and tenacity, but heavy German shell-fire prevented them from being reinforced, just as it prevented Ducrot's force from succeeding in its attack from the right. As dusk fell the troops were withdrawn and ordered to camp in the open during the night before resuming the attack on Le Bourget the following day. The ground was too hard for tents to be erected, and 900 men were frostbitten that night. The next day, under heavy fire, and lashed by an icy north wind, they tried to dig trenches in order to advance on Le Bourget by means of a regular siege. But it was impossible to make any impression on the rock-hard ground, and as the hours and days went by, the shivering troops began to show signs of mutiny. Still Trochu hesitated to withdraw them, knowing that the people of Paris would find it hard to forgive another defeat; but on the 24th he had no option but to order a retreat and the men were marched back into the capital. They were completely demoralized by the difficulties they had encountered: the heavily fortified German positions, the bitter cold, and above all the incompetence of their own superior officers, who had left them for 36 hours without rations and sacrificed hundreds of lives to no purpose. Twenty thousand men were suffering from anaemia, and several battalions of the Garde Mobile, according to General Clément Thomas, were restrained only with difficulty from shouting: "Long live peace!" as they re-entered Paris.

The other major attack of 21 December, to the east of Paris, was more successful, and Vinoy speedily took possession of the important triangle formed by Neuilly-sur-Marne, Ville-Évrard and the Maison-Blanche. But here again, French incompetence brought disaster. After the occupation of Neuilly-sur-Marne, a detachment of engineers was given orders to fortify Ville-Évrard in order to protect the position against enemy sharp-shooters on the opposite bank of the Marne. By eight o'clock in the evening the trenches had been dug, General Blaise had inspected the village, and his troops had settled down for the night in the empty houses. Hérisson, who rode into the village that evening to see a friend on Blaise's staff, has left us this account of the drama that followed:

> The General was there, sure enough, with his officers round a large fire of beams and planks supplied from the debris of the houses blown up by our and the German shells. Sitting astride a straw-bottomed chair, with his steaming boots on the hearth, the General and his officers, cigar or pipe in mouth, were talking over the events of the day, and broke off every now and then to take a mouthful of old rum out of the common flask. I got off my horse and tied him to a tree. The greatest suffering a rider has to undergo is cold feet, and I was not sorry to warm mine at the bivouac fire. A place was made for me in the circle, and the conversation, stirred up afresh by a new arrival, became quite gay. There we were, roasted in front and frozen behind, turning ourselves round at irregular intervals as if we were on a gridiron, and surrounded by sentires, when a strange noise made us leap to our feet.
>
> "That's a Prussian bugle," said the General. "Where the devil can it come from?"
>
> He had not finished his sentence when flames were seen coming up through the air-holes of the cellars of the surrounding houses, and I saw him fall flat on the ground beside the fire.

The explanation was that some of the Prussians occupying Ville-Évrard, unable to leave the village fast enough in the morning of the 21st, had hidden in the cellars. The French had neglected to take the elementary precaution of searching all the houses, with the result that they were taken by surprise when the Prussians emerged from their hiding-places. Blaise himself was wounded in the shoulder and the thigh, and died at one o'clock in the morning. "It is doubtful", wrote Labouchère, "whether a French general who can allow himself to be surprised in this way is of much value", but Blaise was in fact one of the most capable generals in Paris, and in any case, as the *Daily News* correspondent admitted, the French were not so well supplied with officers that they could afford to lose any.

The extent of all these misfortunes was not immediately apparent to the people of Paris. True, a few perceptive citizens read between the lines of the first official bulletin and realized immediately that the sortie had failed. "Why disguise the truth?" Adolphe Michel asked on the 22nd.

> The military operations begun yesterday have brought us fresh disappointment. Le Bourget has not remained in our power; admittedly we were "thwarted by the state of the atmosphere". Monsieur Trochu had not foreseen the mist when he conceived his plan, and now the whole action has been suspended. And what are we to say about those Prussians who "remained in the cellars" and came out at night to attack our posts? Is it possible to make a franker confession of incompetence and lack of fore-sight?

Many Parisians, however, went on hoping against hope that the sortie was proving successful. Even on the 23rd, looking down from Montmartre at the troops at Le Bourget desper-ately trying to dig themselves in, one Frenchman was heard exulting: "At last our generals have understood their work: they are going to carry the Prussian positions one after the other, by a regular siege, as they ought to have done long ago." By the time it became clear that the Le Bourget sortie had failed, Christmas had arrived.

Out at Versailles, there was junketing and jubilation. There were Christmas trees in every post, and lavish Christmas dinners washed down with beer for the men and champagne for the officers. The Prussian commanders were delighted at the ease with which the latest French sortie had been repelled, and confident that bombardment would soon bring Paris to her knees. For the long-awaited bombardment now appeared to be imminent. By passing on to Moltke reports of the clam-our for bombardment in the German press and the Prussian Assembly, Bismarck had finally won his way, and it had been agreed that the shelling of the southern fortifications of Paris should begin as soon as a ten-day supply of shells had been accumulated at Villacoublay. Foreign correspondents were given to understand that only a bombardment of the French forts were envisaged, but Bismarck, like the Nationalist press in Germany, was clearly eager to see shells falling on the "modern Babylon" itself. "At last", he wrote to his wife on Christmas Eve,

> there is a prospect of the bombardment of Paris, we hope before the New Year. ... Owing to the scattering of our army from Tours to Lille, the overhasty wastage of troops, and the sleepy conduct of the war before Paris, there is not one department in France in which we are complete masters, so that we could exact an indemnity. May God better matters, His arm is not flesh. In Him I trust, when I look at these dissolute people. We too are sinners, but not yet so Babylonish, nor so opposed to God. ...

The Babylonians, for their part, had an austere, frugal Christmas. By way of a treat, the Government substituted beef for horseflesh in the meat-ration, and added an ounce of salt butter, a delicacy which most of the population had not seen or tasted since September, but this was the limit of official generosity. Public events matched the Parisian's Christmas fare in austerity. There was a charity performance at the Comédie Française; a lecture at the Conservatoire given by Louis Ratisbonne, who drew a comparison between Christmas in Paris and in Germany; and a bazaar in aid of war victims at the Ministry of Public Instruction. At this last event, according to the *Illustrated London News*,

> the simplest articles of food were exposed for sale side by side with objects of taste and luxury, and, what is not all surprising, commanded hardly inferior prices. One hears of a turkey – set off on a couch of velvet, it is true – realizing a couple of hundred francs; and of bonbonnières, containing fine flour in lieu of sweetmeats, being sold for half this amount; of potatoes priced as high as the choicest truffles; of celery fetching almost its weight in silver; and radishes realizing ten francs, instead of ten centimes, per bunch.

As for the English residents in Paris, most of them gathered on Christmas morning at the little English church in the Avenue Marboeuf, which was hung with holly as in previous years. Talking together after the service, most of them tried to convince each other that they were going to celebrate Christmas in the traditional manner and with the traditional fare. "The English colony", wrote the Oxford Graduate, "*speaks* of roast beef and plum pudding, sniffs from afar the good cheer of Albion, grumbles at Bismarck, and moralizes more wisely about the siege than a leader in *The Times*." But nobody was tactless enough to wish his neighbour a merry Christmas.

Monday 26 December – Sunday, 1 January

The End of the Year

The last week of the year opened with the thermometer marking 12 degrees below zero, men on duty at the outposts freezing to death, and a thousand or more cases of frostbite occurring among the troops. The military bulletin on the evening of Christmas Day announced that because of the hardness of the ground, which was frozen to a depth of 20 inches, work on the trenches had had to be suspended, and it had been decided to install all the troops under shelter except such as were necessary to guard the occupied positions.

If the troops' condition in the severe cold was grim, that of the civilian population, especially in the poorer districts of Paris, was not much better. The Government had requisitioned all the coal in the city, for use in the cannon foundries and to make gas to inflate the balloons, and all the coke, which was being rationed out in infinitesimal quantities. As a result there had been a tremendous run on fire wood, and although the price had risen to 6 francs a hundredweight, about treble the normal rate, the city's stocks had been virtually exhausted. To remedy the situation the Government gave orders to cut down about six square miles of timber in the Bois de Boulogne and the Bois de Vincennes, and to fell hundreds of trees lining the main roads out of Paris and the boulevards in the city itself. Depots of firewood were also set up, with a view, so it was said, to making free distributions of fuel to the poor. But on the 26th and 27th the poor, unable to understand why badly-needed fuel should be locked away if it was due to be given to them anyway, took matters into their own hands. Several of the depots were attacked by bands of men and women and the wood stored in them carried off by main force, while in the Élysée district fences and palings were pulled down, trees and benches torn from the ground, and telegraph poles felled.

The sight of hundreds of unauthorized wood-cutters at work on the boulevards – men sawing at the tree-trunks, the women chopping up the branches, the children filling their aprons and pinafores with twigs and faggots – was of course calculated to send a shiver down the spines of the well-to-do. Edmond de Goncourt, for instance, although sympathizing with the sufferings of the poor, found the spectacle of women and children driven to desperation by the cold sinister rather than pitiful. "In the streets adjoining the Avenue de l'Impératrice", he wrote,

> I came upon a threatening crowd, in the midst of horrible-looking women wearing Madras kerchiefs round their heads and looking like Furies of the mob. They were threatening to flay the National Guards who could be seen on sentry-duty in the Rue des Belles-Feuilles. It was all on account of a depot of wood which was used to make charcoal, and which the mob had begun pillaging. This cold, this frost, this shortage of fuel to cook what little meat there is, had roused these women to a fury, and they rushed at the trellises and fences and tore down everything which came to their angry hands. They were helped in their work of destruction, these women, by horrible children, who gave each other a leg up to climb the trees along the Avenue de l'Impératrice, breaking what they could reach and pulling their little faggots behind them, tied to strings which they held in their hands thrust deep into their pockets.

Similarly, an English correspondent heard a warmly-clad and comfortable-looking grocer telling a fellow bourgeois: "It's a hard thing indeed to die for want of fire, but pillage is a serious matter, and once begun, you don't know where it may not end." And the Government issued a proclamation on the 28th, explaining the measures it had taken to provide the population with fuel, and "calling upon the National Guards and all honest men to arrest the marauders and pillagers who respect neither private nor public property".

Almost the only writer who openly sided with the poor in

this matter was the humane Labouchère. "How could they wait for a week", he asked the readers of the *Daily News*,

until the Government could leisurely carry out its plans? They would do for themselves the work of the Government. So they went forth in all directions to cut down trees, and to pick up sticks. They made no distinction between public and private property. Here they saw a fine tree, which would blaze beautifully; they sawed it down. There were some tempting palings, where the wood seemed dry and cut to size; they pulled these up, and carried them off. Behold an enclosure, walled round with planks and hoardings, on which flourished many advertisements; what could be better for firewood? The poor starving wretches pulled them to pieces, with a sagacity which, if you sympathize with it, you will call practical; and if you have no pity, you will call criminal. Property, no doubt, has its rights; but these are very elastic just now in Paris, in so far as they regard the necessaries of life. In fact, as regards these necessaries, the sole right of property in them belongs to the Government, which has made requisition of everything edible and everything combustible in Paris. If you have money, keep it – it is yours; but if you have a horse that can be eaten, or coals that can be burned, you can no longer keep possession of such valuables. The State will pay you for them, but you must give them up for general distribution. So in Paris we have a restricted communism in full working order; and the poor people, fully appreciating this communism, did not see much harm in seizing upon trees which did not belong to them, and on palings and beautiful trelliswork which they had not paid for, to light themselves fires wherewithal, and to keep themselves from freezing. . . .

The battered morale of the Parisians suffered another blow on the 27th, the hundredth day of the siege, when the Germans began shelling the forts on the north-east front of the city. Twelve heavy siege-batteries were unmasked in the morning, and during the course of the day they fired some 3,000 shells at the Forts of Noisy, Rosny, and Nogent, and at the French positions on the plateau of Avron. The bombardment stopped at five o'clock in the afternoon, but only to be resumed in the night. During the afternoon of the 28th, some field guns were brought up by the Prussians and started shelling the plateau, which was swept by the fire of eight converging batteries. While the advanced forts bore the bombardment stoically, the exposed positions on the plateau, where there was no natural cover, and the frozen parapets of the French batteries were as brittle as glass, proved absolutely untenable, and the order was given to retire. The retreat began at six o'clock in the evening, but as there were something like 100 heavy guns to move along the frosty roads in complete darkness, it was three o'clock in the morning of the 29th before the *mitrailleuses* covering the retreat were able to leave the plateau.

The news of the evacuation of Avron had a profoundly depressing effect on the population of Paris, whose first, baffled reactions were faithfully recorded by the Oxford Graduate. "The National Guard", he wrote on the 29th,

> is at all times fond of musical display, but I never heard its music louder than today, as I passed up the Rue de Rivoli. Surely there is something in the wind, thought I, and on the Place de l'Hôtel de Ville the matter was explained: a war battalion had just returned from the outposts with the news that Avron was evacuated. Great was the concern of the people: the Nationals themselves, the bearers of the news, made light of it, to our great astonishment. "We have left Avron," they said, "but what of it? We did very well to leave it." "Leave it to the Prussians?" indignantly cries a grey-beard. "Ah! Bah! You're an *alarmist*. The Prussians cannot occupy Avron, commanded as it is by the guns of Rosny; it is simply neutral ground, and I give you my word Avron is a position of no importance." "Mon cher Monsieur," observes a cynic, who shall be nameless, "is not that the case with all positions? They are important while they are held, and cease to be so when they are lost." The Nationals were soon marched off with great bustle, loud flourish of trumpet, and beating of drums; the groups thickened in the square, and Babeldom prevailed. A patriot tears and stamps, shrieks that "the heavy naval guns are still at Avron," shakes his fist at contradictors; but a friend pats him on the back, and explains that, although the infantry has been removed from the plateau, the artillery has been left there to bombard the Prussians. "Ha, ha!" cries a merry little man with a round face, "I shouldn't like to be in their shoes: Rosny is warming them well." But a prowling *faubourien* protested with dogged reiteration that Avron was *bel et bien nettoyé* (cleared out), artillery and all, except for two naval guns abandoned to the Prussians. "It's a lie: look at his *red hair* – he's been in at least fifty groups: sieze him, off with him to the guard-house." The red-haired gentleman slunk off, followed by a dozen respectabilities, who muttered something between their teeth about traitors and alarmists. ...

The red-haired gentleman was proved right later in the day, when Trochu issued a bulletin announcing and explaining the evacuation. The terms in which the bulletin was couched only added to the Parisians' irritation, for while admitting that the use of heavy siege-artillery by the Prussians must modify the system of defence, the Governor complacently maintained that "all this has been foreseen since the beginning of the siege". The people of Paris were not so easily comforted. "That the conditions of the defence", wrote one commentator,

> will have to be transformed, as the bulletin tells us, can be well understood, in face of the tremendous cannonading which has been going on now for three days; but I doubt whether it is equally true that the new phase upon which we have entered will not affect either the means or the energy of the defence. If in our sorties we have been invariably driven back by the Prussian field artillery, what hope is there of breaking through the enemy's lines now that the terrible Krupp cannon are at length in position all round Paris, in works which we have all along been assured were being destroyed by our naval gunners as fast as they were constructed?

The *Daily News* correspondent, as if anxious to maintain the British reputation for understatement, reported that "there is a strong undercurrent of feeling rising against General Trochu just now on account of his indecision and many delays". In fact, Trochu had never been more unpopular. He now had not only the growing discontent of the population to face, but also the impatience of his colleagues at the Hôtel de Ville. Already, immediately after the failure of the sortie of 21 December, Picard, Garnier-Pagès and Jules Simon had insisted that the Governor should be placed under control, Picard pointing out that General Le Flô, the Minister of War, was really Trochu's superior and ought to act as such. On Christmas Eve Trochu had offered to resign his command, but the Council, after prolonged discussion, had decided that he should be neither deposed nor allowed to resign; at the same time it had been agreed that the other generals of the Army of Paris should be asked to express their opinion of the situation. A few days later Jules Favre presided over a meeting of the Mayors of Paris, who launched a violent attack on Trochu, and on the 30th nearly all the newspapers in Paris joined together in demanding a clear lead from the Government. "What is to be done", asked the *Temps*,

> with the army of 200,000 men formed in Paris during the siege? This, our last resource, if the city is compelled to surrender,

must at all costs be saved from our ruin to prolong the country's resistance in some more favourable quarter. Let the Government speak out boldly and declare, without hesitation, what means it possesses, and whether it can afford to wait for our deliverance by the provincial armies.

The next day, the last day of the year, the Government spoke out as requested, but far from boldly. In a wordy proclamation Trochu explained that the enemy, "in despair at not being able to present Paris as a Christmas gift to Germany, as he had solemnly promised, had added the bombardments of our forts to the varied processes of intimidation already employed to weaken the defence". This bombardment, "the most violent ever suffered by any troops", had, he said, deprived the army of a much-needed respite; but it was ready for action and, in conjunction with the National Guard, would "do its duty". Finally, rebuffing rumours of divided counsels in the Government, he declared that there had been no differences of opinion in the Council, and that he and his colleagues were "closely united in the thought and hope of deliverance".

This proclamation did nothing to allay the population's anxieties or to calm its impatience: on the contrary. "The Governor", asserted one writer,

> seems to ignore the validity of the objections urged against his temporizing policy; for he meets them with the classical tirade which we thought Ollivier, Palikao and the ex-Empress had worn threadbare – about the necessity of union and concord among citizens: the usual argument with which a Government *in extremis* supports its demands for *carte blanche* to commit its last blunder.

The ornate metaphor of "the sheaf of sentiments of unity and mutual confidence" raised a titter on the boulevards; the clumsy denial of any dissension between the members of the Government provoked murmurs of "*Qui s'excuse, s'accuse*"; and it was generally remarked that the Governor expressed no confidence in victory, but merely spoke ambiguously of "duty" and the "hope of deliverance".

The Council of War which met on the 31st was in fact just as pessimistic as the Governor. After some preliminary remarks from Jules Favre, General Ducrot declared that he had never believed in help from outside, that he did not think any army from either Paris or the Loire could pierce the enemy lines, and that a grand sortie of 200,000 men, such as the *Temps* had suggested, would be an act of folly in his opinion. General Vinoy thought that an attempt to break out with two columns advancing in opposite directions ought to have been made, but considered that in view of the demoralized conditions of the troops, it was now too late. His opinion was shared by Generals Noël, Tripier and de Bellemare, and Admirals La Roncière and Pothuau, who all insisted on the low morale of the troops. General de Bellemare asserting that the Gardes Mobiles, from their commanding officers downwards, were unanimous in their clamour for peace. Three generals, General Schmitz, the Chief of Staff, General Frébault of the artillery, and his colleague General Guiot, were in favour of attempting a sortie, not because they had any hope of success, but simply to avoid the dishonour of capitulating without making a supreme effort. As for General Clément Thomas, Commander-in-Chief of the National Guard, he reproached General Trochu for not having made more use of the citizen soldiers, to whom any "forlorn hope" attack should be entrusted. The Governor replied that he would adopt this last suggestion when the time came. "I have said", he added, "that I would not capitulate, no more will I. At the last moment I will propose to you a final enterprise, which may be disastrous, but which may also have unexpected results. However, we have not yet reached the proper moment for the discussion of this last attempt." After this catalogue of depressing opinions, Jules Favre summed up as optimistically as he could, observing that nobody had proposed capitulation and that on the contrary everybody was in favour of an active defence effort. But he added that only a whole nation could undertake a fight to the end.

Although their morale had been shaken by the evacuation of Avron, the Parisians were really in far better spirits than their rulers. As Labouchère wrote,

> the people submit to their hard fare, to cold and hunger, and long nights void of amusement, with a cheerfulness which is sublime. There is no deception in this. They complain quickly enough about many things. They criticize the Government fearlessly, denouncing its mistakes and blunders. But they make no complaint about their miseries, and accept them with an unpretending fortitude which no people in the world could surpass.

The usual preparations were made to celebrate the New Year, and the traditional stalls were put up on the boulevard, although there were scarcely any sweets to sell. And when the Ministry of Agriculture announced the distribution of a supplementary ration of food, the population greeted the news with wry amusement. "The Government", wrote one commentator,

> contributes its share to the general gaiety (?) – three and a half ounces of preserved meat, a handful of coffee-grains, a few dried kidney-beans, a pound of broken rice, and a cake of chocolate. Enjoy your New Year's Day, Parisians, and fatten yourselves up for the Krupp of Châtillon.

A novel addition to the city's diet, but one which only the prosperous could afford, was provided on the 30th when Castor and Pollux, the two young elephants of the Jardin d'Acclimatation, were shot by order of the director, Geoffrey Saint-Hilaire. The newspapers, taking care to state that they had been killed on account of the high price of forage and not for the sake of their meat, published the following detailed account of their execution:

> Castor fell yesterday morning to Monsieur Devisme's bullet. The rifle which killed him is of 33 mm. calibre and weighs 6 kilogrammes. The explosive bullet is 15 cm. long, cylindrical in form with a cone-shaped end, and fitted at the end of the cone with a steel point on which is placed the firing-cap.
>
> This terrible bullet contains 80 grammes of fine shooting powder and when charged weighs 280 grammes. The charge required to hurl this projectile is 8 grammes of powder.
>
> The shot was fired at a range of 10 metres; entering below the right shoulder, the bullet broke the first rib and exploded in the abdomen. After this terrible discharge, the elephant remained standing, shaking itself but not trying to break its bonds. It was only after a few minutes that the internal haemorrhage caused by the explosion choked the animal. Then he fell, but his death-agony was prolonged. After four large buckets had been filled with his blood, he was still showing signs of life.
>
> Present at this curious execution were Monsieur Geoffrey Saint-Hilaire, director of the Jardin d'Acclimatation, Monsieur Milne-Edwards, Monsieur Bouchel, the retired hunter, some naturalists, etc.
>
> Then came Pollux's turn. Monsieur Devisme was present. But it was the younger Monsieur Milne-Edwards who very skilfully despatched the elephant. He used a double-barrelled sporting-gun and cone-shaped bullets with steel points.
>
> The animal had been securely attached with a strong leather strap. Struck in the right temple, he gave a plaintive cry and fell

on his knees; then he stood up again. A second bullet hit him in the centre of his forehead. He fell on his knees again, and stretched out motionless, as if struck by lightning, on his right side. His trunk moved slightly. His gentle eyes closed. He was dead.

Both animals were bought by Deboos, the proprietor of the Boucherie Anglaise on the Boulevard Haussmann, where on the 31st Edmond de Goncourt saw Pollux's skinned trunk hanging on the wall in a place of honour. "The master-butcher", he wrote,

> was perorating to a group of women: "It's forty francs a pound for the fillet and the trunk . . . . Yes, forty francs. . . . You think that's dear? But I assure you I don't know how I'm going to make anything out of it. I was counting on three thousand pounds of meat, and he has only yielded two thousand, three hundred. . . . The feet, you want to know the price of the feet? It's twenty francs. . . . For the other pieces, it ranges from eight francs to forty. . . . But let me recommend the black pudding. As you know, the elephant's blood is the richest there is. His heart weighed twenty-five pounds. . . . And there's onion, ladies, in my black pudding."

Goncourt fell back on a pair of larks, which he carried off for his lunch on New Year's Day. But that evening he was able to record in his *Journal:* "Found the famous elephant black pudding at Voisin's, and dined on it."

Hundreds of Parisians could have made similar entries in their diaries, according to an anonymous letter-writer quoted by Louis Moland. "Castor and Pollux", he remarked,

> were no doubt a corpulent couple of youngsters; but one meets so many people who have eaten a piece of them or are going to eat a piece of them that the miracle of the multiplication of the loaves seems to have been repeated. There is not a single little restaurant which has not put elephant steak on its menu, and one keeps hearing worthy citizens saying: "We are going to have some elephant black pudding or elephant sausages for dinner." I think they are pushing credulity rather far, if of course they are genuinely credulous. We are living in a city of voluntary or involuntary illusions. . . .

A considerable gift for illusion was required on New Year's Day to see any resemblance in it to the first day of earlier years. The shops were mostly closed, the streets half-empty, the stalls on the boulevards as short of customers as they were of eatables. There was no sign either of the usual stream of carriages taking bearers of *étrennes* on their round of visits. Few New Year presents were in fact given, and then they were generally of a strictly practical nature: tins of sardines, potted rabbits and tiny bags of potatoes. The sky was overcast, the Seine was covered with drifting ice-floes, and all day long the rumble of gun-fire could be heard in the distance. Yet the Parisians' irrepressible humour was displayed once again in New Year wishes ranging from "a victorious plan for General Trochu" to "half the ills which can afflict mankind for William of Prussia, and the other half for Bismarck".

This last wish was reciprocated by the Prussians, but in deadly earnest. Dining next to W. H. Russell at Versailles, the Commandant of the German Headquarters, Major von Winterfeldt, whom the English correspondent described as "a fine hard type of Prussian", expressed the fear that Paris might capitulate too soon, "and thus spare the people the suffering they so richly deserved for their frivolity, wickedness and crime".

Paris Under Fire

During the first few days of the New Year there was much talk in both Paris and Versailles of "the psychological moment". A German newspaper correspondent had explained at great length that since a bombardment could have only a limited physical result, the German leaders "considered it best to defer it until the Parisian mind, being shaken by misery, famine, sickness and despair, was susceptible of the strongest psychological effect". The bombardment of the forts on the eastern side of Paris, which was taken as a prelude to the long-awaited shelling of the city itself, suggested that in the opinion of the Germans the psychological moment had come.

Yet if they thought that the threat of bombardment would demoralize the people of Paris, they were utterly mistaken. On the contrary, it raised the spirits of the Parisians, who were almost relieved to find themselves facing a tangible physical danger after three months of ominous inactivity on the enemy's part. With typical optimism they argued that it showed that the Prussians were growing tired and impatient, and that if they held out a little longer the enemy would have to raise the siege. Some of them even indulged in elaborate calculations to prove that the bombardment of the forts was a crippling expense for the Prussians. "From Tuesday to Sunday", Hugo wrote in his journal, the Prussians hurled 25,000 projectiles at us. 220 railway trucks were needed to carry them. Each shot costs 60 francs: total 1,500,000 francs. The damage to the forts is estimated at 1,400 francs. About ten men have been killed. Thus each of our dead has cost the Prussians 150,000 francs.

But if morale in Paris was high, the fact remained that the physical condition of the population was pitiful. "I have no scruple in telling you this", Labouchère wrote to his newspaper,

which might seem to give hopes to the enemy of speedy surrender, because I have no doubt whatever as to the fortitude of the people, who are indeed ready to hold out to the last crust of bread. The patriotism of the Parisians is unflinching. Whatever murmurs we may hear – whatever complaints against the Government – there is no thought of surrender among those who have the best right to complain. Therefore, in all frankness, I give you the death list of the last week, namely, that ending 31 December: Smallpox, 454; scarlatina, 6; measles, 19; typhoid fever, 250; erysipelas, 10; bronchitis, 258; pneumonia, 201; diarrhoea, 98; dysentery, 51; diphtheria, 12; croup, 16; puerperal affections, 8; other causes, 1,897 – total, 3,280.

As Labouchère pointed out, this was by no means the total mortality of Paris, since the number of deaths in ambulances, hospitals and other public institutions was published only once a quarter. It was a reasonable assumption that the total mortality of Paris during the last week of 1870 was about 4,000, which, considering that the population of the city was just over 2,000,000, implied decimation if the same rate of mortality continued for a year.

Hundreds of deaths a week were, of course, due to starvation or undernourishment. But by far the greatest scourge was the bitter cold. During the previous 50 years, the average temperature for the month of December had been 3·54 C. or 38 F., whereas in December 1870 it had been —1·07 C. or 30 F., and only nine days had shown a temperature above freezing-point. And now, on 5 January, bombardment of the city was added to the privations and sufferings of the Parisian population.

A note written by Lehndorff to Bismarck at 9.30 announced with obvious satisfaction:

At 8.15 the first shot was fired from the battery, more since then. Perhaps you have known this for some time, but I did not wish to miss the opportunity of sending to you at your bedside, as soon as you awake, the news of this final fulfilment of your wishes.

To begin with, the German fire was directed at the forts to the south of Paris, but during the afternoon several shells fell inside the fortifications at Montrouge and in the Latin Quarter. The first shell burst in the Rue Lalande, wounding a turner at work in his shop, and soon others were falling around the Mairie of the 14th Arrondissement, whose clock-tower the Prussians were obviously using as a target. As evening drew on, the bombardment became heavier, and the range of the Prussian artillery widened, its shells tearing up trees in the Luxembourg gardens and shattering tombs in the Mont- parnasse cemetery. A few naïve citizens had at first main- tained that the afternoon's shells came from the French forts, whose gunners were "aiming wide of the mark"; but all doubt was removed by the heavy fire in the evening and by a Govern- ment proclamation which was posted up all over the city, announcing that the bombardment had begun. This procla- mation, couched in the familiar Trochu style, declared that, far from intimidating the capital, the enemy's shells would strengthen it in its resolution to fight and conquer. "Paris", it concluded, "will show itself worthy of the Army of the Loire, which has forced the enemy to retreat, and of the Army of the North, which is marching to our aid!"

The next morning the German guns opened up once more, altering their range slightly, so that fresh districts received their baptism of fire. "An hour ago", the Oxford Graduate recorded in his diary,

> I heard a loud crash at the back of our house and the sudden rush of a crowd gathering close under my windows. ... Our English maid came rushing upstairs from the baker's, and the first words she addressed to my mother were: "Please, ma'am, I've seen the first bomb that's fallen into Paris", evidently very proud of having been an eyewitness of this historical fact. The shell has buried itself in the earth by the new church of St. François Xavier, at a hundred yards from our house; and judging from the direction of the hole, it must have been aimed at the Invalides, though it has fallen some three hundred yards short of the mark.

Over at Versailles, the Germans showed some reluctance at first to admit that they were shelling the civilian population of Paris, and it was left to newspaper correspondents to discover this for themselves. Between nine and ten o'clock on Friday the 6th, W. H. Russell climbed up to the roof of an empty house at Versailles which commanded a clear view of the city. "Paris was burning", he writes in his memoirs.

At least one would say so who was influenced by certain tree-shaped columns of smoke with flagrant bases, which rose up in the still air, reminding one of the engravings in *Bruce's Travels* of dust storms in Africa. ... From my post of observation I could command one of the little windows opening on the roof where the King is wont to stand, and I could make out the uniform buttons on coats glistening in the dark room inside. The house is within easy range of the fort; but as the entrance to it is from a narrow lane with high walls on each side, visitors can mount up without being seen, and the French do not seem to suspect that it is the chosen observatory of His Majesty, General Moltke, and Count Bismarck. I watched to see if the Prussian fire was regulated in accordance with the orders issued, as General Walker stated, by the Crown Prince, that shells were not to be thrown into the city; but I could not see anything to make me doubt that their guns were firing at the very highest angles consistent with safety, and I could watch the explosions far inside the *enceinte*....

The same day, Edmond de Goncourt described in his *Journal* the whining of shells overhead, "like the howling of a high wind in autumn"; told how "on every doorstep, women and children stand, half frightened, half inquisitive, watching the medical orderlies going by, dressed in white smocks with red crosses on their arms, and carrying stretchers, mattresses and pillows"; and added gloomily: "The shells have begun falling in the Rue Boileau and the Rue La Fontaine. To-morrow, no doubt, they will be falling here; and even if they do not kill me, they will destroy everything I still love in life, my house, my knick-knacks, my books." But honesty compelled him to record that the people in his district were behaving with extraordinary equanimity in the face of the bombardment: "Since yesterday, it seems so natural to the population that nobody pays any attention to it, and two tiny children who are playing in the garden next door stop at every explosion, say in their lisping voices: 'That was a shell', and then calmly go on with their games."

The younger generation in particular treated the bombardment lightly, even turning it to their own profit and amusement. Street-urchins took to offering fragments of shells for sale at prices ranging from five centimes to five francs. And those with a mischievous turn of mind exploited the situation to make laughing-stocks of prosperous-looking citizens. At the beginning of the bombardment Labouchère had noted with amusement the "ludicrous unanimity" of the Parisians' reaction to an approaching shell. "They are wonderfully obedient", he had written,

> to rules and recipes. For every situation in life they have a recipe. And as they have been informed that when a shell bursts upon them, the best chance of escape is to fall flat upon their bellies, down they go whenever there appears the slighest symptom of danger. ... When the people are most accustomed to the shells, they will learn to distinguish the cases where the rule is absolutely necessary and where it is superfluous. For the present, they are all obedience within range of the shells and kiss the earth with an alacrity which will no doubt be most effectively reproduced in the comedies, farces and burlesques of many years to come.

The temptation offered to the Parisian street urchins was irresistible. "When they see a man or woman particularly well dressed," Labouchère reported on the 8th,

> say a man glorious in furs, that argue an extraordinary care of his person, they cry out: "Flat, flat! a shell – a shell – à plat ventre! Down on your faces!" The man, gorgeous in fur, falls flat on the ground – perhaps in the gutter – and the Parisian urchin rejoices with exceeding great joy.

However, while the bombardment had completely failed to demoralize the population, it had not yet become sufficiently heavy or widespread to arouse a violent desire for retaliation among the Parisians. As a result, when a self-constituted Communist committee issued an indictment of the Government of National Defence – printed on red paper and posted up all over the city on the 5th – it obtained a poor response from a population fascinated by the novel spectacle of the bombardment. A few hundred people gathered on the Place du Château d'Eau and tried to start an insurrection, but the public did not budge and the meeting broke up. "The appeals for a revolution by the bandits of the Commune have had no effect", the Rothschild agent C. de B. reported: "but everybody blames the Government for being so weak with these miserable allies of the enemy." This was an exaggeration: the Oxford Graduate for one criticized the population for "turning a deaf ear to the warnings of a group of energetic men, whose red placard appeared last Thursday on the walls, summoning the citizens to appoint a Commune"; and he concluded:

> Such is the state of utter prostration into which the people have fallen, partly by physical suffering and exhaustion, partly by the enervating system of falsehood under which the men of 4th September have sheltered their own incapacity; the people are incapable of any resolution, which might either save them at the eleventh hour or – if, as I believe, they are already past all hope of salvation – might arouse their energies for some nobler end than a capitulation patiently waited for by the Government, and connived at by the army.

Trochu's mind was undoubtedly preoccupied with thoughts of capitulation, as was shown by the proclamation which he published in answer to the "Red Placard". This proclamation, which of all the dozens of siege manifestos caused the greatest sensation, read as follows:

> To the Citizens of Paris: At a time when the enemy is redoubling his efforts at intimidation, and endeavour is being made to lead the citizens of Paris astray by deceit and calumny. Our sufferings and our sacrifices are being turned to advantage against the Defence. Nothing will make us lay down our arms. Courage, Confidence, Patriotism. *The Governor of Paris will not capitulate!*

The concluding sentence of this document won for Trochu a brief recurrence of his former popularity. But then the sceptics began to wonder if there was not a touch of casuistry in its wording. As the *Daily News* correspondent reported,

> the Parisian, who is one of the most suspicious people in the world, asks: "Why does he say that the Governor will not capitulate? Why not say that Paris will not capitulate? Does he mean that he personally will not sign a surrender, but will leave that duty to others?" Of course, this is hyper-criticism, but it shows the anxiety of the people to resist to the uttermost.

Meanwhile the bombardment continued, steadily growing in its intensity. During the day the Prussians tended to concentrate their fire on the Paris forts, which were clearly visible, but during the night they aimed their guns at the built-up areas inside the city. Some families took to spending the night huddled in their cellars, while others sought refuge with friends living across the river on the Right Bank. All contemporary reports bear witness to the uncomplaining courage of the poorer people on the Left Bank, who bore the brunt of the department. Lily Ballot, for instance, wrote to her mother, Louise Swanton Belloc: "What is pitiful, while heartening, is to see the very poor who have been bombed showing such courage and *sang froid*. One meets them with all their belongings piled up on handcarts, or in wheelbarrows, and sometimes with little children tied by ropes to their mothers." And she added:

How terrible to think that the world has fallen once more into barbarism! The bombs fall constantly on ambulances filled with wounded, and two large maternity hospitals have been hit, as have also been the Salpêtrière and the Pitié. How right was the Compte de Circourt when he used to say, in his icy voice, that the Prussians are a race of barbarians made of iron, and lacking hearts. Thank God I have never known a Prussian.

Other letters and journals levelled the same accusation of deliberate barbarity at the Prussians. In the first place, the indiscriminate shelling of the civilian population at night was taking an increasing toll of women and children. Hérisson quotes in his memoirs a typical *lettre de faire-part* which he received at this time – "Monsieur and Madame Jules Legendre regeret to have to inform you of the death of their daughters, Alice, aged thirteen years and six months, and Clémence, aged eight years, killed by a Prussian shell" – and soon the King of Prussia was being referred to as "the modern Herod". Public indignation was particularly aroused by the death of four little boys, pupils at the Collège Saint-Nicolas in the Rue de Vaugirard, who were killed in their sleep in their dormitory during the night of 8 January. An official funeral was given to the boys at Notre-Dame-des-Champs, and a huge crowd followed the coffins to the Montparnasse cemetery, where Jules Favre delivered a moving graveside oration.

Even more shocking to the Parisians than the killing of young children, which was inevitable in the wholesale bombardment of a civilian population, was the discovery that the Prussians were deliberately directing their fire at churches and hospitals. The church of Saint-Sulpice, easily recognizable by its towers, was struck several times, while shells rained down on the Panthéon, the parish church of St. Geneviève, where hundreds of people were praying ardently if ineffectually for the protection of the patron saint of Paris. But it was the hospitals, most of them characterized by special architectural features and all of them flying the flag of the Geneva Convention, which suffered most. Shells fell repeatedly, day after day, on the hospital of the Val-de-Grâce, which was full of wounded, on the Salpêtrière, which housed 2,000 aged and infirm women and 1,000 lunatics, on the Pitié and Necker hospitals, on the hospital for young children, and on the asylum for the blind. The protests of the doctors and surgeons of one hospital after another proved of no avail; and when Trochu himself complained to Moltke about the bombardment of the hospitals and ambulances, the German commander merely replied sarcastically that the fog and the distance had so far prevented his gunners from taking accurate aim, but as his batteries closed in they would be able to pick out the Red Cross flags more clearly.

This mocking answer roused one member of the Government to propose that all the German prisoners in Paris should be confined in those buildings most frequently damaged by the bombardment, but the proposal was defeated on the grounds that two wrongs did not make a right. Instead the Government addressed a protest to the representatives of Foreign Powers against the bombardment of Paris, in which they declared that

> Prussian shells have been wantonly launched against hospitals, ambulances, churches, schools and prisons, and that the exigencies of war can never be an excuse for the shelling of private buildings, the massacre of peaceful citizens, and the destruction of hospitals and asylums. The Government of National Defence therefore protests loudly, before the whole world, against this useless act of barbarism.

It was generally believed in Paris that world opinion would be united in its condemnation of Prussia for bombarding the French capital. Labouchère declared that "the King, who affects to represent the most enlightened, the most highly-educated people in the world, assumes a tremendous responsibility in the face of civilization and before the tribunal of history, when he ventures on such a purposeless bombardment." Edgar Quinet described the bombardment as "a great moral victory for France". And C. de B. assured the Baron Lionel de Rothschild that the shelling of Paris "may be put down as a complete failure for Germany, which will gain nothing from it but world-wide reprobation for an odious act".

But this "world-wide reprobation" was a pious hope, not a reality. The neutral countries, impatient to see the war come to an end, shut their eyes to the inhumanity of the bombardment in the hope that it would bring peace nearer. Queen Victoria's only comment on the subject in her diary was the unfeeling entry for 6 January: "The Bombardment of Paris continues and so far with success." *The Times*, which on 30 December had acclaimed the shelling of Mont Avron with the comment that "the Germans are just beginning what they could and should have achieved three months since", felt slight qualms of conscience as news came in of civilian casualties inside Paris itself, but it stifled these qualms by neatly dividing the responsibility for the bombardment between the besiegers and the besieged. "Much as we may feel disposed", it stated, "to denounce the Bombardment of Paris as an outrage upon humanity, we think the Prussians who resorted to it may share the blame with the French who provoked it...."

The Prussians themselves – with the possible exception of the Crown Prince, who had opposed the bombardment of the inhabited districts of Paris, only to be overruled by the King – had no doubts about the rightness of their course of action. W. H. Russell wrote in his Versailles diary on the 8th:

> Another grim and snowy Hussar from Von G— out at Clamart. He says their guns range up to the Invalides, and that they have dropped shells close to the Luxembourg.
>
> General Reed, U.S. Consul, has come out of Paris, and wants to get home. I went to the Château Chapel. His Majesty and Staff there – in fine, devout good spirits. I wrote all day. I dined upstairs. The King, in spite of the snow, drove out in an open carriage to see how Paris was getting on, and came back past Place Hoche with an air of considerable satisfaction. He must see that the end is not far off, and that the fruit of his victories is all but ripe. Before turning in for the night went as far as the gate on the Saint-Cloud road to listen to the bombardment. It was a calm, frosty night – moon shining, stars bright – lights in the windows of Versailles – noise of laughter and tinkling of glasses.

Down below, Paris was burning.

Hope Dwindles

Every day now saw the publication in Paris of a whole literature devoted to the bombardment: lists of people killed and wounded by the falling shells; details of donations given for the aid of shell victims, notably by Richard Wallace, one of the greatest benefactors of the people of Paris; an announcement by the Government that civilian victims of the bombardment would be treated in the same light as soldiers; and protests from surgeons and doctors as one hospital after another was hit by shells. Most of this literature made grim or at least solemn reading, but this was scarcely the case with a document published on 13 January. A protest to Bismarck from those members of the Diplomatic Corps who were still in Paris, it complained that proper notice of the bombardment had not been given through the usual channels, and asked for measures to be taken to enable foreign residents to place their persons and property out of danger. This pathetic document was signed, as one correspondent put it, by "both the minnows and the whales", the signature of the United States Minister appearing between that of the Duc d'Acquaviva, the chargé d'affaires of Monaco, and that of Julio Thirion, the interim chargé d'affaires of the Dominican Republic.

Most Parisians, even in the most heavily shelled districts of the city, found it hard to take the bombardment as seriously as this, "Although war and its horrors have been brought home to our very doors," wrote Labouchère, it is still difficult to realize that great events are passing around us which history will celebrate in its most solemn and dignified style. Distance in battles lends grandeur to the view. Had the charge of Balaclava taken place on Clapham Common, or had our gallant swordsmen replaced the donkeys on Hampstead Heath, even Tennyson would have been unable to poetize their exploits. When one sees stuck up in an omnibus-office that omnibuses "will have to make a circuit from '*cause de bombardement*'; when shells burst in restaurants and maim the waiters; when the trenches are in teagardens; and when one is invited for a sou to look through a telescope at the enemy firing off their guns, there is a homely domestic air about the whole thing which is quite inconsistent with 'the pomp and pride of glorious war'".

Yet this did not mean that the danger or the damage created by the bombardment were any less real, as Edmond de Goncourt remarked after a tour of the shelled districts. "There is no panic or alarm", he wrote in his *Journal*;

everybody seems to be leading his usual life, and the café proprietors, with admirable sang-froid, are replacing the mirrors shattered by the blast of exploding shells. Only, here and there among the crowds, you notice a gentleman carrying a clock under his arm; and the streets are full of handcarts trundling a few poor sticks of furniture towards the centre of the city, often with an old man incapable of walking perched in the middle of the jumble. The cellar ventilators are blocked with bags of earth. One shop has devised an ingenious protective screen consisting of rows of planks lined with bags of earth and reaching up to the first floor. The paving-stones in the Place du Panthéon are being taken up. A shell has taken off the Ionian capital of one of the columns of the Law School. In the Rue Saint-Jacques there are holes in the walls and dents from which small pieces of plaster keep falling. Huge blocks of freestone, part of the coping of the Sorbonne, have fallen in front of the old building to form a barricade. But where the shelling has left the most impressive traces is the Boulevard Saint-Michel, where all the houses on the corners of the streets running parallel to Julian's Baths have been damaged by shell splinters. On the corner of the Rue Soufflot, the whole first-floor balcony, torn away from the front, is hanging menacingly over the street.

At the same time, the food situation was rapidly deteriorating. "The sufferings of Paris", wrote one commentator,

were a joke for two months. In the third month the joke went sour. Now nobody finds it funny any more, and we are moving fast towards starvation or, for the moment at least, towards an epidemic of gastritis. Half a pound of horsemeat, including the bones, which is two people's rations for three days, is lunch for an ordinary appetite. The prices of edible chickens or pies put them out of reach. Failing meat, you cannot fall back on vegetables; a little turnip costs eight sous and you have to pay seven francs for a pound of onions. Nobody talks about butter any more, and every other sort of fat except candle-fat and axlegrease has disappeared too. As for the two staple items of the diet of the poorer classes – potatoes and cheese – cheese is just a memory, and you have to have friends in high places to obtain potatoes at twenty francs a bushel. The greater part of Paris is living on coffee, wine and bread.

Now, although wine and coffee were still plentiful, bread was growing desperately scarce. It was at present made of bran, rice, barley, oats, vermicelli and starch, with a slight admixture of flour, but even this black indigestible substance had become so hard to find that on the 13th an absolute panic occurred in the outlying districts and the bakers' shops were stripped bare. The measures which Jules Ferry, the new Mayor of Paris, had taken to regulate bread supplies, such as prohibiting bakers from selling bread to any but their regular customers, had come at a time when many people were fleeing to the Right Bank from the bombardment, so that the fugitives were obliged to choose between dying of hunger and returning home. Finally the Government was forced to recognize that the only possible solution was rationing. On the 13th, Magnin, the Minister of Commerce, was given permission to requisition all the remaining stocks of flour; and five days later the supply of bread was limited to 300 grammes or 10 oz. per head per diem, children under five to receive only half that quantity.

Yet, incredibly enough, the people of Paris made no complaint about their pitiful rations. Even the aristocratic Goncourt admitted that

this Parisian population has to be given its due – and admired. In front of the insolent display of the foodshops, clumsily reminding the starving population that the rich, with money, can always procure poultry, game, the delicacies of the table, it is astonishing that this population should not break the windows, beat up the shopkeepers. But no! At the most, a joke, a witticism, in which there is not even any anger. . . .

And Goncourt added:

When I used to read in Marat's paper the furious tirades of the *People's Orator* against the grocer class, I thought that was simply maniacal exaggeration. Now I see that Marat was right. Their trade, which has been all *National-Guardized*, is a real trade of robbers and swindlers. For my part I should see no harm in hanging from their shop-fronts two or three of those wily cut-throats, convinced as I am that, once that has been done, the price of a pound of sugar would stop rising by two sous an hour. . . .

The people seemed less concerned about the grim food situation than about the growing shortage of news from the outside world. Because of the cold weather the number of dispatches brought into Paris by pigeon post had dropped, and it was in vain that the Post Office tried to put in practice some more successful system of communication. Already, in December, an attempt had been made to send letters into Paris by way of the Seine, enclosed inside zinc spheres fitted with fins; but although the river was dragged repeatedly, none of these zinc balls had come to light. A more promising system using small glass balls resembling water bubbles had since been devised, and a number of these crystal vessels had been taken out of Paris by balloon; but just as this method was about to be initiated, the river froze. Turning frantically from glass bubbles to trained dogs, the Post Office authorities sent five *chiens de bouvier* out of Paris by the *Général Faidherbe* balloon on 13 January; but this last system was no more successful than the others. Instructions were given to all the French outposts not to fire at these dogs if they appeared, and it may be that these instructions fell into the hands of the Prussians, for none of these dogs succeeded in crossing the German lines.

The only sure method of communication during these last few weeks of the siege – though it was, of course, strictly limited to diplomatic messages – was the American Minister's bag, which was regularly allowed across the Stygian passage at the Pont de Sèvres. It was through Washburne's good offices that the French Government was able to communicate at this time with Earl Granville on the subject of the Black Sea Conference in London. The British Foreign Secretary had invited Jules Favre to this conference, and after protracted hesitation Favre finally applied to Bismarck for a safe-conduct, a request which the German Chancellor promptly rejected.

Bismarck gave as his reason for refusing a safe-conduct the form in which Favre's demand was phrased, for it implied that the Government of National Defence was the legal government of France, an implication the Prussian Government did not accept. After raising Favre's hopes again by suggesting that a plan might be devised to allay German scruples on this point, Bismarck finally dashed them to the ground with a concluding paragraph in his most ironical vein.

"But", he wrote,

> even if such a plan can be devised, allow me to ask if it be advisable that your Excellency should leave Paris, and your post as a member of the Government there, in order personally to take part in a Conference about the Black Sea, at a moment when interests are at stake in Paris which are more important for France and Germany than Article XI of the Treaty of 1856? Your Excellency would also leave behind in Paris the diplomatic agents and subjects of neutral States who have remained, or rather have been detained there, long after they had received permission to pass through the German lines, and who are, therefore, so much the more under the protection and care of your Excellency as the Minister for Foreign Affairs of the *de facto* Government. I can, therefore, scarcely suppose that your Excellency, in the critical position of affairs in the establishment of which you so materially assisted, will deprive yourself of the possibility of helping to effect a solution, the responsibility of which rests on you.

Humiliated by Bismarck in the eyes of the world, the Government of National Defence cut just as sorry a figure in the opinion of the Parisians. The military operations carried out in the first fortnight of January had been either futile or unsuccessful, or both. For instance an attack aimed at the German positions at the Moulin-de-Pierre, threatening the Fort of Issy, was at first reported to have been completely successful; but later it was admitted that the officer in command had lost his way and attacked the wrong post. Again, in the night of the 13th the German positions at Le Bourget were attacked once again, with the object of destroying the batteries threatening Saint-Denis; but the only result was that the French troops suffered heavy casualties and severe discouragement, and the next day the Germans started shelling Saint-Denis according to plan.

The population shared its displeasure evenly between

Trochu and his generals. When the *Général Faidherbe* balloon left Paris and it was rumoured that Trochu was travelling with it, unkind citizens suggested that this might be his famous Plan; and accusations of treason as well as of incompetence were repeatedly levelled at the High Command. Some idea of the poor opinion which Paris held of the army's conduct of the siege can be obtained from Edmond de Goncourt's record of a conversation which took place at Brébant's Restaurant on 10 January.

"The talk", he wrote,

> was all about the despair among the big pots in the army, about their lack of energy and determination, about the discouragement they are spreading among the troops. Somebody mentioned a meeting at which, in the face of the cowardly or undisciplined attitude of the old generals, poor Trochu threatened to blow out his brains. Louis Blanc summed the thing up by saying: "The army has lost France and doesn't want her to be saved by the civilians."
>
> Tessié du Motay told us two things illustrating the stupidity of our generals, which he claimed to have witnessed himself. During the sortie of 21 December he saw General Vinoy, who had been ordered to take Chelles at eleven o'clock, arrive on the battlefield at two o'clock, surrounded by a fantastic, rather tipsy staff, and asking where Chelles was. Du Motay was present, I think, the same day, at the arrival on the plateau of Avron of General Le Flô, who, likewise, asked if that really was the plateau of Avron. The same Du Motay declared that after our complete success on 2 December the army had received the order to advance when Trochu was told there was no ammunition left.
>
> This led Saint-Victor to proclaim somewhat wordily the need for a Saint-Just. Somebody spoke of the threat, which had apparently reached the Government today, to burn Paris down if it did not capitulate. In a corner Berthelot produced a comically exaggerated indictment of Alphand, declaring that he was the author of all our misfortunes – this in quite an original way, by refusing nothing that was proposed to Ferry, but by doing it himself and as badly as he could. He cited the salting of meat which was spoilt, the installation of ambulances in the Luxembourg, where the wounded were frozen, the trench-works at Avron and a great many other depressing cases, which, he said, in his ferociously unjust antipathy, would earn Alphand the name of the Haussmann of William of Prussia.

The unfortunate Trochu did not merely have the suspicion and contempt of the population to bear with: he was now at

loggerheads with many of the members of the Government.
Cabinet meetings were marked by lengthy recriminations,
with Favre in particular reproaching the Governor for his
lack of military success or his promise never to capitulate.
For by now it was obvious that Paris could not hold out much
longer, and the only problem was how to arrange a capitulation without losing face too badly and without provoking an
insurrection inside Paris which might lead to civil war.

At one cabinet meeting General Clément Thomas urged his
colleagues to tell the truth to the population, declaring that if
it rose in arms and slaughtered the Government, the latter
would die just as gloriously as if it fell in battle. Not surpris-
ingly, this proposal found little support, and it was rejected
in favour of a more pleasing and less dangerous plan. As
Maurice d'Hérisson tells us in his memoirs,

> there entered into the minds of the leaders that cruel, impious and
> yet logical idea, that the mob would not keep quiet until a certain
> amount of slaughter was allowed, and that, in order to cure Paris
> of her fever and reduce her excitement, some pints of blood must
> be taken from her.

Trochu and Ducrot were well aware that the *sortie en masse*
which Paris had been clamouring for for so long had no
chance of success, but they and the Staff felt that "those
scoundrels in the clubs will not be content until we have
proved to them *ad hominem* that they are incapable of extric-
ating themselves from the mess, and that the time has come to
lay down our arms." The army's honour, too, would be saved
by a last great attack, or, as Trochu put it: "It cannot succeed,
but Paris must die on her feet."

And so, coldly and dispassionately, preparations were made
for the futile, bloody slaughter of Buzenval.

Buzenval

On Wednesday, 18 January, while the final measures were being taken in Paris for the last sortie of the siege, Versailles was celebrating a historic event, the acclamation of King William of Prussia as Emperor of Germany. The ceremony took place at noon, in the Hall of Mirrors, with the King standing under a gigantic allegory of Louis XIV inscribed: "*Le Roy gouverne par luy-même*", in the presence of a host of splendidly-uniformed officers and black-robed Lutheran pastors. "Psalms were sung", wrote W. H. Russell that day,

and prayers were said, and Court Preacher Roggé preached a sermon, its burthen "*Mene! Mene! Tekel! Upharsin!*" – "God hath done wonders in this land, and we have done them for Him"; and then amid much waving of swords and helmets, hurrahs as meetly greet great conquerors, Wilhelm, King of Prussia, was hailed Emperor of Germany, and with tearful eyes received the congratulations of Princes, Dukes and Lords of his Empire. And the rest of the day – for it is the Orden's Fest – there was nothing but rejoicing, feasting, revelling and State dinners in Versailles.

Meanwhile, in Paris, the Government was busily engaged in drawing up a series of proclamations to be published the next day. All but one of these concerned draconian measures which the rulers of Paris had timorously postponed from week to week and which they had now summoned up the courage

188

to take only because, as Picard put it, "the voice of the guns would drown the mutterings of the people". The other proclamation referred to the imminent sortie, which Favre described in the first draft as a "supreme struggle" and a "final effort". But in spite of his insistence that the Government could not decently lead the people to the final extremities without a word of warning, his colleagues clung to the policy of deceit and pretence they had always followed, and Jules Simon was instructed to draw up a more hopeful document.

Trochu was not present at this meeting on the 18th, for he was supervising the marshalling of the city's forces for the the sortie. About half the assault force of 90,000 men consisted of National Guards, whom Trochu and his Staff had at last decided to use in large numbers, and they formed a striking contrast to the battle-tested regular troops. "The soldiers of the Line", reported the Besieged Resident, after watching them on their way to the Porte de Neuilly,

> were worn and ragged; the marching battalions of the National Guards spick and span in their new uniforms. All seemed in good spirits: the soldiers, after the wont of their countrymen, were making jokes with each other, and with everyone else; the National Guards were singing songs. In some instances they were accompanied by their wives and sweethearts, who carried their muskets or clung to their arms. Most of them looked strong, well-built men, and I have no doubt that in three or four months, under a good general, they would make excellent soldiers. In the Champs-Élysées there were large crowds to see them pass. "Pauvres garçons," I heard many girls say, "who knows how many will return?" And it was indeed a sad sight, these honest bourgeois, who ought to be in their shops or at their counters, ill-drilled, unused to war, marching forth with stout hearts but with little hope of success, to do battle for their native city, against the iron legions which are beleaguering it.

Edmond de Goncourt, who saw the National Guards marching past the Arc de Triomphe at about three o'clock in the afternoon, was deeply moved by the sight, despite all his prejudices against the citizen soldiers. "The monument to our victories", he wrote in his *Journal*,

> lit by a ray of sunshine, the distant cannonade, the immense march-past, with the bayonets of the troops in the rear flashing beneath the obelisk, all this was something theatrical, lyrical, epic in nature. It was a grandiose, soul-striking sight, that army

marching towards the guns booming in the distance, an army with, in its midst, grey-bearded civilians who were fathers, beardless youngsters who were sons, and in its open ranks women carrying their husband's or their lover's rifle slung across their backs. And it is impossible to convey the picturesque touch brought to the war by this citizen multitude escorted by cabs, unpainted omnibuses, and removal vans converted into army provision waggons.

On the morning of the 19th, Paris awoke to find the walls covered with official posters. First there was Jules Ferry's decree ordaining the rationing of bread. Then came an announcement that the homes of absentees would be requisitioned for the accommodation of the wounded and of victims of the bombardment, followed by a decree commandeering the food and fuel left behind by these "non-residents" for the use of the general public. A fourth notice called on all husbandmen who possessed secret stocks of seed to give them up within three days, on pain of imprisonment, and a fifth offered a reward of 25 francs per quantial to anybody informing the authorities of hidden stocks of cereals. Finally there was Jules Simon's proclamation, signed by all members of the Government except the President, informing the Parisians that a fresh sortie was about to be attempted, and concluding:

> Those among us who can offer our lives on the battlefield will march against the enemy. Those who remain, eager to prove themselves worthy of the heroism of their brothers, will submit, if need be, to the bitterest sacrifices, as a means of helping their country. Let us suffer, let us die if necessary; but let us conquer. *Vive la République!*

The sortie was to consist of a triple attack on the German lines from Saint-Cloud to La Jonchère by three *corps d'armée*, under Generals Vinoy, Carré de Bellemare and Ducrot. Vinoy was to attack the redoubt of Montretout, between the park and the village of Saint-Cloud; the central column, under Bellemare, was to march against the German positions east of the Château of La Bergerie; while Ducrot's forces, on the right, were to attack the Château of Buzenval before linking up with Vinoy in the vicinity of Garches.

These operations, which were due to begin simultaneously at 6 a.m., were dogged with bad luck from the start. The marshalling of the three columns during the night was delayed by the barricades at Neuilly and Asnières and by the heavy rain which had turned the fields and roads into quagmires. None of the columns was in position at 6 a.m., and Ducrot's column, held up by an artillery regiment which had lost its way in the foggy night, was actually four hours late. As a result, it was impossible to launch a simultaneous attack along the whole front; and although the columns on the left and in the centre captured the Montretout reboubt and occupied Buzenval Park, Ducrot's dilatory forces could make no impression whatever on the German defences. The Germans, moreover, followed their usual practice of abandoning their forward line and falling back to fixed positions from which they kept up a heavy, demoralizing fire on the French troops.

Trochu directed the whole frustrating operation, as far as he was able, from the terrace of Mont Valérien. "It was a unique position", the admiring Hérisson wrote later,

> which permitted him to follow with eye and glass the movements of his army – a superb pedestal such as probably no commander-in-chief, no conqueror had ever had. Surrounded by his entire Staff, he had only to give an order and the officer concerned saluted, went down the steps, found his horse at the postern gate, mounted, and, followed by the Governor's eye as far as the spot indicated, directed the movement of the troops in full view of the man who had just ordered the manoeuvre. It was a marvellously impressive sight.

Unfortunately, seen from closer quarters, what was happening on the Buzenval ridge was far less impressive. The National Guards, whose marching battalions received their real baptism of fire in this battle, fought bravely for the most part; but some hundreds of them were shot down by their comrades in the rear as they advanced through the orchards of La Bergerie, blazing away haphazardly at the trees. Again, the French advance at Buzenval was halted for three hours because the National Guards refused to go through a breach in the park wall which was covered by German guns; and it was not until a lieutenant of the Line had almost pushed his own men through the breach that the Prussians could be dislodged. And finally, when, as night was falling, Trochu came down from Mont Valérian to encourage his troops to make a last, supreme effort, a grotesque incident occurred which nearly proved fatal to the Governor.

"Leaving the battlefield in the darkness", writes Hérisson,

after recognizing that he must once more abandon the positions he had taken and the heights he had scaled, seeing that they were threatened by fresh German reserves, the General, surrounded by his officers and followed by an escort, was crossing a field where a disorderly bunch of National Guards were marching on their return to Paris. Suddenly a voice cried out: "The Uhlans! the Uhlans!" and several shots were fired straight away.

"It is I, Trochu!" shouted the General, riding forward. It was all in vain. The firing went on in greater strength than before, and the Staff had to receive, almost point-blank, the fire of a hundred men before the latter saw their mistake and recovered from their panic. The darkness, fortunately, made their aim uncertain, but one of the General's Orderly Officers, Lieutenant de Langle, fell dead on his horse's neck. A chassepot bullet had hit him full in the chest and gone right through him.

And so it happened that the last words which the Governor heard from the lips of his army were contained in the sinister shout: "The Uhlans!"

Back in Paris, every vantage-point had been crowded since soon after dawn, and orderlies and ambulance waggons returning from the battlefield were constantly pestered for news. The first reports were good, and during the afternoon Government stocks rose by 40 centimes. But at half-past ten a message from Trochu reached the Hôtel de Ville, informing the Government that the French forces were in retreat, and advising it to tell the population the facts. The Government, dreading the consequences if it followed this advice, sent Favre, Ferry and Le Flô to Mont Valérien to discover the precise state of affairs from the Governor himself. It was 4 a.m. when they returned with confirmation of the news of defeat, and within a few hours the whole population was aware that the last sortie had failed.

Labouchère, who went out to Neuilly in the morning of the 20th, found the French troops tired and demoralized. "Every house in Neuilly and Courbevoie", he reported,

was full of troops, and regiments were camping out in the fields, where they had passed the night without tents. Many of the men had been so tired that they had thrown themselves down in the mud, which was almost knee-deep, and thus fallen asleep with their muskets by their sides. Bitter were the complaints of the commissariat. Bread and *eau de vie* were at a high premium. Many of the men had thrown away their knapsacks, with their loaves strapped to them, during the action, and these were now

192

the property of the Prussians. It is impossible to imagine a more forlorn and dreary scene. Some of the regiments – chiefly those which had not been in the action – kept well together; but there were a vast number of stragglers wandering, about looking for their battalions and their companies. At about twelve o'clock it became known that the troops were to re-enter Paris, and that the battle was not to be renewed; and at about one the march through the gate of Neuilly commenced, colours flying and music playing, as though a victory had been won. I remained there some time watching the crowd that had congregated at each side of the road. Most of the lookers-on appeared to be in a condition of blank desapir. They had believed so fully that the grand sortie must end in a grand victory that they could hardly believe their eyes when they saw their heroes returning into Paris, instead of being already at Versailles. There were many women anxiously scanning the lines of soldiers as they passed by, and asking every moment whether some relative had been killed. As I came home down the Champs-Élysées it was full of knots of three or four soldiers, who seemed to consider that it was a waste of time and energy to keep up with their regiments. ...

The gloom into which the Parisians were cast by this final failure was deepened by the news, which had arrived by pigeon post the previous day, that General Chanzy had suffered a crushing defeat at Le Mans. They were appalled by the list of distinguished men who had been killed at Buzenval – a list which included the scientist Gustave Lambert, the venerable Marquis de Cariolis, who had volunteered for service at the age of 67, the young painter Alexandre Regnault, who had scored a great triumph in the Salon of 1870, and the actor Seveste, who was carried that afternoon into the green-room of the Théâtre-Français, mortally wounded, during a performance of Molière's *Le Médecin Malgré Lui*. And the finishing touch to their despair was added by the evening papers, which printed a message from Trochu to his Chief of Staff which had clearly not been meant for publication:

You must now urgently demand at Sèvres an armistice of two days in order to pick up the wounded and bury the dead. This will require time, energy, vehicles with good horses, and a great number of men to act as stretcher-bearers. Lose no time.

This unfortunate dispatch was immediately seized upon by Trochu's enemies as evidence that he had planned the sortie in the certainty of defeat, and with the object of getting his troops slaughtered; and the demand for his resignation became a frenzied clamour. At a meeting between the Government and the arrondissement mayors in the afternoon of the 20th, Trochu was urged to retire, but refused to do so unless a general with greater faith in victory could be found to take his place. He also pointed out that his various functions of Governor, President and Commander-in-Chief were linked to one another, and that he could not resign from one office without abandoning the others. But at a Council meeting held in the evening of the 21st he finally agreed to resign his command, though still retaining the Presidency of the Council. The appointment of General Vinoy as his successor was being discussed when news arrived at the Hôtel de Ville that an armed mob had broken open Mazas Prison and released Flourens.

This was a development which the Government might have been expected to foresee and forestall. Already, at 11 p.m. in the evening of the 19th, the *rappel* had been beaten throughout Belleville and Menilmontant by order of the revolutionary leaders, in the hope of persuading the local National Guards to march on the Hôtel de Ville and overthrow the Government; but most of the citizen soldiers were still outside the ramparts, returning from Buzenval, and the intended rising had to be called off. Then in the afternoon of the 21st, a Communard demonstration had been improvised at the funeral of Colonel Rochebrune, several companies of Belleville National Guards marching down into Paris shouting for Trochu's resignation and the establishment of the Commune. Now, a little after midnight, some 800 of the same National Guards and former Sharpshooters had descended on Mazas Prison, cowed the guard of 30 men into submission, and released Flourens and seven other political prisoners.

This time the Government, terrified of a more violent repitition of 31 October, took swift action. Several battalions of loyal National Guards were sent to the Mairie at Menilmontant, where Flourens and the rioters were celebrating, and drove them into the street. At the same time precautions were taken to protect the Hôtel de Ville, in front of which the rioters had sworn to meet at noon that day. General Blanchard was ordered to send three battalions of Breton Mobiles into Paris; General d'Exéa was instructed to occupy the Lilas district with infantry and artillery, with a view to making a flank attack on Belleville if necessary; General Courty, at Puteaux, was called back into Paris and told to stand by with his troops in the Champs-Élysées; and all the infantry posts throughout the city were reinforced.

That morning Paris awoke to find in the *Journal Officiel* the formal announcement of Vinoy's appointment as Commander-in-Chief; and on the walls proclamations from Vinoy and Clément Thomas calling for the support of the army, the National Guard and all loyal citizens against "the party of disorder" which was fomenting trouble inside the walls.

The early part of the day passed off quietly, but about noon crowds of Sunday sightseers as well as Communards made their way to the Place de l'Hôtel de Ville, where there were some 5,000 people by two o'clock. Two deputations of malcontents were received in turn by Gustave Chaudrey, the adjoint to the Mayor of Paris, who explained to them that the Government was in Council "elsewhere"; and it seemed that the demonstration was going to come to nothing when suddenly about 100 National Guards, mostly belonging to the 101st marching battalion, emerged from the Rue du Temple, with a drummer at their head beating the charge. What followed then is not clear, but it seems that first one then several shots were fired by the newcomers at the officers of the Mobiles walking about behind the railings of the Hôtel de Ville. The Mobiles inside the building then poured a volley of shots into the huge crowd, and absolute panic ensued, hundreds of men, women and children fleeing for their lives into the adjoining streets and cafés. "For about twenty minutes", reported the ubiquitous Labouchère, who had taken refuge in a house on the Square,

> we heard muskets going off. Then, as the fight seemed over, the door was opened and we emerged. The Place had been evacuated by the mob, and was held by the troops. Fresh regiments were marching on it along the quay and the Rue de Rivoli. Wounded people were lying about or crawling towards the houses. Soon some *brancardiers* arrived and picked up the wounded. One boy I saw evidently dying – the blood was streaming out of two wounds. The windows of the Hôtel de Ville were broken, and the façade bore traces of balls, as did some of the houses round the Place.

Five people, including two children, had been killed, and about 20 seriously wounded. It was clear that the riot, if such it could be called, had never had the slighest chance of success, for there had been far more sightseers than insurgents on the Place de l'Hôtel de Ville. Certainly it had not been organized by the real leaders of the Communards, who however much they called for *résistance à outrance* must have known that the end was near; and Flourens was not even present. But it had one unexpected result: it actually strengthened the Government's hand.

While the crowds had been massing on the Place de l'Hôtel de Ville, a strange meeting had been going on at the Ministry of Public Instruction across the Seine, between members of the Government, arrondissement mayors and Staff officers. The officers, pressed to say if there was the slighest hope of raising the blockade, admitted that there was none; and the mayors, who as late as the 20th had been calling for yet another sortie and insisting that they would rather starve than capitulate, finally bowed to the Army's views. The news of the bloody but brief shooting affray on the Place de l'Hôtel de Ville gave added force to the argument for surrender: it convinced the Government, the mayors and the Army that only a tiny, violent minority favoured continued resistance – in which opinion they were mistaken – and also that with a "whiff of grapeshot" any opposition from this minority could be easily suppressed.

Capitulation was now not only inevitable but possible.

Capitulation

"I am struck more than ever", Edmond de Goncourt wrote in his *Journal*,

> by the silence, the deathly silence, which disaster creates in a great city. Today you can no longer hear Paris living. Every face looks like that of a sick person or a convalescent. You see nothing but thin, drawn, pallid features, faces as pale and yellow as horse-flesh.
>
> Opposite me, in the omnibus, there were two women in deep mourning: a mother and daughter. Every few moments the mother's black gloves clenched spasmodically and moved automatically to her red eyes, which could not weep any more, while a tear, slow to flow, dried from time to time on the girl's lower eyelid.
>
> On the Place de la Concorde, near the crumpled flags and the already rotten immortelles of the City of Strasbourg, a company was camping, blackening the walls of the Tuileries garden with its fires, and, with its heavy sacks, forming a sort of screen for the balustrade. Passing through their midst, you heard phrases such as this: "Yes, we're burying the sergeant-major tomorrow."
>
> Another curious, very symptomatic phrase. A prostitute splashing along behind me in the Rue Saint-Nicolas, called out to me: "Monsieur, will you come up to my room, for a piece of bread?"

Paris was indeed not only in a state of deep depression but on the verge of starvation. There were constant disturbances outside the bakers' shops, for often the bakers could not honour even the wretched ration of 300 grammes per head per diem: and at the Council meeting of 23 January Magnin reported that the dwindling stocks of wheat, rice, oats and other cereals would provide bread only until 4 February. True, the rumours of surrender which were circulating in Paris had led some shopkeepers to bring out their hidden provisions; but only the rich could pay the exorbitant prices demanded by these profiteers, and the rest of the population were growing weak from lack of food. Cases were reported of people dropping dead in queues outside food-shops, and undernourishment, cold and disease took their toll of thousands more. Week by week the death-rate had risen alarmingly: from 3,680 in the first week of January to 3,982 in the second and 4,465 in the third. "The mortality among children is fearful", wrote one observer; "at every step you meet an undertaker carrying a little deal coffin." And as a grimly sardonic afterthought he added: "Adults are conveyed to the cemetery in handcarts; only one horse is allowed by Government decree for the most sumptuous funerals, the sable steeds have been requisitioned for the meat-market together with the Cuirassiers' chargers. . . ."

Faced with the imminent prospect of famine on a horrifying scale, the Government decided that it could not delay negotiating an armistice any longer. Jules Favre was accordingly instructed to go to Versailles to discover what terms the Germans were prepared to offer, while concealing the desperate food situation in Paris. He was to say that the Government wished to bring the war to an end, but that the population was so eager to continue the struggle that any knowledge of the Government's negotiations was likely to provoke an insurrection. Above all, he was to do his utmost to obtain swift pre-provisioning of the capital and to dissuade the Prussians from entering Paris, imprisoning the garrison in Germany, or disarming the National Guard.

Favre left Paris in the late afternoon of 23 January, with his son-in-law, Martinez del Rio, and Maurice d'Hérisson. The Foreign Minister's two companions took elaborate precautions to conceal his identity from the National Guards on duty in the Bois de Boulogne, for Favre was convinced he would be lynched if the citizen soldiers guessed his mission; and night had fallen by the time they reached Sèvres. There they embarked in a small boat which had been pierced by so many bullets that they had to bale out the water with a saucepan as they paddled across the inky river, trying to avoid the drifting ice-floes and lit by the sinister glare of the fires at Saint-Cloud. On the other bank of the Seine a group of Prussian officers and a detachment of Uhlans were waiting for Favre with an old closed carriage, and they immediately escorted him to Versailles.

There he was seen by an Englishman, who promptly told W. H. Russell. In his memoirs Russell wrote later:

> I was going after dinner to look in at the Casino, where the Duke of Coburg receives his friends in the evening, when I ran up against Mr. R— in the street. He was agitated – his eyes filled with tears. "Tell me, for God's sake, what it is all about," he gasped. "What? I don't understand what you allude to." "Why should Jules Favre be here? What can he be doing unless Paris is doomed?" "Jules Favre here!" I exclaimed; "that is impossible." "But I swear it. I know him as well as I do myself. Not five minutes ago he passed me in a carriage, going towards the Rue de Provence. The light was on his face. I could not be deceived." This was news indeed. I said not a word to a soul, hurried off to the Chancellerie and Les Ombrages, had the news confirmed, saw him with my own eyes, sent off a telegram – and London next day read in *The Times* that Jules Favre was in Versailles, and that the negotiations for capitulation had commenced.

They began inauspiciously, about midnight on the 23rd, with Bismarck quite truthfully informing Favre that he was in negotiation with the Empress, and observing that he saw no reason why he should deal with a government which had no legal authority. In fact the Empress's envoy, Clémont Duvernois, had so far failed to arrive at Versailles, and Bismarck had decided to ignore the dynastic issue, but his bluff had the effect of completely unnerving Favre, who was reduced to expounding the virtues of a Republic and imploring the Chancellor not to bring back the Emperor.

The next morning Bismarck followed up his advantage by reluctantly agreeing to negotiate with the Government of National Defence, provided that that government proved amenable to reason. In return Favre agreed that the armistice should apply to the whole of France, and not just to Paris – a point which his colleagues had left to his discretion – and that Gambetta's Delegation should not be allowed to interfere with its implementation. The Chancellor then proceeded to outline his terms for an armistice – terms very different from the harsh conditions which Moltke had unsuccessfully urged on the Kaiser: the garrison was to surrender its arms and colours but would not be sent as prisoners to Germany: the guns on the ramparts were to be thrown into the ditches and the forts were to be surrendered to the Germans, but the latter would not enter the *enceinte* during the armistice; the bourgeois battalions of the National Guard were to be allowed to keep their arms, to help in the preservation of order, but all the other battalions were to be disarmed; Paris was to pay a war indemnity, the amount of which would be settled by negotiation; and finally, parliamentary elections were to be held to return an assembly which would decide the question of peace or war.

When Favre returned to Paris that day to consult his colleagues, they not unreasonably greeted these terms as "better than they had dared to hope", but even so they urged him to try to improve on them. Accordingly, during the next few days, the frail old lawyer used all his eloquence and skill in an effort to wring further concessions from the Iron Chancellor. Hérrison, who acted as Favre's secretary at all the Franco-Prussian meetings except the first, has left us a vivid impression of the contrast presented by the two negotiators. "Count Bismarck", he wrote in his memoirs,

> wore the uniform of the White Cuirassiers – white tunic, white cap and yellow band. He looked a giant. In his tight uniform, with his broad chest and square shoulders, and bursting with health and strength, he completely overshadowed the tall, thin, stooping, miserable-looking lawyer, with his wrinkled frock-coat and his white hair falling over his collar. One look at the pair was sufficient to distinguish between the conqueror and the conquered, the strong and the weak.

But Favre knew how to make use of his pitiful appearance to play on an opponent's sympathy, as Bismarck was well aware. "He is a fine little fellow," the Chancellor wrote to his wife, "white-haired, dignified, and amiable, with good old French manners, and it is very difficult for me to be as hard with him as I have to be. The rascals know this, and consequently push him forward."

Despite Bismarck's clearsightedness and the occasional rage into which he flew, the concessions Favre wanted were nearly all granted. Garibaldi, who from an Italian free-lance had become the general of a French army, and whom Bismarck wanted to exclude from the armistice – "I mean to parade him through Berlin", he said, "with a placard on his back saying: 'This is Italy's gratitude' " – was included after all. The war indemnity, which Bismarck suggested putting at a milliard, saying that Paris was such a fine, rich lady that it would be an insult to ask for less, was eventually fixed at 200,000,000 francs. Two of the Prussian conditions which the French Army found particularly mortifying – that the guns on the ramparts should be thrown into the ditches, and that the garrison should surrender its colours – were withdrawn by Bismarck after Hérisson, in a little impromptu negotiation of his own, had pretended that otherwise the French Government would refuse to sign the armistice agreement. As for the provisions respecting the National Guard, Favre insisted that any attempt to disarm any part of that body would lead to civil war; and Bismarck finally gave way – though not without uttering a prophetic warning. "So be it," he told the French Minister, "but, believe me, you are making a blunder. And sooner or later there will be a heavy reckoning for you with the rifles you are rashly leaving in the hands of those fanatics. . . ."

The negotiations very nearly broke down on the 26th, when military representatives of both sides were called in to settle the technical details of the armistice, and the generals found it hard to accept the demands made by the diplomatists. On the German side Moltke, smarting from a recent reproof administered by the Kaiser, sulked unpleasantly and was openly chided by the Chancellor. The French military representative was neither Trochu, who had sworn that he would never capitulate, nor Ducrot, whom the Germans accused of having escaped from Sedan while on parole, but an old general called Beaufort d'Hautpoul, who not only wept like a child when told of the mission he had to perform, but burst into a violent tirade against the Prussians while lunching as Bismarck's guest at Versailles. Subsequently the Germans uncharitably alleged that the general had been drunk, but Hérisson maintained that he had drunk only three glasses of water and that this explosion had been due simply to outraged patriotism. Whatever the truth of the matter, Bismarck took Favre aside after the meal and said that if the French intended to bring Beaufort d'Hautpoul to Versailles again, they might

201

as well break off the negotiations at once. The next day the old man's place was taken by General de Valdan, Vinoy's Chief of Staff.

After this incident the negotiations went ahead smoothly, and in the evening of the 26th, as Favre and Hérisson were getting into their carriage, Bismarck suggested that the bombardment and counter-bombardment should cease at midnight. Deeply moved, Favre promptly agreed, asking only that Paris should be allowed to fire the last shot, a request which the Chancellor granted. Hérisson, although very tired, decided to stay up that night for the solemn moment, and midnight found him walking along the quays listening to the Meudon and Châtillon batteries thundering in the distance. "I remember hearing the first stroke of midnight", he wrote later,

> as I was standing beneath the Palais de Justice clock. The watches or the German army must have been well regulated, as well as our own, for before the second stroke of the bell sounded from the old tower, an imposing, mournful, eerie silence reigned everywhere. You may believe me or not, but it seemed to me that something was wanting. And I am not sure but that a goodly number of Parisians, already asleep in the gas-bereft city where nobody stayed up late, did not awake, roused by the silence from their first sleep. . . .

The Parisians were not, of course, unprepared for this sign that capitulation was imminent. On the morning of the 26th the *Journal Officiel* had informed them that, in view of the hopeless situation of the capital, the Government had entered into negotiations for an armistice, and all day excited, angry or simply dispirited groups of people had been discussing the latest rumours on the boulevards. "You can see everybody", Goncourt wrote in his *Journal*,

> performing the painful mental operation of accustoming the mind to the shameful idea of capitulation. Yet there are some strong-minded men and women who go on resisting. I have been told of some poor women who, even this morning, were shouting in the queues outside the bakers' shops: "Let them cut our ration again! We're ready to suffer anything! But don't let them surrender!"

It was too late, however, to go back now, although several battalions of the National Guard protested to the Government and the Communards made an unsuccessful attempt to seize the guns stationed around Notre-Dame. The Government, fully aware of the danger that an insurrection might take place when the news of the armistice negotiations was announced, had taken stringent precautions to guard the Hôtel de Ville and other public buildings, and advocates of *résistance à outrance* found that there was nothing they could do but fulminate helplessly against their rulers. This they did with a vengeance, ably abetted by the Press, which poured out a spate of caricatures vilifying the leaders of the Government and the Army. The most hurtful of these cartoons was probably one entitled "The Lying Triumvirate", which showed Trochu, Ducrot and Jules Favre hanging from a wall with placards hung round their necks – placards bearing the three most famous phrases of the siege, all three now belied by events: "The Governor of Paris will not capitulate" ... "Dead or victorious" ... "Not an inch of our territory, not a stone of our fortresses".

On the 27th a fresh proclamation was issued by the Government giving the terms of the armistice agreement and promising to publish particulars of the capital's provisions which would prove beyond all doubt that "resistance has lasted to the uttermost limits of possibility". The next day, at eight o'clock in the evening, the armistice – called a Convention rather than a Capitulation in order to spare French susceptibilities – was duly signed, and came into effect immediately: the siege was over.

Although it had been known since the 26th that capitulation was only a few hours away, the news, when it came, was a shock to the population. "Some few, whose sufferings had been intense", wrote an English correspondent, "greeted the tidings as a deliverance from bitter misery, but the aspect of Paris was generally one of mournful agitation."

In an attempt to console the people of Paris, the Government and Press lavished praise on them, the former extolling their "moral energy and courage", the latter assuring them that only famine and the ineptitude of their leaders had forced them to surrender. The Line, declared one writer, had fought magnificently at Champigny and La Malmaison; the gunners and the sailors had defended the forts admirably; the Mobiles had shown their courage at Bagneux, Rueil and Bry-sur-Marne; the marching battalions of the National Guard had conducted themselves bravely at Buzenval; while the noncombatant population had endured cold, hunger and bombardment with wonderful stoicism. And if Paris had fallen, wrote another, what a fall it was! "There is nothing like it in the history of sieges", he maintained,

> for the capture of Constantinople by the Mahometans fades into insignificance when compared with the beleaguerment and doom of the Queen of Cities, the most beautiful of capitals, the centre of European culture, the Mecca of luxury for the whole civilized world, the scene of all that is most brilliant and tragic in the history of France, the dwelling-place of two million people, the greatest fortified camp ever constructed by engineering skill, garrisoned by the largest army that ever defended a stronghold.

It was all in vain. Paris could indeed be proud of her resistance, but that resistance had been futile, and the taste of defeat was bitter.

Epilogue

"Oh, how fearfully unhappy we are!" Lily Ballot wrote to Madame Belloc on the day of the Capitulation.

> Ten days ago our black bread still tasted so good. Moral distress counts for so much more than any physical pain. As for the people of Paris, they don't perhaps feel as we, the so-called educated, do. All the same, their silence today has about it something frightening. It is as if the city were enveloped in a shroud. The sky is dark and grey, and so in harmony with what fills our hearts. ...

This torpor of despair lasted for two or three weeks; and not even the revictualling of the capital, the restoration of communications with the outside world, or the elections of 8 February – which returned republicans for Paris and monarchists for the provinces – succeeded in rousing the Parisians from their apathy. The only question which seemed to interest them during this period was whether or not the Prussians intended to inflict a final humiliation on them by parading through their city. Surely, they argued, no French statesman worth his salt would allow the enemy to add this insult to the injury they had suffered during a long winter of physical and moral hardship.

They were soon to be disillusioned. Adolphe Thiers, who as the most ardent advocate of peace at any price in an Assembly full of pacifists had naturally been chosen as the head of the new Government, had no love for a city which had

205

already interfered with his statesmanship on 31 October, and he was determined to ignore the capital's susceptibilities if they conflicted with the interests of the country as a whole. Accordingly, when, during the peace negotiations at Versailles, Bismarck pulled one of his habitual bluffs, and offered Thiers the choice between surrendering Belfort – a fortress dear to French hearts but comparatively unimportant to the Germans – and allowing the German Army to stage a triumphal entry into Paris, there could be no doubt as to the French statesman's answer.

In the *Journal Officiel* of 27 February the Parisians learned the terms of the Peace preliminaries which had been signed at Versailles the day before: Alsace and the northern part of Lorraine were to be transferred to German sovereignty, France was to pay a war indemnity of five milliard francs within three years, and – by far the bitterest blow for the people of the capital – the Germans were to stage a ceremonial march into Paris and occupy part of the city until the preliminaries had been ratified. The area which the German forces were to occupy was that bounded by the Seine, the Place de la Concorde, the Rue du Faubourg Saint-Honoré and the Avenue des Ternes – a rich quarter which corresponded to German ideas of the French capital and which at the same time was at a safe distance from the turbulent, patriotic working-class districts.

The entry of the German troops took place at ten o'clock in the morning of Wednesday, 1 March. Thiers had previously urged the population to "forget its resentment and think only of the maintenance of order"; but resentment was not so easily forgotten, and the Parisians had decided on measures calculated to show their hatred of the triumphant enemy. Houses along the route of the march-past were to be shuttered, shops and cafés were to remain closed to the Germans, and no newspapers were to appear during their occupation of the capital. The result was that when the German troops marched down the Champs-Élysées they were greeted by an eerie silence, broken only by occasional jeering from the crowds massed in the side-streets. Some indication of the feelings of the population towards the Germans was given later by W. H. Russell, who tried for some time to emerge from the Champs-Élysées to take a report of the march to the Gare du Nord, and found his way barred by a crowd which, with his pro-German sympathies, he described as a rabble of howling savages.

"I managed to get to the Arc", he wrote,

before the troops entered, except the detachment which had been sent on in advance early in the morning to take possession of the Palais de l'Industrie, and guard the barriers at the end of the Place de la Concorde and the bridges. Here there was a large troop of Staff Officers, principally Bavarians, who were drawn up waiting for the troops, not liking the looks of the crowd, which was packed along the side-walks, and jeering the soldiers. Of course, I had to stop and chat with one or two of my friends; but time was pressing, and as soon as I could I sidled off, and continued my course down the Champs-Élysées. But the crowd – some of them – had seen me with the Staff, and as I rode down I heard "*Voilà un Prussien déguisé!*" "*Hola! voici un espion!*" "*À bas les Prussiens*", etc., which were of no consequence as long as one was near the aforesaid *Prussiens* and on horseback out of reach of the crowd. I assumed an air of profound indifference and a cheerful demeanour, and smoked my bad cigar, and tried to put life into my broken-down horse from the end of my spur, till I saw an opening near the Rotonde, and turned to the left, down a street leading to the Rue du Faubourg Saint-Honoré. At the far end there was drawn up a guard of troops of the Line, behind whom there was a mass of people pushing and striving to get through and have a look at the enemy. I rode up to the officer, who advanced to meet me with "You must not pass here", and was explaining that I was an Englishman, and wanted to go to the Embassy, when a little wretch squeaked out: "*Non! Il est Prussien. Il est entré tout à l'heure avec les Prussiens. J'ai vu ce monsieur.*" Enough; a roar burst from the mob – "Down with him! kill him!" etc., and they made a desperate rush to get through the soldiers; but the officer, calling to his men, and motioning to me with his hand to retire, turned the rear rank right about, and kept off the howling savages with the line of bayonets, whilst I briskly fell back on the Champs-Élysées, and keeping down by the avenue near the back wall of the Embassy garden, avoiding the Prussians and the rear of the crowd, trotted as fast as I could go without attracting attention, to the Rue Boissy d'Anglais, and turned down it to the main line of the Rue du Faubourg again. Here there was another military post and another crowd behind it, and as I approached, I heard the same words from the officer, "*On ne passe pas ici*", and the same savage cry from the mob. ...

The Kaiser did not take part in the ceremonial entry of 1 March, intending to march in with his Guard on the 3rd.

However, he was cheated of this satisfaction by the French National Assembly, which ratified the preliminaries on the very day of the German entry, and sent Favre to Versailles on the 2nd to demand the immediate withdrawal of the German forces. As a result, instead of marching into Paris with his troops on the 3rd, the Kaiser had to be content with reviewing them at Longchamp as they marched out.

Strangely enough, this brief occupation of the French capital, though it aroused fierce resentment against the Germans, had a far more profound effect on relations between the French themselves, widening the gulf which the siege had created between the poorer and richer classes of Paris on the one hand, and between Paris and the provinces on the other. For four months the poor people of Paris had borne increasing hardship and even starvation with incredible patience while the well-to-do had bought themselves comparative immunity from hunger and cold; they had been constantly lied to and deceived by a government of incompetent lawyers and soldiers who had never dared to take the brutal but essential measures which Gambetta had implemented in the unoccupied departments; they had been involved in a humiliating capitulation without the 300,000 members of the National Guard ever having been fully committed in battle; and now, when what Thiers called "the decent people of Paris" had left the city to join their families in the country and "breathe some fresh air", they had been obliged to watch the enemy parade arrogantly through their streets. Again, for four months Paris had held out against the enemy and pinned down a huge investing army which might otherwise have ravaged the rest of France, while the provinces had done little or nothing to help her; and now, with monstrous ingratitude, those provinces had saddled her with a reactionary Assembly of country squires and aristocrats which had trampled her pride in the dust.

As if this were not enough, the Assembly proceeded to take a whole series of measures which suggested that the provinces, in alliance with the prosperous classes of Paris, intended to impose their will on the capital and restore the monarchy. A law was passed declaring that all debts and rents, which had been postponed during the war, had to be paid within 48 hours – a measure which plunged all the workers and small tradesmen of Paris into bankruptcy; the Assembly voted to move from Bordeaux, where it had been sitting, to Versailles, instead of Paris; six newspapers were suppressed at one fell swoop, in the kind of attack on the Press which had provoked the Revolution of 1830; and finally the Army was ordered to remove the cannon which the National Guard had installed on the heights of Montmartre and refused to surrender to the Germans. The result was inevitable: on 18 March revolution flared up in the capital, the Government fled to Versailles, and the Commune of Paris – that pipedream of the lower classes during the siege – was proclaimed.

The events which followed are well known: the second siege of the city by the Versailles forces, lasting well into May, and the notorious "Bloody Week" in which the defeated Communards fired public buildings and shot hostages such as the Archbishop of Paris, while the Government troops, for their part, massacred 20,000 men, women and children, shooting and bayoneting until the gutters ran with blood and the mortuaries were filled with corpses.

The name of the Commune, with its resemblance to Communism, the red flag which it took as its symbol, and Lenin's description of it as "the greatest example of the greatest proletarian movement of the ninetenth century" have combined to create a widespread belief that it was a proletarian revolution based on Marxist principles. In fact, although the Commune was a lower-class movement and during its brief spell of power passed some measures in aid of the workers, it was patriotic and radical rather than socialist and Marxist, and its origins are to be seen, not in any political textbook, but in the circumstances and consequences of the siege of Paris.

Back in January 1871, the Oxford Graduate had made an eloquent and perceptive prophecy regarding the Paris which would emerge from the siege.

"Capitulation", Markheim had written,

will soon restore order, with all its shams and hollowness – that is, a despotism which will pander to the vices of the moneyed classes, deliver them from Belleville by grape-shot, and from the Prussians by self-humiliation, and restore for another period of twenty years the life of selfishness and Sybaritism, the prelude in France of a social earthquake, in which the whole nation may some day be swallowed up, and disappear, like Sodom and Gomorrha, from the face of Europe. I must say that the working classes, against whom I was prejudiced at the commencement of the siege, have gradually risen in my opinion during these last two months of suffering to which they have so cheerfully submitted. Perhaps their vices were more skin deep than those of the bourgeoisie, and they have been to some extent disciplined by misfortune and by the consciousness of a genuine determination to defend their city; but they are essentially unsteady, disorganized, impetuous, and they had been quacked ever since the Great Revolution of '93, till their case has become well-nigh hopeless. In them, however, I fancy I can recognise some germs of life which Fortune may develop for the salvation of France, while the rest of French society is a corpse, for which the only remedy is lime, to arrest putrefaction.

In the event, it was the corpses of the thousands of workers shot down by the Versailles troops which were treated with lime, and the "selfish, sybaritic society" which the English observer had known under the Second Empire was soon restored. Indeed, confronted with the gay, glittering Paris of the World Fair of 1878, the journalist George Augustus Sala entitled a book he wrote at that date: *Paris Herself Again.*

He was mistaken. Divisions had been created between working class and bourgeoisie, between capital and provinces, which have not been closed to this day. After the great siege of 1870–1871, neither Paris nor France could ever be the same again.

Bibliography

The following list is a selection of the most interesting or useful works or articles consulted in the preparation of this book.

Achard, Amédée, *Récits d'un soldat*, Paris, 1871.

Adam, J., *Mes illusions et nos souffrances pendant le siège de Paris*, Paris, 1906.

Alméras, Henri d', *La vie parisienne pendant le siège et sous la commune*, Paris, n.d.

Anon, *La cuisinière assiégée ou l'art de vivre en temps de siège par une femme de ménage*, Paris, 1871.

Arsac, Joanni d', *Mémorial du siège de Paris*, Paris, 1871.

B., C. de, *Letters from Paris* (1870–5), edited by Robert Henrey, London, 1942.

Benjamin, Hazel, "Official Propaganda and the French Press during the Franco-Prussian War", *Journal of Modern History*, IV, 1932.

Bismarck-Schoenhausen, Otto Eduard von, Prince, *Bismarck's Letters to his Wife from the Seat of War, 1870–1871*, London, 1915.

Bizot, Victor, *Souvenirs de la guerre franco-allemande en 1870–71*, Lyons, 1914.

Blume, Carl Wilhelm von, *Die Beschiessung von Paris 1870–71 und die Ursachen ihrer Verzögerung*, Berlin, 1899.

Borel d'Hauterive, M., *Les Sièges de Paris, Annales militaires de la capitale depuis Jules César jusqu'à ce jour*, Paris, 1881.

Bourgin, Georges, *La Guerre de 1870–1871 et la Commune*, Paris, 1939.

Brunel, Georges, *Les Ballons au siège de Paris, 1870–1871*, Paris, 1933.

Brunet-Moret, Jean, *Le Général Trochu (1815–1896)*, Paris, 1955.

Cartier, Vital, *Un Méconnu: Le Général Trochu*, Paris, 1914.

Chuquet, Arthur, *La Guerre 1870–1871*, Paris, 1895.

Claretie, Jules, *Histoire de la Révolution de 1870–71*, Paris, 1892.

Cresson, E., *Cent jours du siège à la Préfecture de Police* (*2 novembre 1870–11 février 1871*), Paris, 1901.

Daily News, *Correspondence of the War between Germany and France 1870–1*, London and New York, 1871.

Dalsème, A.-J., *Paris pendant le Siège*, Paris, n.d.; *Paris sous les obus*, Paris, 1883.

Decante, E., *Souvenirs de la campagne, 1870–1871, et du Siège de Paris*, Melun, 1914.

Ducrot, Auguste-Alexandre, *La Défense de Paris (1870–1871)*, Paris, 1875.

Duveau, Georges, *Le Siège de Paris, septembre 1870–janvier 1871*, Paris, 1939.

Favre, Jules, *Le Gouvernement de la Défense Nationale du 30 juin 1870*, Paris, 1871–1875.

Fischer, Georg, *König Wilhelm und die Beschiessung von Paris* Leipzig, 1902.

Forbes, Archibald, *My Experiences of the War between France and Germany*, London, 1871.

Gallet, Louis, *Guerre et Commune: Impressions d'un hospitalier 1870–1871*, Paris, 1898.

Guatier, Théophile, *Tableaux de Siège: Paris, 1870–1871*, Paris, 1871.

Goncourt, Edmond et Jules de, *Journal: Mémoires de la vie Littéraire*, Paris, 1956–1959.

Grouard, Auguste-Antoine, *Blocus de Paris*, 1889–1894.

Guéniot, Dr. A., *Souvenirs parisiens de la Guerre de 1870 et de la Commune*, Paris, 1928.

Guillemin, Henri, *L'héroïque défense de Paris, 1870–1871*, Paris, 1959.

Hans, Ludovic, *Siège de Paris: Le comité central et la Commune, Journal anecdotique*, Paris, 1871.

Hérisson, Maurice d'Irisson d', *Journal d'un officier d'ordonnance, juillet 1870–février 1871*, Paris, 1855.

Heylli, Georges d', *Journal du Siège de Paris*, Paris, 1871–1874.

Howard, Michael, *The Franco-Prussian War*, London, 1961.

Hugo, Victor, *Choses vues*, Paris, 1913.

Jollivet, G., *Souvenirs d'un Parisien*, Paris, 1928.

Kranzberg, Melvin, *The Siege of Paris, 1870–1871: A political and social history*, New York, 1950.

Labouchère, Henry, *Diary of the Besieged Resident in Paris*, London, 1872.

Lacretelle, Charles-Nicolas, *Souvenirs*, Paris, 1907.

Larchey, Lorédan, *Mémorial illustré des deux sièges de Paris 1870–1871*, Paris, 1874.

La Roncière Le Noury, Émile de, *La Marine au Siège de Paris*, 1872.

Leclerc, Louis, *La Garde Nationale à cheval pendant le Siège de Paris*, Paris, 1871.

Lowndes, Mrs. Belloc, *I too have lived in Arcadia*, London, 1942.

Maillard, Firmin, *Histoire des Journaux publiés à Paris pendant le siège et sous la Commune*, Paris, 1871.

Michel, Adolphe, *Le Siège de Paris, 1870–1871*, Paris, n.d.

Moland, Louis, *Par ballon monté: septembre 1870–10 février 1871*, Paris, 1872.

O'Shea, John Augustus, *An Iron-Bound City*, London, 1886.

Oxford Graduate [Henry William Gegg Markheim], *Inside Paris during the siege*, London and New York, 1871.

Pflugk-Hartung, Julius von, *Krieg und Sieg 1870–71: Ein Gedenk-buch*, Berlin, n.d.

Russell, W. H., *My Diary during the last Great War*, London and New York, 1874.

Sarazin, C., *Récits sur la dernière guerre franco-allemande*, Paris, 1887.

Sarcey, Francisque, *Le Siège de Paris: Impressions et souvenirs*, Paris, n.d.

Segretain, Alexandre, *Souvenirs d'un Officier du Génie 1845–1891*, Paris, 1962.

Sheppard, Nathan, *Shut up in Paris*, London, 1871.

Steenackers, François, *Les Télégraphes et les Postes pendant la guerre de 1870–1871*, Paris, 1883.

Tissandier, Gaston, *En Ballon! Pendant le siège de Paris*, Paris, 1871.

Trochu, Général, *L'Empire et la Défense de Paris devant le jury de la Seine*, Paris, 1872.

Victoria, Queen, *The Letters of Queen Victoria, 1862–78*, London, 1926.

Vinoy, Général, *Campagne de 1870–1871: Siège de Paris*, Paris, 1874.

Vizetelly, Ernest Alfred, *My Days of Adventure: The Fall of France, 1870–71*, London, 1914.

Vizetelly, Henry, *Paris in Peril*, London, 1882.

Index

About, Edmond, 99, 101
Acquaviva, Duc d', 181
Adam, Edmond, 84
Allix, Jules, 58, 59
Alméras, Henri d', 31
Alsace, 36, 39, 87, 88, 89, 97, 206
Alton-Shée, Edmond, Comte d', 65
Amazons of the Seine, 58, 61, 62
Ambigu, Théâtre de l', Paris, 95
Amiens, 52, 101
Arago, Étienne, 30, 64, 80, 84, 85
Arc de Triomphe de l'Étoile, 25, 32, 70, 92, 143, 189
Archimède (balloon), 111
Argenteuil, 33
Armand Barbès (balloon), 46
Arnold, Matthew, 152
Arsac, Joanni d', 155
Asnières, 191
Aubervilliers, 19, 125
Aurelle de Paladines, General Louis-Jean-Baptiste de, 75, 102
Austria, 78
Auteuil, 33
Avrial, 81
Avron, 126, 157, 165, 168, 180, 186

B., C. de (Rothschild agent), 52, 53, 114, 149, 155, 176, 179
Bagneux, 56, 57, 125, 203
Ballot, Lily, 19, 178, 205
Barbot (hotelier), 71

Barreswil, Charles-Louis, 105
Bastille, Place de la, 25
Bazaine, Marshal Achille, 39, 75, 76, 77, 78, 80, 82, 103
Beaufort d'Hautpoul, General, 201
Beaugency, 149
Belfort, 206
Belle-Île, 111
Bellemare, General Carré de, 77, 168, 190
Belleville, 30, 44, 53, 81, 114, 141, 142 194, 209
Belloc, Louise Swanton, 19, 28, 178, 205
Belly, Félix, 60, 61
Bercy, 43
Berlin, 18
Berthelot, Marcelin, 186
Besieged Resident, *see* Labouchère
Bibesco, Prince Georges, 48
Bibliothèque Impériale, *later* Bibliothèque Nationale, Paris, 18–31, 93
Bicêtre, 19, 123
Bismarck, Otto Edward Leopold, Count von, 17, 26, 30, 35, 37, 45, 46, 67, 75, 86, 88, 89, 94, 95, 98, 99, 115, 144, 149, 151, 159, 160, 161, 171, 173, 175, 181, 184, 185, 199, 200, 201, 202, 206
Blaise, General, 158
Blanc, Louis, 35, 36, 81, 82, 186
Blanchard, General, 194

215

Blanqui, Adolphe, 50, 81, 82, 83, 85

Bondy, Forest of, 72, 103

Bordeaux, 25, 47, 106, 135, 144, 149

Boucherie Anglaise, 170

Bouffes-Parisiennes, Théâtre des, Paris, 86

Bougival, 69, 71, 157

Boulogne, Bois de, 17, 20, 64, 121, 162

Bourbaki, General Charles, 76, 101, 149, 155

Bourges, 135

Bourget, Le, 76, 77, 78, 80, 82, 153, 157, 159, 185

Boyer, General Napoléon, 76

Brare (postman), 28

Brébant, Restaurant, 75, 186

Brie, 127

British Embassy, Paris, 44

Brittany, 53

Bry-sur-Marne, 203

Burke, Edmund, 116

Burnside, General Ambrose Everett, 45, 46

Burty, Philippe, 57

Buzenval, 69, 125, 187, 190, 191, 193, 194, 203

Capoul, Victor, 18

Cariolis, Marquis de, 193

Castelze, 111

Castor (elephant), 169, 170

Celle-Saint-Cloud, La, 157

Chaillot, 143

Cham, *alias* Amédée de Noé, 31

Champigny, 125, 127, 128, 129, 131, 203

Champs-Élysées, Paris, 32, 92, 114, 189, 193, 195, 206, 207

Chant du Départ, 23, 143

Chanzy, General Antoine-Eugène-Alfred, 149, 155, 193

Charenton, Porte de, Paris, 19, 75, 92, 140

Chartres, 101, 104

Château-Thierry, 26

Châtillon, 19, 29, 41, 56, 93, 117, 169, 202

Châtiments, Les (Hugo), 23, 65, 96

Chatou, 28

Chaudrey, Gustave, 195

Chennevières, 133

Cherbourg, 135

Chevet (caterer), 73

Chevilly, 41

Choisy-le-Roi, 41, 74, 126

Churchill, Arabella, 59

Circourt, Albert, Comte de, 178

Clermont-Ferrand, 107

Coeuilly, 125, 127, 157

Combat, Le, 75, 76, 77, 94, 141, 142

Comédie Française, 160

Constitutionnel, Le, 102

Corbeil, 144

Corneil-en-Parisis, 103

Cornélie, *see* Courmont

Coulmiers, 102, 103, 108, 113

Courbevoie, 32, 192

Courmont, Cornélie Le Bas de, 55

Courty, General, 194

Creil, 47

Cresson, Guillaume-Ernest, 85

Créteil, 127, 140, 142

Dagron, René, 107

Daguerre (balloon), 104, 110, 135, 136

Daily News, 24, 36, 148, 153, 159, 164, 166, 177

Dampierre, Comte Picot de, 57

Danton, Georges-Jacques, 35

Daumier, Honoré, 94

Deboos (butcher), 170

Delescluze, Charles, 81, 82, 83

Dominican Republic, 181

Dorian, Pierre-Frédérick, 81, 84, 85

Duboscq, Jules, 107

Ducloux, Maître, 68

Ducrot, General Auguste-Alexandre, 27, 69, 70, 120, 142, 167, 187; courage 69, 130–31; and insurgents, 85; rejects Prussian terms, 89, 90; and Trochu's Plan, 102; 'dead or victorious', 124, 131, 203; and the great sortie, 125–27, 130, 131, 133; and Le Bourget, 157, 158; and the last sortie, 187, 191; accused by Germans, 201

Dupanloup, Félix-Antoine-Philibert, Bishop of Orleans, 34

Dupuy de Lôme, Henri, 104

Duvernois, Clément, 199

Électeur Libre, L', 87

Emperor of the French, *see* Napoleon III

Empress of the French, *see* Eugénie-Marie de Montijo de Guzman

Épineuse, 52

Evans, Dr. Thomas Wiltberger, 20, 137

Eugénie-Marie de Montijo de Guzman, Empress of the French, 19, 20, 75, 94, 167, 199

Exéa, General Antoine-Achille d', 151, 194

Faidherbe, General Louis, 156

Farcy (gunboat), 38

Favre, Jules, 24, 37, 46, 49, 98, 142, 166, 167, 168, 178, 189, 192; 'not an inch, not a stone', 24, 87, 99, 203; at Ferrières, 30; and insurgents, 49, 83, 86, 88, 89, 142, 202; meets Thiers, 89; protests to Bismarck, 115; humiliated by Bismarck, 185; at Versailles, 198, 199, 200, 201, 202, 208

Fère, La, 156

Fernique (photographer), 107

Ferrières, 46

Ferry, Jules, 48, 53, 64, 76, 80, 84, 85, 183, 190, 192

Figaro, Le, 99, 135

Fitz-James, Charles, Duc de, 59

Fleuriot de Langle, Admiral Alphonse-Jean-René, 143

Flourens, Gustave, 44, 45, 52, 53, 77, 81, 82, 83, 85, 140, 142, 194, 196

Fontainebleau, Forest of, 128

Fonvielle, Arthur de, 141

Frébault, General Charles-Victor, 151, 168

Frederick Charles, Prince, 37, 75, 149, 155

Frederick William, Crown Prince of Prussia, 18, 26, 37, 153, 175, 180

Froeschwiller, 19

Galilée (balloon), 110

Gambetta, Léon, 21, 46, 47, 52, 70, 101, 103, 104, 108, 115, 120, 128, 149, 151, 199, 208

Garches, 190

Gare de Lyons, Paris, 19

Gare d'Orléans, Paris, 19

Gare du Nord, Paris, 19, 23, 110, 206

Garibaldi, Giuseppe, 201

Garnier-Pagès, Louis-Antoine, 166

Gautier, Théophile, 72

Général Faidberbe (balloon), 184, 186

Gennevilliers, 69, 103, 125

Geoffroy Saint-Hilaire, Étienne, 169

George Sand (balloon), 47

Gien, 120

Gironde (balloon), 104

Gladstone, William Ewart, 37

Goncourt, Edmond Huot de, 18, 20, 21, 25, 29, 39, 42, 43, 53, 55, 57, 63, 72, 73, 81, 84,

Goncourt, E. H. de-*contd.*
93, 97, 119, 120, 121, 123, 132,
134, 136, 138, 143, 147, 163,
170, 175, 182, 183, 186, 189,
197, 202
Goncourt, Jules Huot de, 18
Gondreville, 104
Goujon, Jean, 92
*Grande Duchesse de Gérolstein,
La* (Offenbach), 17
Granville, Earl, *see* Leveson-
Gower
Great Britain, 78
Gros, Jean-Antoine, 64
Guérin, Dr., 105
Guilhem, General Pierre-Victor,
41
Guiot, General, 168

Haussmann, Baron Georges-
Eugène, 17
Havre, Le, 102
Hay, L', 41, 126
Hérisson, Maurice d'Irisson d',
31, 41, 45, 46, 48, 69, 77, 78,
83, 124, 125, 128, 156, 158,
178, 187, 191, 198, 200, 202
Hoff, Sergeant, 95
Hôtel de Ville, Paris, 21, 23, 30,
44, 47, 48, 49, 53, 58, 76, 78,
80, 81, 82, 84, 85, 86, 87, 119,
165, 166, 192, 194, 195, 196,
203
Hôtel-Dieu, Paris, 93
Hugo, Victor-Marie, 21, 23, 24,
25, 31, 34, 35, 42, 65, 81, 96,
172

Illustrated London News, 49,
137, 148, 160
Invalides, Hôtel des, Paris, 174,
180
Issy, 19, 123, 185
Italy, 78
Ivry, 19, 125

Jardin des Plantes, Paris, 105

Joinville-le-Pont, 125
Jonchère, La, 69, 190
Joséphine (cannon), 63
Josnes, 149
Journal de Rouen, Le, 54
Journal Officiel, Le, 37, 78, 83,
84, 90, 98, 140, 154, 195, 202,
206
Jules Favre (balloon), 111

Kératry, Émile, 66, 101, 102
Kock, Paul de, 98
Krupp, Alfred, 109, 110, 166,
169

Labouchère, Henry, *alias* the
Besieged Resident, 24, 28, 29,
32, 37, 39, 50, 66, 70, 74, 82,
86, 87, 90, 98, 101, 114, 117,
126, 137, 142, 146, 148, 149,
151, 158, 164, 168, 173, 176,
179, 181, 189, 192, 195
Ladreyt de la Charrière,
General, 127
Lafollye (civil servant), 105,
106, 107
Lagrange, Joseph, Comte de,
118
Lambert, Gustave, 193
Lampérière (National Guard),
141, 142
Langle, Lieutenant de, 192
Lapommeraye, Henri de, 95
La Roncière-Le Noury, Ad-
miral Bon de, 168
Laurent, Marie, 96
Lavertujon, André-Justin, 135
Ledru-Rollin, Alexandre-
Auguste, 81, 82
Le Flô, General Adolphe-
Emmanuel-Charles, 166, 186,
192
Legendre, Jules, 178
Lehndorff, 173
Lemoine (aeronaut), 110
Lenin, Vladimir Ilyich, 209
Lesseps, Ferdinand de, 124

Leveson-Gower, Granville George, 2nd Earl Granville, 184

Liberté, La, 126, 154

Lidfjild, 111

Lille, 25, 156, 160

Loire, Army of the, 101, 102, 103, 104, 111, 120, 125, 128, 134, 135, 150, 156, 167, 174

Longchamp, 208

Lorraine, 34, 36, 39, 87, 89, 97, 206

Louvre, Musée du, Paris, 19, 78, 83, 85, 92, 128, 145, 155

Luxembourg, 119, 174, 180, 186

Luzarches, 111

Lyons, Richard Bickerton Pemell, 1st Earl, 92, 138

MacDowall, C. Stuart, 112

MacMahon, Marshal Marie-Edmé-Patrice de, 20, 25

Madeleine, Église de la, Paris, 155

Magnin, Joseph, 145, 183, 198

Malmaison, La, 203

Mans, Le, 52, 193

Manteuffel, Edwin, Freiherr von, 156

Maréchal, Lieutenant, 65

Marion de Lorme (Hugo), 96

Markheim, Henry William Gegg, *alias* the Oxford Graduate, 29, 43, 51, 66, 83, 86, 114, 125, 131, 135, 141, 147, 165, 174, 176, 209

Marles, 71

Marly-le-Roi, 92

Marne, River, 125, 126, 127, 133, 158

Marseillaise, 18, 23, 115, 148

Marseilles, 25

Martin, Henry, 143

May (diplomat), 47

Mazarine, Bibliothèque, Paris, 93

Mazas Prison, Paris, 194

Menilmontant, 114, 194

Mercadier (civil servant), 107

Metz, 75, 76, 77, 80, 103

Meudon, 38, 117, 153, 202

Meurice, Paul, 23, 65

Mézières, 25

Michel, Adolphe, 159

Michel, Louise, 58

Millière, 83

Milne-Edwards, Henry, 169

Mirabeau, Honoré-Gabriel, Marquis de, 35

Moland, Louis, 170

Moltke, Helmuth, Count von, 26, 37, 88, 134, 142, 149, 159, 175, 179, 200, 201

Monaco, 181

Moniteur, Le, 105, 106

Moniteur de l'Armée, Le, 105, 150

Montgolfier, Adelaide de, 21, 28

Montmartre, 28, 46, 159, 209

Montmartre, Club de, 72

Mont-Mesly, 127

Montparnasse, 174, 178

Montretout, 70, 191

Montrouge, 19, 56, 174

Mortemart, 63, 121

Mottu, Jules-Alexandre, 81, 83

Moulin-de-Pierre, 185

Nadar, *alias* Félix Tournachon, 28, 47

Napoleon III, Emperor of the French, 17, 20, 37, 58, 75, 94, 95

Necker, Hôpital, Paris, 179

Neptune (balloon), 28

Neuilly, 127, 158, 189, 191, 192, 193

Niepce (balloon), 104, 107

Noël, General, 168

Nogent, 19, 156, 164

Noisy, 19, 164

Norway, 111

Notre-Dame, Paris, 84, 178, 203

Nouvelles, Les, 36

Ollivier, Émile, 17, 167

Opinion Nationale, L', 154

Orléans, 101, 102, 104, 108, 110, 111, 113, 114, 115, 134, 135, 149

Oxford Graduate, *see* Markheim

Palikao, Charles-Guillaume, Comte de, 167

Panama Canal Company, 60

Panthéon, Paris, 28, 35, 178, 182

Paris, *passim*

Paris-Journal, 119

Passy, 143

Pavillon Henri IV, Hôtel du, Saint-Germain, 71

Pays, Le, 154

Paysans Lorraine, Les, 95

Pearl, Cora, *alias* Eliza Emma Crouch, 44

Pelletan, Eugène, 64

Petit Créteil, Le, 92

Petit-Journal, Le, 87

Phalsbourg, 30

Picard, Louis-Joseph-Ernest, 68, 80, 81, 83, 142, 166, 189

Pierrefitte, 55

Pinaigrier, Robert, 93

Pitié, Hôpital de la, Paris, 178, 179

Pius IX, Pope, 94

Place Saint-Pierre, 46

Point-du-Jour, 51

Polhès, General, 70

Pollux (elephant), 169, 170

Pontoise, 102

Pope, *see* Pius IX

Portalis, Albert-Édouard, 67

Pothuau, Admiral Louis-Pierre-Alexis, 168

Pré Catalan (restaurant), 121

Prussia, Crown Prince of, *see* Frederick William

Prussia, King of, *see* William I

Puget, Comte de, 135

Puvis de Chavannes, Pierre-Cécile, 108

Pyat, Felix, 76, 78, 81, 82, 83

Quinet, Edgar, 34, 179

Rampont (civil servant), 110

Ranvier, Gabriel, 81

Raspail, Eugène, 81

Ratisbonne, Louis-Fortuné-Gustave, 160

Raynal (magistrate), 115

Reed, General, 180

Regnault, Alexandre, 193

Renan, Ernest, 34

Renault, General, 127

Revillon, Tony, 54

Revue des Deux Mondes, 139

Reynolds (diplomat), 47

Ricord, Philippe, 138

Rio, Martinez del, 198

Rochebrune, Colonel, 194

Rochefort, Henri, 21, 31, 44, 52, 56, 64, 77, 81

Romainville, 19

Rosny, 19, 164, 165

Rothschild, Lionel de, 53, 149, 155, 176, 179

Rouen, 25, 102, 120, 135, 149

Rueil, 203

Russell, William Howard, 70, 171, 175, 180, 188, 199, 206

Russia, 78

Sadowa, Battle of, 18

Saint-Cloud, 27, 38, 56, 69, 121, 157, 180, 190, 199

Saint-Denis, 19, 122, 185

Saint-François-Xavier, Paris, 174

Saint-Germain, 71

Saint-Lazare, Gare, Paris, 72

Saint-Quentin, 156

Saint-Sulpice, Paris, 178

Saint-Victor, Paul de, 108, 136, 186

Sainte-Chapelle, Paris, 93

Saisset, Admiral Jean-Marie-Joseph-Théodore, 55, 126

Sala, George Augustus, 210
Salpêtrière, Hôpital de la, Paris, 178, 179
Sasse, Marie, 18
Saxony, Crown Prince of, 26
Schmitz, General Isidore-Pierre, 41, 83, 128, 129, 168
Schneider, Hortense, 17, 95
Schoelcher, Victor, 85
Sedan, 20, 37, 54, 98, 201
Seveste, Jules-Didier, 193
Sèvres, 27, 89, 193, 198
Sèvres, Pont de, 27, 89, 184
Simon, Jules, *alias* François-Jules Simon-Suisse, 30, 142, 166, 190
Soir, Le, 37, 99, 101
Sorbonne, 182
Spandau, 35
Spicheren, 19
Spuller, Eugène, 47
Standard, The, 67, 71, 75
Steenackers, François, 106, 107
Strasbourg, 28, 30, 35, 42, 43, 63, 197
Strauss, Dr. David, 34

Tamisier, General François-Laurent-Alphonse, 44
Tannhäuser (Wagner), 133
Temps, Le, 166, 168
Tessié du Motay, Cyprien-Marie, 186
Théâtre-Français, Paris, 193
Thiais, 41
Thiers, Adolphe, 76, 78, 88, 89, 98, 205, 206, 208
Thirion, Jules, 181
Thomas, General Jacques-Léonard-Clément, 141, 150, 157, 168, 187, 195
Times, The, 35, 161, 166, 180, 199
Toul, 30, 42, 43
Tours, 30, 52, 79, 105, 106, 107, 110, 111, 135, 155, 160

Triat Gymnasium, Paris, 58, 59-
Tripier, General Émile-Jules Gustave, 168
Trocadéro, Paris, 143
Trochu, Armand, 112
Trochu, General Louis-Jules, 31, 39, 45, 53, 57, 65, 70, 74, 77, 89, 92, 120, 126, 134, 142, 156, 157, 171, 187, 189, 191; and Empress, 21; proclamations, 23, 26, 30, 41, 57, 68, 99, 103, 123, 150, 165, 166, 174, 177; reviews, 25, 26, 85; criticized, 44, 51, 68, 117, 159, 167, 168, 186, 194, 203; and insurgents, 48, 84, 85; appearance, 51; on battlefield, 56, 131, 191, 192; and Trochu Plan, 68, 80, 102, 103, 116, 117, 125, 186; resign, 167; 'the Governor will not capitulate', 177, 201, 203; protests to Moltke, 179; resigns, 194
Tuileries, Palais des, Paris, 20, 57, 197

Uhrich, General Jean-Jacques-Alexis, 28, 110, 111

Valdan, General de, 202
Val-de-Grâce, Hôpital du, Paris, 179
Valérien, Mont, 56, 63, 71, 125, 143, 157, 191, 192
Vanves, 19, 29, 56
Vauban (balloon), 103, 110
Verdun, 103
Vérité, La, 67
Versailles, 37, 45, 71, 76, 89, 92, 94, 115, 151, 153, 159, 170, 171, 180, 188, 193, 199, 201, 206, 208, 209, 210
Victoria, Queen, 36, 56, 180
Villacoublay, 159
Ville de Châteaudun (balloon), 104

Ville d'Orléans (balloon), 111

Ville-Évrard, 157, 158

Villemessant, Jean-Hippolyte-Auguste Cartier de, 99

Villette, La, 141

Villiers, 125, 127, 157

Vincennes, 155, 156

Vincennes, Bois de, 162

Vinoy, General Joseph, 25, 56, 57, 125, 126, 151, 157, 168, 186, 190, 194, 195

Vizetelly, Ernest, 59

Vizetelly, Henry, 49, 59

Voisin (restaurateur), 151, 170

Volta (balloon), 144

Walker, General, 175

Wallace, Richard, 181

Washburne, Elihu Benjamin, 23, 92, 149, 184

William I, King of Prussia, Emperor of Germany, 17, 24, 31, 37, 75, 88, 94, 98, 99, 112, 154, 171, 175, 178, 179, 180, 186, 188, 201, 208

Winterfeldt, Major von, 171

Wodehouse (diplomat), 92